FRANKLIN

JEFFERSON.

for transporting us beyo
for abolishing the free system
and enlarging it's boundaries

THE MYSTERYE
of the
LOST TITLE--

The Declaration of Independence

The Mysterye

of the Lost Title --

This Work at last shall speak about a Mysterye -
Of Principles in conflict, -- from our Ancestry: -
Of men, in Games, with Guile & shadowed Sophistry
Embattling men of Character Unmixed, & deceptively
O'erturning Axioms fixed.   These things -- writ truly -
Were hidden, veiled and stilled, - then lost in History...

THE MYSTERYE

of the

LOST TITLE ---

The *Declaration* of *Independence*

by

Robert Hull Savage

Designing for Illustrations

by

Ingeborg Schlingloff

Sources from the Best Authorities

This Work never before Extant

First Edition

NEW YORK

Printed by Cosmos Communications
for Ionian Pictures

2 0 0 2

Cataloguing Data

Savage, Robert Hull
The Mysterye of the Lost Title - *The Declaration of Independence*
[48] 282 [18] pages, 8 vo, case bd., 220 Illustrations, Book List, Glossary, Jefferson's Lost Original MS.(= 54" x 43"):its abridgment *&* disappearance; 49 Portraits Cnt. Congress, 56 Sigs, 6 flags , Committee of 5; Orig. Title ; { 41 photo-plates of MS; 31 Authentications; Genealogy T.J.'s MS copies.}
Illustr. Design:- I. Schlingloff. Printing : Cosmos Communications, NY

1. Declaration of Independence 2. History British America 3. Liberty

ISBN: 0-9722107-0-9
Printed in the United States of America 2002 First edition Ionian Pictures
Published in Fort Ticonderoga, NY, July 4th 2002 - 226th Signing Anniversary

The Mysterye of the Lost Title -
-- *The Declaration of Independence*

General Contents

Book II - A Sequel (*in Preparation*)

The Lost Original Manuscript
-- *The Declaration of Independence*

The Recompense of Errors
The Loss of British America
A Constitution fixed in Secret
Immigration & the Tower of Amnesty
The Muscle of the Gods
The Deluge

JEFFERSON

DEDICATION

To the Memory
of
Thomas Jefferson

Originations

✠ ——————————— ✠

THE ENGLISH TEXT & POETRY, editing, ornamentation & layout, & the genealogy of the Jefferson manuscript Declarations, with thirty Authentications of the Original Manuscript, are by the Author, as are the photographic negatives for the illustrations, including light micrographs, and also the pre-press computered layout of the text.

The Archival organization of the photo-negatives, with their special selections, optical printing, arrangement, & scanning are by the Designing Illustrator, Ingeborg Schlingloff, as are translations of German & French texts relevant to the research. Her accredited translation of the Work into the German language is in preparation.

The scientific and historical research of the Work, and the book-design, are by the Author and the Designing Illustrator. The relevant reference books, manuscripts, old engravings and woodcuts are located in their Libraries except as otherwise noted.

These Libraries were enriched at mid-century from collections of Professor Charles Albert Savage, a scholar in Greek, & Father of the Author; & in the 1980's from the *New York Auction House* of the late William Doyle, Esq.; and still further - through the 1990's- from the *New York Auction House of* Swann Galleries *(Rare & Early Printed Books)*, with valuable advice from the distinguished President, Mr George Lowry, and from the specialists, especially Mr Tobias Abeloff.

Large photographs of Jefferson's Lost Original Manuscript were made in the security of a Private Library, directly from the Manuscript. No prior description or photographs of it have ever been found - except Jefferson's references to it in 1776 and after,- which are detailed, explicit, and evidently incontrovertible.

The Author was educated in Science, Literature and the Arts, with a later specialty in Electricity and Magnetism; & was on the Scientific Staff of the General Electric Research Laboratory, in Schenectady, New York, for 31 years, attaining 27 patents, 3 of which were applied *for reasons essential* to all high flying U. S. aircraft, and then applied *out of necessity* to the unique U-2 Spy-plane and to the Pioneer space crafts through the 10th, hurtling out of the solar system in 1997 for the Constellation Taurus, 2 million years away.

————————✠————————

‡————————‡

Deep appreciation is hereby expressed to the following, for generous access, with kind assistance, to invaluable source material found essential for this work :--

-To Archibald MacLeish, late Librarian of the Library of Congress, with Professor Julian Boyd, who inspired researchers, with a Limited Edition in 1943 of - *"The Declaration of Independence - the Evolution of the Texts in Facsimile..."* Their photographs, mostly at a scale of 1 : 1, are unsurpassed in quality, definition *&* importance, and provide necessary perspectives with commentary on the numerous texts which have gradually appeared out of unrecorded hiding-places, without continuous provenances or even a genealogy.

- To the New York Public Library, for use of important background sources in the Annex, the Emmett Collection, and the Main Reading Room, as traced in the *invaluable* Black Book Card Catalog.

-To the New York Historical Society, for permission some years ago to photograph and to publish our original portrait views of the authentic busts of Jefferson, Franklin, *&* Washington.

-To the Cooper-Hewitt Museum some years ago for permissions to photograph and to publish our original views of an Egyptian Royal mask from 2000 B.C.

-To Fort Ticonderoga, for permissions to photograph special scenes.

-To Carl Zeiss, Oberkochen, Germany, for examination by Micro-X-ray, Scanning *&* Transmission Electron Microscopy of tiny fragments of the paper of Jefferson's Unknown Manuscript *&* for specialized commentary, arranged through the courtesy of Mr Rudolf Partsch.

-To the Deutsche Museum of Muenchen, Germany, for permission to photograph and to publish certain works in their restricted collections, including miniature models of early paper-making, and an original Gutenberg Press; and access to their early and rare book collections in a special private library room, with exceptionally generous permissions.

-To the Ingolstadt Stadt-Museum, for permissions relating to Christopher Scheiner's unique inventions and original pictures, relevant to this research.

Preface

—

History stands on Truth from a distant past
But oft is twisted, torn to shreds at last,
So Readers should not plunge in unknown waters
When first 'tis apt, to read the Foreword matters --
Discovering both the Argument and Plot
So often vilified by what is not...

As History soon unfolds upon this stage
The Characters - as bright and dark - do rage
In turmoil over differing ambiguous ends
While Greed with Lust resists and darkly sends,
For Unanimity, a Blackmail for support,
Concealing Inconsonance which Lies distort.

From Discovery within a strangely unknown History,
In sequence read each word to reach the Mysterye.

ᛉ ᚢ

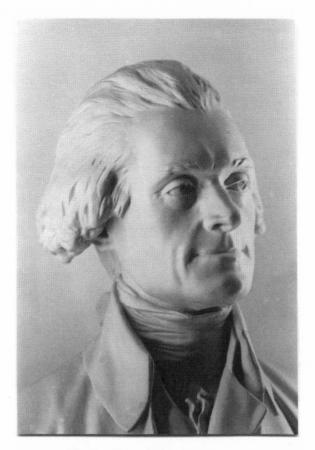

Houdon Bust of Thomas Jefferson
Jefferson stated that he wrote on paper a "Fair Copy",
also called the "Original Draught", - -
that it was debated on the 2nd, 3rd and 4th days of July,
and on the evening of the last... "was agreed to by the House,
AND SIGNED BY EVERY MEMBER PRESENT
except Mr. Dickinson."

- But it vanished two centuries ago...

Thomas Jefferson's manuscripts of the Declaration of Independence show confusion of identity and uncertainty of provenance: --

The American Philosophical Society owns four small pages of manuscript in Jefferson's handwriting, once mistakenly claimed to be the Original, - but mutilated from later notations & underlinings, and badly damaged from improper storage and apparent restorations.

The New York Public Library owns four manuscript pages of similar text, once claimed to be the Original, but showing scars by plastic tape and faded density with color changes from tampering.

The Massachusetts Historical Society has similar manuscript pages but with major parts of the text lost from pages 3 and 4.

The Library of Congress has four small pages stated by some historians to be the Original, and known as the *"Rough Draft"* from vertical designations - not by Jefferson - written down the edge of page-4 together with *"Independance Declaration",* of a contrary word - order. Unlike the above texts, this Rough Draft shows authentic revisions in stages, found also in the printed text of Jefferson's Autobiography; but this Draft has a few nearly illegible sentences, written too small, with smudging of impermanent ink, and with one paragraph on a strip of paper pasted by Jefferson upon lines 40 - 43, obscuring basic text underneath.

None of these four manuscripts is signed or dated, and none contains the intended title or corresponds precisely to the first printed version of the Declaration which is known as the *Broadside,* dated July 4, 1776. Without signatures none of these manuscripts can be considered to be Jefferson's Original.

The National Archives in Washington have a Declaration written on parchment in larger format & often cited as the Original, - but it *is not a Jefferson manuscript nor is it entitled "Declaration of Independence".* It is styled -- *"The Unanimous Declaration of the 13 united States of America",* and dated July 4th before the Colonies were unanimous. It was not authorized by Congress to be written until July 19, nor completed until August 2, as copied by a scribe evidently from a printed Broadside. Visitors may look at this Parchment Copy unaware that it is not the Original nor even the full text.

No manuscript of 1776 had been found with Jefferson's title when in 1976 the eminent historian Julian Boyd published a startling work in the Pennsylvania Magazine of History (October 1976) - -

"The Declaration of Independence -
The Mystery of the Lost Original"

—⟶

Professor Boyd therein wrote, in reference to copies of the Declaration, "All of them including the enshrined engrossed copy (or Parchment Copy) have in common the fact that they are derivatives of the prototype which was adopted in Congress on the evening of July 4 1776, & which unhappily disappeared from history almost at the moment of its creation... It is the purpose to attempt to describe that missing document and to identify its several derivatives ..."

As is now known, Jefferson's first text for the Committee was an incomplete paper, existing later only in fragments, which led in stages to *"The Original Draught of the Declaration of Independence"*, - frequently referred to as "The *Fair Copy*", - and it is this lost Manuscript that was the prototype for all the derivatives. As completed, and presented to Congress on June 28, it was ordered temporarily "to lie on the table".

That Jefferson's Fair Copy *"disappeared* on the night of July 4th... not to be seen since", engendered disbelief: - denial that it had a title, oaths that it was not signed, & assertions that it never existed. In its absence some scholars confined their studies to the Rough Draft or to the several interim copies, calling each one of these *The Declaration*. But none of these small copies was signed - and signatures are indispensable for the validity of a state Document.

Signatures are unique as hallmarks of persons, - intricate motifs with mutations. Letter-shapes of varied stress form original designs through thrust or sweep of quill. A signature suggests partly of authenticity, but alone this may not be enough as one may be copied. Would Jefferson not have foreseen the exigency for full authentication of a validly signed Document? - he who foresaw & secured for us the Mississippi River, the Louisiana Territory, the Bill of Rights, a Statute of Religious Freedom, our Decimal coinage system, the University of Virginia, the initial Library of Congress, the Declaration of Independence, a legal stop to Virginia's slave imports, - and sought, & almost secured - the Abolition of Slavery?

Jefferson said that he wrote, on paper, a *Fair Copy* (or *Original Draught of the Declaration of Independence)*, *that he submitted it to Congress for debate on July 2, 3, and 4, and that* " *it was signed on the evening of the last by every member present except Mr Dickinson".* But that signed paper Document vanished two centuries ago & all questions of its title, history and whereabouts have never been resolved. In the face of continued historical denial Boyd's perception of historical truth stands as reasoned and increasingly prophetic.

Thomas Jefferson's Concept and Architecture - The University of Virginia

PART II

Prologue--
Contents

On the settlement of the English Colonies...
from *David Ramsay:(History of the American Revolution,1789):-*

"The extensive Continent which is now called America, was 300 years ago unknown to three quarters of the globe. The efforts of Europe in the 15th century to find a new path to the rich countries of the East, brought on the discoveries of a new world in the West. Christophoro Colombo (Columbus) acquired this distinguished honor in the year 1492, but a later navigator Americus Vespucius who had been employed to draw maps of the new discovery robbed him of the credit he justly merited of having the country called by his name.

"In the year 1493, Pope Alexander VI, with a munificence that cost him nothing, gave the whole Continent to Ferdinand and Isabella of Spain. This grant was not because the country was uninhabited, but because the nations existing there were infidels; and therefore in the opinion of the infallible donor not entitled to the possession of the territory in which their Creator had placed them. This extravagant claim of a right to dispose of the countries of heathen nations was too absurd to be universally regarded even in that superstitious age; and in defiance of it several European sovereigns though devoted to the See of Rome undertook & successfully prosecuted further discoveries in the Western hemisphere.

"Henry VII of England, by the exertion of an authority similar to that of Pope Alexander, granted to John Cabot (Caboto) & his 3 sons a commission, "to navigate all parts of the ocean for the purpose of discovering Islands, Countries, Regions or Provinces... which have been hitherto unknown to all christian people with power to set up his standard to take possession of the same as Vassals of the crown of England." By virtue of this commission, Sebastian Cabot explored & took possession of a great part of the North American Continent in the name & on behalf of the king of England.

"The country thus discovered by Cabot was possessed by numerous tribes or nations of people. As these had been unknown to all other Princes, they could not possibly have owed allegiance or subjection to any foreign power on earth; they must have been independent communities and capable of acquiring territorial property in the same manner as other nations. Of the principles on which a right to soil has been founded, there is none superior to immemorial occupancy - a state no Prince could derive a title to the soil from discovery, because that can give a right only to lands which either have never been owned, or which after being possessed have been deserted. The right of the Indian nations to the soil in their possession was founded in nature. It was the free and liberal gift of Heaven to them and such as no foreigner could rightfully annul."

CHRISTOPHORO COLOMBO

70

CHRISTOFORO *Colombo, di fama pari a qual si vo-glia de' chiari Heroi, apportò alla sua patria, & al-l'Italia, co'l ritrouar gran parte della terra a noi ignota, gloria singolarissima. Nacque sì memorabil' huomo in Cogoreo, Villa vicina a Genoua: e, perche egli si ve dea dalla natura inclinato all'arte del nauigare, a quella tutto si diede, e diuentato Pilota d'una Naue, nel Mare Oceano, venne in consideratione consef-*

...

The primary New World discoveries were neither Portuguese
nor Spanish but were the creation of Christophoro Colombo, the Italian
navigator and mathematician; his concepts were extended in North
America primarily by the Italians Vespucci and Cabato (John Cabot).
It took the Spanish monarchy 7 years to penetrate even vaguely the wisdom
of Colombo whose visions were drawn partially from achievements in the
13th century of Marco Polo, a Venetian. The Italians gave us not only the
Renaissance itself but the inspiration and execution of
our greatest scientific discoveries in exploration.

Original Map, London 1797
showing North and South America. Here in detail from it:
The 13 United States with the Indian tribes.

Features of map: "6 nations" of Northern Indians, Cherokees and Creeks
in the South, strategic waterways from the North: St. Lawrence River
into Richelieu River (not designated), Lake Champlain, Hudson River.
The map shows early borders to Canada, Florida and the West.
Of historical interest is the inscription along a line running through the
Atlantic or Western Ocean slightly West of a 200 Meridian:
"Line of Demarcation 470 Leagues to the Westward of the Canaries,
Awarded in 1493 by Pope Alexander VI to separate
the Discoveries of the Portuguese and the Spaniards..."

Anno Regni

GEORGII III.

REGIS

Magnæ Britanniæ, Franciæ, & Hiberniæ,

S E X T O.

At the Parliament begun and holden at *Westminster,* the Nineteenth Day of *May, Anno Dom.* 1761, in the First Year of the Reign of our Sovereign Lord *GEORGE* the Third, by the Grace of God, of *Great Britain, France,* and *Ireland,* King, Defender of the Faith, *&c.*

And from thence continued by several Prorogations to the Seventeenth Day of *December,* 1765, being the Fifth Session of the Twelfth Parliament of *Great Britain.*

L O N D O N:
Printed by *Mark Baskett,* Printer to the King's most Excellent Majesty; and by the Assigns of *Robert Baskett.* 1766.

The most obnoxious Act authorized by King George III - as part of a long stream of abuses

The colonies and Plantation in *America* declared to be subordinate unto and dependent upon the Imperial Crown and Parliament of *Great Britain*; and the Legislative Authority of *Great Britain* declared to extend to, and bind the Colonies and People of *America* as Subjects, in all Cases whatsoever. All Resolutions and Proceedings of the said Colonies denying, or calling in Question the said Power, declared null and void

by the Authority of the same, That the said Colonies and Plantations in America have been and of Right ought to be, subordinate unto, and dependent upon, the Imperial Crown and Parliament of Great Britain; and that the king's Majesty, by and with Advice and Consent of the Lords Spiritual and Temporal, and Commons of Great Britain, in Parliament assembled, had, hath, and of Right ought to have, full Power and Authority to make Laws and Statutes of sufficient Force and Validity to bind the Colonies and People of America, Subjects of the Crown of Great Britain, in all Cases whatsoever.

And be it further declared and enacted by the Authority aforesaid, That all Resolutions, Notes, Orders, and Proceedings, in any of the said Colonies or Plantations, whereby the Power and Authority of the Parliament of Great Britain, to make Laws and Statutes as aforesaid, is denied or drawn into Question, are, and are hereby declared to be, utterly null and void to all Intents and Purposes whatsoever.

Detail of preceding map showing theatre of action

The Roots of Discord

Under British colonization Liberty as an ideal was early established through certain charters of English kings, and with it a full freedom of religion had a most essential place for the retaining of Liberty, because archaic religions in the Old World by falling under their corrupted leaderships had become tyrannical and monstrously cruel.

British Colonial policy after 1620 had demonstrated that in its pure form it is based on industrious cultivation of purchased land, by English and European peoples, with representative governments of their own and full encouragement to advance economic growth through prosperous agriculture, manufacturing and trade. But this peaceful condition had suffered from British wars against France, Holland and Spain, - waged in India, the East and West Indies, parts of Europe including Gibraltar, and especially in the New World where seven years of wars with France from 1755 had been mortally costly, - devastating the British Treasury.

Britain had wrested from France enormous territorial gains on the North American continent and in the West Indies, although these lands *had not belonged to these powers, nor to the Pope or any other power, & foreign* granting of lands must be defined as sheer theft, unless recompensed. British acquisitions had stretched to India, nearly 5000 miles distant *&* seemingly remote, but in that case the British gave great protection to India against devastating barbaric Eastern conquests, -introducing modern government *&* western principles. English influence in restraining *the evils of superstition* has been superb.

But the British treasury had steadily overrun its staggering debt, and the obdurate ministry *&* misadvised king sought expansion of the Empire by squeezing payment from the Colonies, thereby bringing on 14 years of increasing anger and alienation by the colonists.

Thus the British Empire had outgrown its capacity for self-support under unlimited expansion overseas and had resorted to avaricious wringing of monies from the thriving Colonies. With the British debt standing above 150 million pounds at high interest, an expansion of foreign wars forced excruciating crises.

By 1775 a rising unrest pervaded the air, pointing toward bloody revolt, - a thundercloud shadowing towns and villages primarily of New England and the middle Colonies, -- but also the Southern Colonies which through slavery were not models of British-American policy, -- but were caught in the same ambiguity as the British in their promotion of *slavery* for their Royal Navy, through *Impressment* of needed seamen , - *by kidnapping.*

George III

"Let him remember that force cannot give right."
- Thos. Jefferson, 1774

Empire builders

Thoughtful members of Parliament, especially Messrs Pitt, Burke, & Fox had opposed Colonial abuses to the limit of eloquence, but were outvoted by a ministry obsessed with Empire building & Trade monopoly. Franklin, in London, had labored exhaustively, with the same wise restraining aims under humiliations by an obdurate & belligerent House, - all these voices confirming that against military & monarchial authority, sound reason may be fatally strangled.

As the Colonies in North America were proud and ingeniously industrious they resisted British demands and trade restraints, perceiving that to be denied self-government and taxed for distant wars and plunder was unfair, yet the means of forcing the demands became more crushing. -- These included the *invasions of privacy* under the guise of *writs of Assistance*, followed by the quartering of standing armies at the Colonists' expense, and also a succession of Restraining acts, - featuring the odious *Declaratory Act of 1764: -- To Bind the Colonies in All Cases Whatsoever*. Thence hostilities charged forward toward explosion.

Thus the root cause of the American War for Independence had become the *subjections, oppressions, & invasions of privacy*, imposed to a ruinous extent on the Colonists by a regime that had grown to be arrogant and martial - to raise monies in the Colonies for the purpose of *Empire-building* and securing *monopolies of trade* in far distant parts of the world, - against France, Holland and Spain, - all at prodigious expense, as the theatres were scattered over thousands of miles of tempestuous oceans.

Against this background, the rising temper in the Colonies had by 1775 come to a boil. The patriots, -while inventing a new form of government,-- saw the necessity for proclaiming their ideals of *Liberty & Independence*, with condemnations of oppression - and of its origin in *Tyranny*, - which are the subjects of this story. A letter of George Washington to his brother (May 1776) concludes: "...Things have come to such a pass now, as to convince us, that we have nothing more to expect from the justice of Great Britain... that she is capable of the most delusive arts; that no commissioners ever were designed, except Hessians and other foreigners; that the idea was only to deceive and throw us off our guard. The first has been so effectually accomplished as many members of Congress are still feeding themselves upon the dainty food of reconciliation..."

And then he fired a bolt of plain-spoken self-evident truth:

" The Parliament of Great Britain have no more right to put their hands into my pocket, without my consent, than I have to put my hands into yours." -- Geo. Washington.

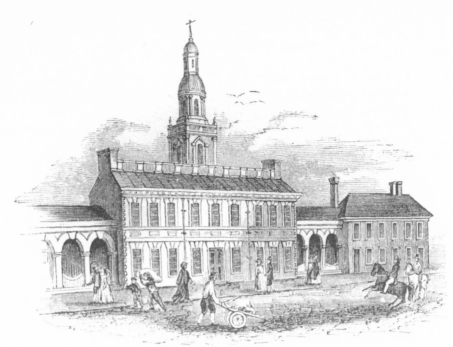

THE STATE HOUSE AS IT APPEARED IN 1774.

From a vignette on an old map of Philadelphia.

One frequently cannot find in modern historical accounts an adequate emphasis on the Secrecy that necessarily surrounded the work on the Declaration. The American War for Independence, a most disastrous and ruinous cataclysm amongst kindred people, was haunted by spying and deception, and became a great promoter of hidden transactions. Security was a phantom, existing only by invisibility, which is the cloak of Secrecy. Without habitual consciousness of the nature and extent of the Secrecy which veiled discussions in the Continental Congress, questions concerning the Declaration may not be fully grasped.

When the Continental Congress began deliberations, oaths of Secrecy were taken from all of the members:

"Continental Congress
Agreement of Secrecy

In Congress, Nov. 9th 1775
"Resolved that every member of this Congress considers himself under the ties of virtue, honor and love of this country not to divulge directly or indirectly any matter or thing agitated or debated in Congress before the same shall have been determined, without leave of the Congress; nor any matter or thing determined in Congress which a Majority of the Congress shall order to be kept secret, and that if any member shall violate this agreement, he shall be expelled from this Congress and deemed an enemy to the liberties of America and liable to be treated as such, and that every member signify his consent to this agreement by signing the same."

In 1776 it was necessary to secure all windows against opening during the meetings in the State House, -- and to make sure that Secrecy oaths were followed. All of the names of the signers of the Declaration except one were held from publication until late 1777.

Secrecy originated in the simple fact that the colonists were widely split among themselves in their attitudes toward the Crown and Parliament of Great Britain, --- for protection, on the one side, or through their own aspirations for independence on the other; and this fervent desire for independence had for a very long time been nurtured following centuries of religious persecutions, -- featuring the horrors of fire and brimstone *in Satanic vaults of the Inquisition* - which had driven the colonists' distraught ancestors to escape to America. Absolute freedom of religion was then paramount -- as it is necessarily today -- in the perpetual presence of *superstition* and the *tyranny* behind that, which overlooks and dictates behind the inevitable *shadows of torture,* to shackle the mind and will of man.

The Tower of London

English Bronze Cannon
This 24 pdr. dated 1762 bears the monogram of
of George III & the arms of Field Marshal
Viscount Ligonier, Master General of the
Ordnance 1759-63. It was cast from metal by
melting down French cannon captured in 1758.

Those aspirations had seemed necessary for many who knew too much of tyranny and did not fear a life without excessive protection. But loyalty to the Crown inspired the loyalists with a zeal that yielded not to persuasion or coercion. They considered it as their duty to report to the British whatever they saw or suspected as being rebellious; -in a word they spied, surreptitiously and frequently, - but with sinister consequences.

Owing to large numbers of spies & their circumspect maneuvers, their identity was not evident; and since many loyalists depended on English trade they could not imagine a sensible severance of ties.

The non-loyalist *rebels,* as patriots, were more open in their actions and intentions. The hidden practices of the spies were revolting to them, - but also dangerous. - Dissension and distrust spread to such an extent that in some Colonies it led to the brink of civil war. As a result, when the committees of correspondence began to send information from one Colony to another, strict rules and practices were imposed to keep transactions confidential.

In all of the turmoil, the Shadow of the Tower fell as far as from London to distant British America simply through *a bounty*, placed upon the heads of all those conspicuous patriots who displeased the King or Parliament, - and this occurred very often. When caught, the assumed culprits were taken to stand trial in England far from their own courts and people, with no possibility of redress, and only the most melancholy future in view, in the Tower of London.

On the perilous night of April 19 1775, John Hancock and Samuel Adams were being sought under this fatal threat. As they were known to be in Lexington at a certain time, when British troops made a night march to seize the powder & ammunition stores at Concord their mission was also to secure these two rebels. It was then that Paul Revere in a night ride brought a last hour's warning so that they escaped both the British and the Tower prison, where they would have entered by the *Traitor's Gate*, a one-way street.

One near-fatal breach in Secrecy occurred in the case of Dr Church, the chief physician of a military hospital near Boston, where wounded Colonial soldiers were taken during the siege, after the burning of Charlestown. Dr Church was in a position to purloin critical military plans, and he passed these to the British through the ruse of a hiding place in the bosom of his kept mistress, - until it chanced that one such report fell into the hands of Washington's officers, - leading to the doctor's immediate imprisonment without access to pen, paper, or solace. -- ꧁꧂

Battle of Breed's Hill
(misquoted as Bunker Hill)

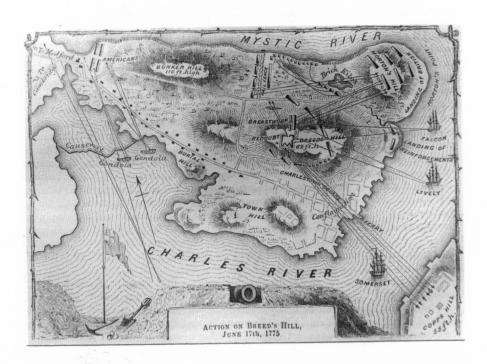

ACTION ON BREED'S HILL,
JUNE 17th, 1775.

> <

With bloodshed on April 19, 1775 at Lexington and Concord, a fair chance of peace with King George III and Parliament was virtually crushed. Opinion in the Colonies prevailed that the provincials could not resist the British unless assisted by a European power, and that an alliance for support could not be had unless the Colonies declared their independence.

Intelligence from Lexington spread furiously, with grave alarm in South Carolina where the Colonists found the militia had less than 3000 pounds of powder, and they resolved to seize the royal arsenal which was intended to reverse British thefts at Concord.

It was fortunately known that East Florida was still neutral, and on the night after the revelations from Lexington a dozen patriots with a crew sailed from Charleston to St. Augustine, where by surprise they boarded a British vessel, carrying off 15 000 pounds of powder with military stores, and leaving a bill of exchange with the captain. They returned by inland waterways, avoiding pursuit ships; and powder was thus stored for defense and projected excursions.

Colonial anger intensified in June with the battle at Breed's hill, when the British without warning burned the entire town of Charlestown, - its stately houses consumed in a gigantic sea of flames. Congress also could not reach accord with the King through the Olive Branch Petition, to which Lord Dartmouth said coldly, - *There will be no answer.*

During the year, before Lee's *Resolution* for Independence would be voted, British guns also destroyed Falmouth, and Congress then published the "Causes for the Taking up of Arms". George Washington had been named Commander-in-Chief of the Continental armies, to take his post near Boston, where oppressions and conflicts with Red-coats had been intensifying.

Late in 1775 it became known in the Colonies that England was forging plans for a brutal conquest, -- with strategies to divide northern & southern sectors in a pincer: -- downward from Quebeck and upward from New York on the Hudson-Champlain water ways, through Fort Edward, Tyconderoga, and Crown Point. A *geographical Rift* in Colonial unity was thus to be forced, -- dividing the land along natural barriers, and quelling resistance piecemeal while cutting communications between isolated sections of the Provinces.

But this in effect was a mere paper plan, which failed to reckon with supply problems in the isolation and fury of the wilderness -- with the unseen terror of its Indian menace.

In the dead of winter Colonel Henry Knox had brought nearly 100 cannon, confiscated from the Fort by Allen and Arnold

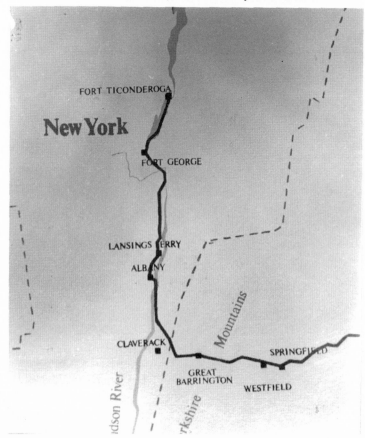

Henry Knox had urged that the capture of Tyconderoga would yield a large supply of heavy French *&* English cannon for General Washington near Boston, then at an impasse with the British Army investing the city, - and Knox offered to transport the cannon through wilderness so that Washington could distract the enemy by bombardment from high ground and then imperil the entire British Fleet in the Bay. All of the other officers objected that to transport the cannon under these circumstances would be impossible, but Washington seized the chance, - sensing that the success of the war for independence hinged on executing this crucial stratagem before the British Fleet obliterated Boston.

"To Henry Knox: (from General Washington)
"Instructions: 16th day of November 1775
"Sir,
        "After you have procured as many of these necessaries as you can there (New York) you must go to Major General Schuyler and get the remainder from Tyconderoga (*&* Crown Point...). The want of them is so great, that no trouble or expense must be spared to obtain them... General Schuyler will give every necessary assistance."

Colonel Knox had enormous obstacles to overcome because of the late season, and after sailing the length of Lake George, he wrote to General Washington on the 17th of December: -

" I return from Tyconderoga to this place on the 15th instant and brought with me the cannon, it having taken nearly the time I conjectured it would to transport them hither. It is not easy to conceive the difficulties we have had in getting them over the lake, owing to the advanced season of the year and contrary winds. Three days ago, it was very uncertain whether we could get them over until next Spring. But now, please God, they shall go. I have made 42 exceedingly strong sleds and have provided 80 yoke of oxen to drag them as far as Springfield, where I shall get fresh cattle to take them to camp."

His cannon train of hearty men and oxen had to cross the frozen Mohawk and Hudson rivers on failing ice, then struggle through hundreds of miles without roads, pulling staggering loads of up to a ton, through mud, and in blizzards, - to the exhaustion of men and animals, - but by ingenuity, raw courage, *&* patriotism he overcame all obstacles to reach the hills around Boston, unseen, and with most of the heavy cannon required for Washington's design.

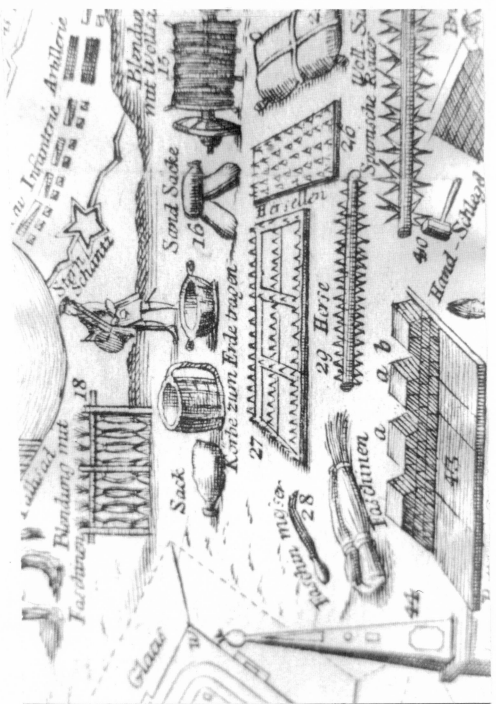

Fortification gunnery
siege instruments

With the object of gaining the strategic hills overlooking Massachusetts Bay around Dorchester Heights, by stealth under cover of darkness, Washington and his staff determined to make the Boston environs suddenly untenable for the British army - and especially for their heavily armed ships in the Bay. To divert the enemy's attention so as to conceal their new strategy, a heavy play of cannon began an intermittent thunder, and for three nights the distracting cannonade continued. To the British it must have seemed fantastic that the Americans could have many huge weapons for bombardments, for they had not discovered that Henry Knox had brought nearly 100 cannon, mortars and howitzers from Fort Tyconderoga, confiscated by Ethan Allen and Benedict Arnold in the previous spring, and the cannon train had reached the camp in secrecy. Without this foresight & ingenuity Boston could not have been relieved - but Washington's army had been strengthened and he had stealthily become an uncompromising menace. Although the bombardment did little damage, it kept the enemy under cover for these opening scenes described by William Gordon. (see pg-039: Hist...)*

"On March 4th all things being ready on that Monday, as soon as the evening admits, the expedition goes forward. The covering party of 800 men lead the way; then come the carts with the entrenching tools; after them the main working body of about 1200 men under General Thomas...

"There are no bad roads requiring an exertion as the frost having been of long continuance, they are so hard frozen as to be quite good. The wind lies to carry into the harbor between the town and the castle what noise cannot be avoided by driving the stakes and picking against the ground, frozen to 18 inches - so that it cannot be heard by any who have no suspicion of what is carrying on. Many of the carts make three trips, some four, for a vast quantity of material has been collected.

"By 10 o'clock at night the troops have raised two forts, one upon each hill, sufficient to defend them from small arms and grape shot. The night is remarkably mild, a finer for working could not have been selected out of the 365. They continue working with the utmost spirit, till relieved Tuesday morning about 3. It is so hazy below the heights that the men cannot be seen, though it is a bright moon-lit night above the hills. It is after daybreak before the enemy in Boston can discern the newly erected forts which loom to great advantage, & are thought to be much larger than is the case.

"General Howe is astonished upon seeing what has been done. 'I know not what I shall do; the rebels have done more in one night, than my entire army would have done in months'. "

A storm descends...in a fury of admonishment

"The Admiral assures General Howe that, if the Americans possess those heights, not one of His Majesty's ships can be kept in the harbor, & a council of war determines to attempt to dislodge the Americans and take the heights by assaults." *

William Gordon, D.D.,"History-Rise of the 13 Colonies... to Independence". 1788, v-2 *

Decisively General Washington had settled a plan of ambiguous offense. Boston was surrounded on every land-side by clustered hills so that nothing sinister could originate on the wharfs or near the water without detection by telescope above. Coded signals were contrived to transmit across the gaps in the hills & intelligence was conveyed from Dorchester Heights. Washington's plan was - -

But on the night of the 5th a storm descends, such as few remembered ever having known, and toward morning torrents of rain lashed the scene in a fury of admonishment. Nor was this the first counter-plot of Nature; for late in 1775 Howe's army in investing Boston had run very short of supplies, especially of food.

The desperately needed stock had been unseasonably delayed in leaving England and, when launched for the Atlantic crossing, all Nature conspired to delay and spoil the vital replenishments. On departure the ships were blown back against the British coast and those which continued were blown off course, in many cases to the West Indies. Others were delayed by winds repeatedly so that huge supplies of animals were lost overboard or died on the decks and had to be abandoned. Of the remaining ships some arrived, only to fall into American hands, as the provincial privateers were swift and more agile in the waters than the supply vessels, and the harbor was menaced from all sides.

On March 6th the design by General Howe was thereby again foiled and copious bloodshed artfully prevented. In councils of war it was decided to evacuate Boston and to sail for Halifax, - first plundering though not devastating the town. But in the ensuing withdrawal the British forces were distraught & baffled by hundreds of loyalists -- seeking asylum from the rebels, -& demanding to sail with Howe's army, with all their furniture & necessaries aboard.

Although it was foreseen during the ominous darkening of the colonial relation to English rule that open conflict would be impossible of success without support from France, it was thought that as long as the Colonies acknowledged the English sovereign and parliamentary authority they could not be trusted if entering into European alliances. It had been assumed that the gaining of decisive support from France would depend on certain colonial initiatives which were not evident in that year. But this assumption was guess-work, and counter-plots were in the making ...

Louis XVI

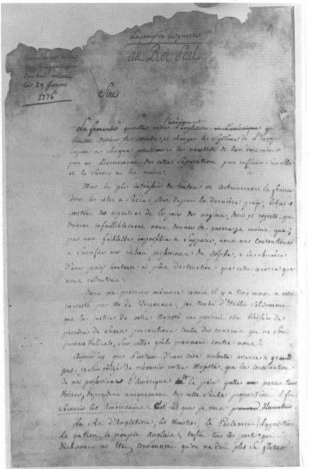

"I am obliged to present to your Majesty it is necessary to help the Americans"

Secret Letter by Pierre Augustin-Caron de Beaumarchais
February 29, 1776 (4 months before the Declaration of
Independence was written)

Fortunately all men were not yet equal in France. The brilliant and the scientific had not yet lost their heads on the bloody altar of Egalité and the great intellectuals of that creative century were at their zenith. Among these was an ingenious inventor who had devised a new mechanical escapement for watches and for navigation instruments, and he was evolving intricate devices for a chromatic pedal system in the harp, - all of which had fascinated the royal family, including the King. Soon this imaginative creator, the persuasive and famous writer Pierre Augustin Caron - was drawn to the Palace with the attention of the King in his favor.

France already in repeated conflict with Britain could seize an opportunity to disrupt the British-American colonial ties with England through *revolution*, and this soon became the plan which Pierre Augustin Caron (Beaumarchais) proposed to Louis *XVI* of France, very early during the British-American crisis. In a secret note of late February 1776, directed intimately to the King, ---- *La Paix ou la guerre-* , Beaumarchais wrote (Secret letter, 29Feb. 1776) -

The quarrel of England & America will soon divide the entire Western World -- and this will change the balance of power in Europe ...

He indicated explicitly the need to examine the nature of the hypothetical separation between those separate peoples, *&* warned -

" This day advances a violent crisis by huge increments. It is therefore essential that I emphasize for your Majesty, that the protection of the American possessions and the much besought peace does rest specifically on one unique proposition, - which is – *that to assist the Americans is essential.* And this I shall demonstrate..."

Beaumarchais then rendered his concept of power balance between France and England in North America *&* in the Caribbean, and he showed the advantages of supporting the Americans, in secret, -- all in an extremely persuasive text.

He indicated that the situation could provide a means for France to secure control over the profitable trade with the *Sugar Isles*. He suggested that the fundamental separation in the political arena under conflict indicates weak support for the coercive suppressions by the British. Beaumarchais further claimed that the colonial agent in London despaired of obtaining military supplies from France, and he added that the Minister of Foreign Affairs, M. de Vergennes, would name the agent separately.

That person turned out to be Arthur Lee, apparently a secret agent in an ambiguous role.

In Philadelphia... something incredible happens...

Beaumarchais also described   the possible outcome of the conflict: - if England were to suppress and conquer America, it could only be done under a ruinous sacrifice of men and material. And he argued that a colonial war with England fought then by the Americans with clandestine help from France   would cost but a fraction of a large-scale conflict between France and England later. Already he was arranging for the Spanish government to join in a project of aid with each country agreeing to contribute equally.

Thence, if it turned out that America won, Britain would be obliged to make up for her losses and would probably try to seize the French Caribbean possessions to gain monopoly of the sugar trade. Finally Beaumarchais reminded Louis that in politics, -

An opportunity not seized is an opportunity lost.

By *May 1776*, Louis had agreed to the proposed plan for secret aid. A fictitious trading firm, *Hortalez et Cie,* was organized, to be run by Beaumarchais, and funded jointly by France, Spain and a few of the rich business associates of Beaumarchais. The Americans would exchange war supplies against shipments of grain and tobacco.   This agency was operative until 1783, and huge amounts of war material were thereby exported to the Americans.

The uniquely influential letter of Beaumarchais was written 4 months before the colonists first proposed *Independence* in the Continental Congress. Yet little seemed known to Congress of the mastery of Beaumarchais over the French court.

Thus even before a declaration of independence had been urged in Congress, Beaumarchais had forseen the importance for France to support the Americans against England and had persuaded Louis *XVI* to approve enormous secret military aid - nearly a year before Franklin settled in Passy to open negotiations with the French ministry.   In all of this intricate plotting Louis insisted on secrecy.

In Philadelphia, agitation advanced with consensus in Congress that resistance to the British would fail unless the Americans became independent and were initially supported by a foreign power.

After stormy sessions for several days, from June 28, 1776, Congress approved the Declaration of Independence.

- But then something incredible happened...

The distinguished historian, Professor Julian Boyd, editor of more than twenty volumes of Jefferson's writings, has written - *that* the *Original Declaration of Independence disappeared on the night of July 4, 1776, and has not been seen since.* -- The existence of that Lost Original has been an unresolved mystery. -

Had it a Title, - - or Signature? - - and where is it?

THE LIBERTY TREE.

Some years ago an unknown colonial Manuscript was found in an abandoned safety deposit box of a bank vault. It had been stored there for a lengthy period under costly security, as obviously of great value. Under state laws as abandoned property it could be sold... and it was publicly sold.

The Manuscript had been written before there was a United States Government or even a Confederation, and has never been the property of any government nor has it been in the public domain. It is a Secret Document released through accident.

This is a search into the origins and meaning of that strangely forgotten Manuscript surviving from the Lost Secrets of the 18th Century, and falling into the hands of this writer as though through *Destiny,* -- he as a Scientist, not a Historian.

This unknown and startling Work has been studied through historical sources and by scientific methods. While it indisputably authenticates itself through more than four dozen original portraits, hand-drawn in black ink, with their corresponding signatures, there seem to be too few present-day Americans who would believe what it is and would care. In the meantime it has been generating a book about itself, a book originating and growing out of the shadows of the Manuscript's soul; *&* as the research developed into documented orderly form, this book has unfolded strange long-buried narratives, clarifying the nature of the subject within its fringes.

The following account is essentially new and is based on the Manuscript itself while the background is drawn primarily from original sources, written by those then witness to the events and qualified in testimony; - but conclusions have been formed also from obscure but related writings, with deep concern here shown over grave errors arising from modern misconceptions of old principles.

To the reader for whom the past seems old and shabby hat, there are lessons in this book, disquieting in tone and requiring sober reflection upon the changing character of our people, *&* leadership, now adrift and disuniting under the burden of diversity, *&* avarice.

For older true Americans, sensing in the image of their vanished forebears an ideal of *Unity in Character & Language* and an unselfish devotion resulting in rare blessings undiminished through seven generations, -- these pages offer an authentic and intimate Portraiture of those souls who gave to posterity the great and nearly imperishable Tree of Liberty, *&* withal, the reasons why the legendary title -- *Declaration of Independence* -- became a *Mysterye.*

On Legend & Reality

A Work concealed from sight in deep Obscurity
By prolonged Absence may have been forgotten; --
Were it cloistered for the sake of its Security,
One could have said, "It vanished - when begotten".

And whenever - if it ne'er appeared again -
Some question would arise of its Reality,
Shrewd Historians without evidence might explain
'Twas only Legend, revered in false Totality.

Yet Scientists, peering through an unseen Aether,
Should say, Historians cannot in truth foretell
Nor conclusive narratives write, foreseeing neither
Unknowns hid, nor Secrets in the Well...

Authorities denying written accounts from the past
May fail to sense the hidden Truth at last...

!

Concerning enigmatic silences

Following the discovery of the unknown Jefferson Manuscript and numerous older references to it, together with its self-authentication through 56 original Signatures and an unheard-of contemporary Portraiture of the second Continental Congress, some guarded disclosures were made to Directors & Curators in Americana at a number of distinguished Institutions in the Eastern States.

In reaction to these disclosures, there came Sphinx-like unresponses...
Was this incredulity?   Or incommensurability?

However, one Curator looked forward with evident appreciation to a proposed book on the subject of the lost Declaration, and it was concluded from that positive response that an extensive authenticating documentation of physical evidence would create interest within an Institution for safeguarding the Document for posterity - & cherishing it.

The following, Parts III and IV, contain the result of this effort to provide substantiation for a future possessor of the Document, while also correcting some errors noted in present-day historical opinion.

PART III

On Jefferson's Lost Original

Contents

Contents
(continued)

—⁂—

*How a Rare Thing could be rescued
from the Winds of Chance*

———————   ⚓   ———————

During the period marking the two-hundredth anniversary of the close of the American Revolution an unusually exciting auction of jewelry was being held, which was noteworthy for its timing and location, and especially for its richness: - emeralds, diamonds, rubies, pearl, topaz, amethyst, moonstone; gold, in white, yellow, rose, -and platinum: - all were being bid in, by an aggressive crowd of speculators feverishly bent for prize.

In the midst of these tumultuous proceedings there quietly appeared at the block a folded Document listed inconspicuously as a copy of a declaration, without note of provenance.

Preoccupied with the sparkling and brilliant jewelry, few seemed prepared for this intrusion and evidently had not sought to review the unknown article during the prior exhibition where it had slumbered unnoticed, - but available. Raised aloft, and unfolded, it excited a universal gasp. The fabric-like paper was luminous under the spotlights, - an ancient browned skin of huge dimension, framed along its borders by decorative embroidery-like figures in the manner of old heraldic deeds or covenants. It stood forth like a huge sheet of money, bank note-of-fortune, strange and magnificent in its sombre haze of mystery. Scarcely did anyone move, as stunned they could not. Few offers were made, the gavel fell, the purchase was sealed, the thing vanished.

Other auctions have gone on, - this went on, - but the new owner as purchaser having prepared himself in his own cloak of anonymity, set forth in time, as though a duplicate of himself to be designated his agent, and he it was who received title as interim. How this was managed, no matter: the incident was at once forgotten, the jewelry rose and fell with the hammer, while the Document made a discreet exit - *in a paper bag.*

One commentary easily overheard came from the disquieted voice of a startled young woman who had been listing her companion's extravagant antique jewel purchases. After she had stared at the Document some restless after-thought flickered by : - said she, --

"It isn't real... It *can't* be real ! ...*or is it?"*

"You will know it by its face", - had been written two centuries before; and still a faint trace of ancient gun-smoke seemed yet lingering over the Document's title - - unnoticed or unknown.

———————⁊   —⋖⋗

The hot excitement of the atmosphere

... knowledge gained through studied observation.

Whence came this unknown Thing from the paper bag I cannot say. That which lies hidden in the security of ownership for many years or generations may be studied and cherished in privacy, but at length through a twist of fate or of a failed inheritance it is found without a home, to be thrust upon the *winds of chance*. In the face of a disaster the lost treasure may have the prospect of a new relation by adoption, but more elusive objects as creations of mind are easily extinguished.

Some of those who frequent the auction room are attracted by opportunity and the enhancement of wealth through trading, while others are in search for the recovery of some fragile work which eludes price but offers a different kind of reward in ownership, together with a satisfying sense of responsibility. The hot excitement of the atmosphere once the pulsations of vigorous enterprise have commenced are known only through experience. Tingling anticipation is generated through sharp uncertainties of outcome in conflicts between unknown assailants of unbridled desire, especially seeking objects of high value.

All of the secret cravings suppressed in taut silence are pitted in contest between a curious mixture of personal aspirations & peculiar lusts of the bidders. The sharp tensions are heightened by stifled disappointments and quashed hopes, softened only by the rhythm of the sequences. One certainty is that the loss of an artwork of an original mind will be a haunting experience for the defeated bidder who will encounter the lost image of his longing in endless dreams.

But the Manuscript's appearance amongst jewelry had broken the rhythm in this theatre so that - whether by celestial guidance or by the pushfinger of luck, - it fell to this waiting hand to guide decisively the prospective agent for the owner, in true purpose toward that obscure treasure, the Document, - so that it could pass through the perils of an auction room & be retrieved unrecognized.

This came about by means of a certain remote knowledge, and a digression here must trace influences unexplainable, but rooted in reality, for it was the knowledge gained through observation and study of original work, with imitation by copying to gain its intricacy as the artist copies the master, that made a sense of recognition of authenticity possible in the face of dubious expert opinion. The Document was said to have been appraised by one with formidable credentials, - but withal, apparently a *neo*-expert, *who knew not that he knew not*. Thence deftly was a rare Document secured and carried off to an unseen person, leaving no trace of recognition, nor of the true value.

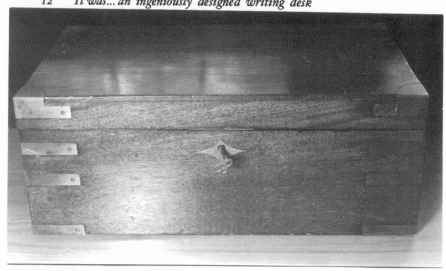

...*an inkwell of exquisite
clear blue glass like
an Aquamarine*

...*the Circle -
as the origin of
Time and Earth measure*

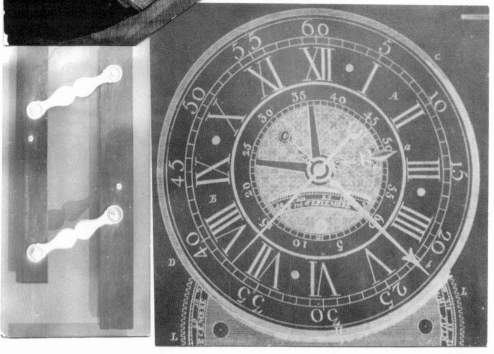

When a Mirror reflected on the Past...
.....

It was long ago said, - that *writing* makes the start for all meaningful existence, - and it was the sensing of this which impressed itself tenaciously upon my small horizon in the earliest years. There came then with that unspoken sentiment, slowly as through an awakening, an antique chest.

It was in the form of an ingeniously designed writing-desk. Having come down from an honored ancestor of Massachusetts it contained, as though intended for one with sense for enigmas, a collection of unusual things for use with a pen, - but also a packet, in a secret drawer, which held a distant message.

The things of use with a pen were unfamiliar by age and their purposes had to be discovered: -a ruler of polished ebony, cylindrical and without numbers; an ink-well of clear blue glass, like a jewel with a gold hinged lid, made for a dwarf; a pen with retractive nib in an embossed tube of lustrous black; a book, "to be sold in Paul's Churchyard at the sign of the Black Bear, London 1632".

Next of all was a flag-cloth, an old browned fabric having printed and colored rectangles or symbols of far-away places, unknown or fanciful one thought with names archaic, forgotten countries long since invaded, -smothered under a diversity of peoples, incompatible with each other when thrown together, never understanding their separate tongues nor communicating, and so in disharmony the invader grinding down the staid old country, - remaking it in a benighted image, -and lost in the memory of a shattered civilization left in flag-cloths of broken peoples.

And last a strange worn device: - in form, two flat strips of polished ebony, hinged together by a pair of silver S's. When the strips were slid in opposition they separated as the pivots turned, the edges remaining parallel in all positions.

The pair formed thus a parallelogram... the straight edges securely parallel at adjustable distance in the range of the S-hinges; - yet this device was not to yield its secret for many a year, though often remembered with a curious lure.

To the geometrical mind the circle may be of first importance, as the origin of our Time- and Earth-measure, for instance, but the parallelogram has the special fascination of harboring laws of shape and proportion, a flexible rectilinear field showing progressive changes of area when squeezed, arranged as an elusive riddle.

What is it? --- It does not tell.

At length, charting a new course...

And then in the chest, what was the Object not of use with the pen but as though formed by it? This forgotten paper was lying in a disguised drawer, to be slid open from the side of the chest after release by retraction of a brass pin under the lid. It was a folded packet, old and wrinkled, which could be unfolded to a single large sheet of writing. It had been signed, not once but many times, with such flourishes that I found copying of the signatures to be absorbing, and learned to repeat the designs with a swing of the pen, and at length adopted the ending loops of one, Hancock, to my own name. But this when shown to an incognizant teacher brought icy silence, so that after detailed memorizing of the shapes of illustrious 18th Century signatures my fabricated art did perish.

All of these little treasures from boyhood had later *vanished*, but their images remained clearly in memory, with new meanings. Amongst this treasure two things held strange fascination; - the riddle of the parallelogram, and the message discovered in the paper, hidden in the secret drawer.

From those distant days there lingered the image of a mysterious figure, who had shown interest in my commentary and in such little discoveries as I could describe.

- Could they be recognized, the tell-tale signatures, and is duplicate shape of signature like fingerprint identification? And would I sell my little chest?

- But I would not... Yet I remembered his face which had first appeared in my Open Mirror, an image falling securely into the recollections of many years.

Times brought change. After long readings of Robinson Crusoe with his deep absorption in adversities, and impressed by his power of imagination to overcome obstacles in *Crusoe-style*, - the lesson of self-reliance became inextinguishable. Those arts of observation essential for personal progress grew from details - minutiae - of the things we secure - taken as it were to shore on our raft, - how they find use through reflection directly aimed at possibility, thereby forcing necessity of effort toward positive achievement. Thus was the singular gift of observation, practiced and polished, - leading to that school of self-teaching wherein *we learn to do all things , make way against all opposition, ask for no favors, forge our native strength and finally gain our independence;* - and so when shipwrecked as it seemed on an island of trade for many a year, I could store self-earned knowledge through observation, at length charting a new course without the yoke of direction-ordering masters.

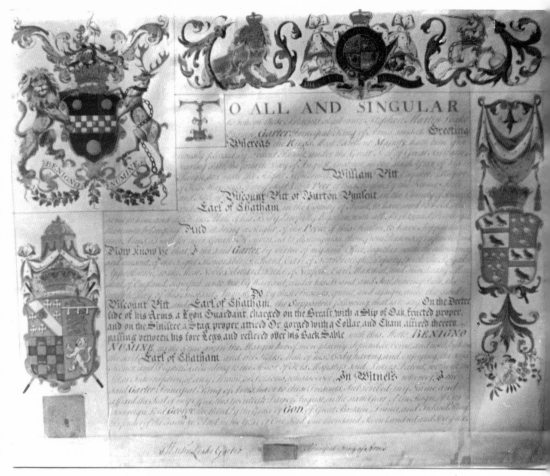

*...Whether symbolism in the 18th century
was an essential feature in documents*

"... the graveyard on the North Slope"

Wherein some early Recollections
were drawn from the Well of Time

Some years later it happened that I could see in the Open Mirror
the strange figure from a misty past. When it was known that I had
the chest, he asked of it, and whether symbolism in the 18th
century still close to the age of heraldry and chivalry was an
essential feature in documents then drawn.

There is connection sure to time-worn thought, tenuously held.

---The presence of symbolism suggests an older reflective mind.

"Applying micro-analytical methods, can duplicating superposed
photos prove authentication, & possibly also suggest origin?"

*Yes... a fragile connection, but sure, the science invaluable, - necessary ,
since Historians may know little of science - and Scientists may know little
of history, - the twain rarely meeting.*

"Then Knowledge from a scientific realm may prove peerless?"

Physical experiments & demonstration speak uniquely in authentications.

"Can the Document truly be secured, within our limit of time,
and can you then authenticate it and write a bookful of it? - yet -
you must understand - you may not play as though Owner."

My role will be as a Candle held against the Darkness.

"Then you should best not be blown out by a *draught*."

I appeared as the Scientist, by profession, and he the real Owner.
Later speaking briefly of the Document he said with emphasis, --

"That it existed was known from history, that it had been hidden
was the secret of the 18th century, that it had been lost and
forgotten was the problem of our own time."

Do you now believe it to be real -- genuine? - I had asked.

"You need not ask. Look upon it: - what do you *see* - or recognize?
Let me relate to you the first impression I had of it...
I was alone in a room when I first began to unfold it. The paper
was old and thick with broken edges. The unfolding had to be done
with greatest care. There was a linen back - unusual stiffness in the
paper, the folds much rounded. The first shock was the enormous
size of the paper when fully unfolded. No such size of manuscript
was ever known to me: -not even Magna Charta is half this size."

The new Owner had given me a scribbled paper to keep as a guide
to a presumed provenance, but now only partially legible: -

Look into the graveyard on the North Slope : --

-- He grew more reserved, having thrown on his dark cloak: and
then came the final note: - I was to receive the bag, close by a
certain wall which he named, with hour and place.

Through a slot in the wall...

In which an Unknown Manuscript appears
-- after two Centuries of Oblivion

⊠

Through a slot in the wall it was handed to me with the expressed warning: -- *Don't lose this!* - It had been folded four times upon itself, then stuffed into a stiff paper bag, and was lying darkly in its own shadows. The bag held restless questions which seemed to whisper:

Who wrote it? -- who hid it? -- who lost it?

With illumination from overhead and partly from behind, this massive Document had shown a luminous brownish skin-like character, as though light were coming through chamois; and yet the markings in ink, both of writing and the penned figures along the borders, were an opaque black, nowhere faded, although the paper had darkened, - if it were paper. When removed to the quietness of a secret place, withdrawn from the bag and unfolded, it seemed muted. The inner luminosity had gone, and the light falling upon the sheet was revealing of aged dusts, archaic of color, the tones distant.

As suspended it had been like a flag, a splendid banner for battle if necessary, - heavy and thick with a lustrous gleam, a latent life within. Unfolded now it lay in mystical silence.

The size when spread covered a grand piano. It was 54 inches of length, 43 of width, seemingly a single sheet. From the underside it was backed by finely woven old linen, holding together the entire mass. Where it had been folded once vertically, once horizontally, then twice again in each direction there appeared the recurrent fold-lines where the paper had become embrittled, cracked and loosed fragments. Where thus weakened there was not continuity remaining to hold the weight closely knit, - yet everywhere else it was firmly together, though stretched and sometimes swollen.

This huge linen-mounted Manuscript bore the signs of private display where nailed within some unknown room, the rusty scars of the nail holes from its escape yet showing where it had been ripped from some unremembered wall to be carried off in flight of desperation. No markings of any kind, nor designations as of extraneous labeling or printing were to be found anywhere upon its margins. The paper though darkened after ages of obscurity must have been of a sterner stuff, originating in rarer papers, enduring from the 18th century whose test of time came from the durability of their honest rags.

The first Quad (quarter part) with 9 portraits on the left margin to the broken foldline & a portion of the second Quad with 2 portraits on the left margin

When first unfolded the Manuscript had the impact of a thunderbolt. On the face was the rare penmanship as from a giant hand: - huge pen lines, - bold, fearless, plainly spoken, which together with searching changes and interlinings showed a work in progress under exacting scrutiny of several critical minds. There appeared thus the unspoken history of the evolution of the text, - what had been written initially, how tentatively revised, then refinished - until the meanings had become increasingly more clear, decisive and complete.

Nor was the design common but appeared as found in ancient Charters, with portraiture at the borders for decoration and authentication. The faces designed to surround and accent the text still seemed to be pondering the meanings, still questioning, even the reader; and thence, as though to tie together in a harmonious completion an urgent message there followed a brace of impassioned signatures, -fifty six of them -colliding and overlapping with staccato definition and swirling flourishes. This was a message that men surely had believed deep into their souls, and must have cherished. It forced attention, defined, and declared. It almost vibrated.

Interwoven round about, and encompassing the faces with harmonious interweaving and kindred knots was a concordant wreath as of a unanimous shared feeling. At the forefront as the masthead five confident faces offered the message in presentation of a courageous work for principle, for posterity. Backing their determination were six partially unfurled flags, unmistakably the signs and signals of the American Revolution.

The symbolism was everywhere, rampant and daring: - a naval ensign for the first ships, the pine tree of Massachusetts Bay, the last British flag diminishing to only a surviving canton in a striped field, the celestial Earth devoid of religious myth, the rattlesnake of Franklin, and last a truly original unknown flag, - a modello for all that might follow.

This Document had been much folded and seemingly much traveled. Its lines of division, oft-repeated as in an old map long in use, were irretrievably broken along boundaries. Yet like a map it could be valued for intrinsic worth as existing uniquely from a time of original inception. Along the lower border a jagged strip of paper had been broken off or taken off and probably lost.

But now appeared an enigma: this Manuscript in unique form, size and design seemed to be totally unfamiliar, yet bore in its penned lines the handwritten text of *the Declaration of Independence*.

V. Jefferson's Rough Draft, page one

V. Jefferson's Rough Draft, page three

V. Jefferson's Rough Draft, page two

V. Jefferson's Rough Draft, page four

The "Rough Draft" laid bare, & what was discovered

--- --- ---

That so large, majestic and important a Manuscript of so familiar a Document had been *concealed* unknown – for two centuries --- was astounding. Knowledge of the Declaration points to several small loosely defined packets of four-pages each in Jefferson's handwriting, - all of letter-size format, drawn in dark brownish ink, - and unsigned. They show the headline *A Declaration by the Representatives...* and are interim copies sent by Jefferson to colleagues, mainly in Virginia, --- Richard Henry Lee, Edmund Pendleton, George Wythe and others. Three of these copies have finally reappeared in libraries. (Pg- 013)

Superior to the interim copies is the *Rough Draft*, -- termed by some the Original, - but mistakenly, as it is simply a Declaration - without title, signatures, or full legibility, and inadequate for the printing of Broadsides of July 4, 1776. It is valued for its indisputable provenance, having been transferred from Jefferson's grandson to the Government after 1830. (Ch- 17)

The Rough Draft was written in 1776 during stormy events in the Colonies under an oppressive Monarchy 3000 miles away. A Committee of Five had been appointed to draft a declaration of independence, comprised of Thomas Jefferson, John Adams, Benjamin Franklin, Roger Sherman and Robert Livingston.

Adams gave the following brief account of the drafting in his Autobiography: -- *"The committee had several meetings, in which were proposed the articles of which the Declaration was to consist, and minutes made of them. The committee then appointed Mr Jefferson and me to draw them up in form... Mr Jefferson desired me to take them to my lodgings and make the draught. This I declined ... He accordingly took the minutes & in a day or two produced to me his Draught."* -- Jefferson however gave a rather different account later: He wrote to Madison in 1823, *"the committee of five met... they pressed on myself to undertake the draught... I consented; I drew it; but before I reported it to the committee I communicated it separately to Dr Franklin and Mr Adams requesting their corrections and you have seen the original paper now in my hands with corrections interlined in their own handwriting. I then wrote a fair copy, reported it to the committee and from them unaltered to the congress"*. According to Carl Becker, -- " that *original paper* of which Jefferson speaks with corrections... interlined in their own handwriting, is commonly known as the Rough Draft."

-- Unexpectedly, that term proves to be an error in identity,-- between two sets of papers having similar textual contents but neither one dated or signed.

    ⦠—< 4-page Rough Draft, Copy of a missing Original Manuscript .

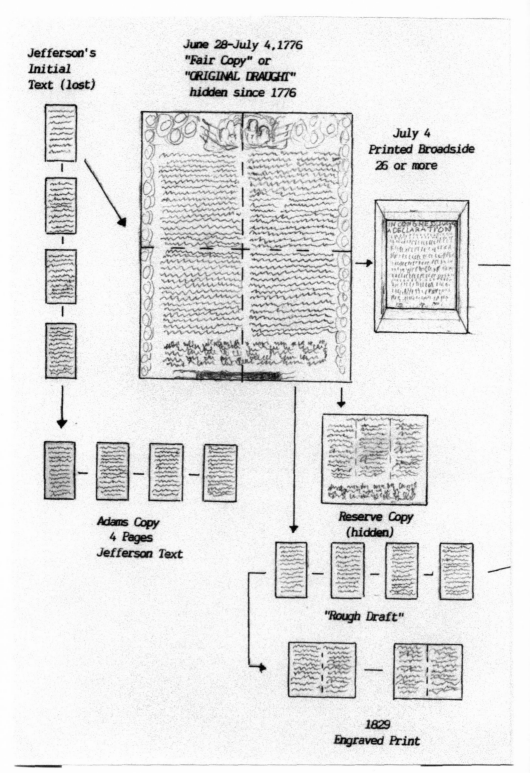

Genealogy of Original Draught

Evidently there were two interlined small copies, with entries by Adams & Franklin on only one, but after Jefferson's demise the term *Rough Draft* was seemingly given to the wrong copy. (Ch- 17)

As already described - the Committee met several times, after which Adams gave the minutes to Jefferson to draft a declaration, which he then wrote as the initial paper, - incomplete, scratched, fragmented and retained by him privately. But that unknown paper does not appear to be the Rough Draft, - rather the paper with interlines by Adams and Franklin, and later apparently lost.

Confusion of identity fell upon the *two* small similar drafts:
  a) Jefferson's initial paper interlined by Adams and Franklin;
  b) a later similar text with all interlines by Jefferson only.

These two different versions should not be mistaken by error of designation. Jefferson referred to an original paper with interlines in different handwritings and cited to Madison, whereas the *Rough Draft* is the term given by historians to the copy now found to have all writing in Jefferson's hand. It is actually a copy-text. It could be termed a *Shadow-copy*.

The early Manuscript texts of the Declaration formed a series:
  1) The initial lost paper, read by Franklin, copied by Adams,
     then annotated by the committee and "copied fair" as
  2) The Fair Copy, or Original Draught from (1), showing all
     corrections, alterations, excisions (then disappearing),
  3) The Adams copy of the initial paper (1) (Ch- 28).
  4) The Rough Draft - or small duplicate of the Fair Copy (Ch- 9).

Historians in appraising the interlines of the Rough Draft, without analysis, have attributed them to different hands, but by photo-enlargement they are evidently by one hand (Ch- 29).

The *corrections* have been confused with the *alterations* and Jefferson has been faulted as to numbers of each because of critics' failures later to distinguish his corrections from alterations, - terms which are not synonymous. *Alteration* adverts to a change of direction or emphasis, and Jefferson was referring to three new paragraphs, - lines 41+, 71+, and 92+, the latter moved to 85 as shown in a marginal note, pg-4 of the text.

The *corrections*, not to be confused with *alterations*, were mainly improvements in wording. They were numerous, and Jefferson did not say otherwise. He showed them by leaving deletions & changes visible as only partially crossed out, & confirming revisions between Adams, Franklin, & Jefferson, - an example of forthright thought in metamorphosis. Later, *all these manuscripts vanished:* -the committee's notes, the initial paper, and even the *Original Draught*.

Four Quads were revealed by cracked boundaries along the midlines

In which four Quads are traced in the Manuscript
◻ ◻ ◻ ◻

It soon became clear that the Unknown Manuscript is much larger than many renowned documents but that a single sheet of paper 54 x 43 inches was probably not available in the 18th century. However several sheets could have been abutted & backed, then glued to form one single composite sheet.

Proof of this possibility came when a fine horizontal ink line was found between lines 34 and 35 of the left column where edges had been joined. Evidently the left column of the text comprised two vertical panels, each 27 inches in height.

The right column also comprised two similar panels, and thus the Manuscript consisted of four contiguous parts with a narrow vertical decorated border running down along the central fold, not interfering with text. The folds could have been set with the intention of avoiding damage to text by isolating it from the folds. The Manuscript had to be compactable for travel, or even for sudden escape.

After the discovery of a four-part composite format, each quarter-part of the Manuscript was designated a *Quad*. Each line of text was numbered so that the 156 lines were apportioned between the four parts, the text reading downward as a book through Quads 1 and 2, then on the right half through 3 and 4. The dimensions of the initial sheets or quarter parts were close to the 18th Century *Elephant folio size*, 28 x 23 inches (71 x 59 cm), with surfaces of unmarred smoothness but increased thickness for durability.

Since Jefferson normally used small thin sheets of common writing paper for notes and correspondence, it seemed probable that his first thoughts on a declaration would flow over several such sheets, - advancing his arguments so as to convince his countrymen of the wrongs of oppression and the *injustices from arbitrary power*. With clarity and sharp example he would thus point to the *necessity for independence*.

The line-length in a script is of basic importance for continuous reading, and depends on the number of letters or words the eye assimilates consecutively in scanning each line, which ranges from about nine to fifteen words in an excellent format. If the length is much greater than this the eye may *double*, that is, may re-read a line because of confusion in returning to the next starting point. Jefferson evidently knew this well, as shown in all of his copies of the Declaration. - Only at the final stage would the text require enlargement of the handwriting.

Quad 1 from Original Manuscript ca. 12% of actual size

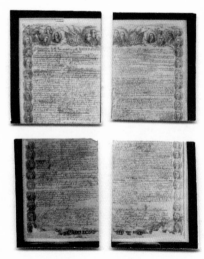

4 Quads from Original Manuscript ca. 3% of actual size each

In the case of important documents the small size of sheet was inadequate for presentation to a Congress of forty-nine members. Jefferson would have seen that a packet of four separate sheets would entail too much shuffling when referring to different parts. As a surveyor and an architect familiar with map-making and drawings on large paper it would have been natural for him to set together four small sheets as a composite, and then estimate requirements for a large presentation copy for the Congress.

An effective arrangement would show the sheets -one and -two of four in a first column, adjoining sheets three and four in a second column. This display could be seen all at once, - but would require also as stated, that the size of writing be increased several fold for readability, thus increasing the paper size. The entire text would then appear as one large composite of four sections, to be easily read by a congressional group around a table.

The Magna Charta in its several versions in the 13th century (*1215 & 1225 AD*), was written on large sheets, as were other Charters later for reading by numbers of people simultaneously. This single sheet form also includes the legal advantage that one set of signatures sufficed for one large document, but not easily with several separate sheets.

Important state documents were usually *engrossed,* a term meaning to make a large copy of a legal instrument in careful formal handwriting. *The Fair Copy* (= a copy *in a large clear hand*) was the term Jefferson used to characterize his *Original Draught* from the various primitive papers handled in committee and the later small interim copies drawn for his colleagues after the initial printing of the Broadside on the night of July 4th 1776. (Ch- 25)

The Quads of the Manuscript were seen to be framed panels with decorated portraiture in the side columns, a row of olive branches as a dividing border, a masthead along the top, and a brace of signatures in a large section above the lower border.

Division of the Manuscript into four Quads was useful for photographic precision wherein the recording of original text on large negatives (4 x 5 inches) was necessary for printing of full-scale (1 : 1) photo-facsimiles. Two negatives were used to cover each Quad, or eight large negatives for the entire Manuscript.

To calibrate the huge size of the Manuscript, several rulers were mounted flat along each side during the photography, so that in the enlarging process from the negatives the true size could be adjusted to the proportion exactly 1 : 1 , -- or so that one inch of true scale appeared in the print as exactly one true inch.

Enlarged oblique view of Manuscript, lower right section

The arrangements for photography were of crucial importance for representation of the Manuscript's readability, and also for true representation of its damaged areas, including correct rendering of its swollen contours, folds and weathered surface character, - thus to reveal a very old & for mysterious reasons, a much hunted and besieged fugitive document even from its inception. When fine details are faithfully magnified photographically some secrets may be revealed of the methods & purposes applied during the creation.

The handling of the illumination in the photography of this old Manuscript was varying in character. It was intended to reveal the message and the display as clearly and as perfectly as possible, for which purpose the illumination was diffused and spread inward from all sides so that shadows of irregularities would not show. With this type of lighting the Manuscript appears flat and not properly venerable, while the true state of its deterioration may not be emphasized. This method was used initially for large photo facsimiles for test analysis.

The disadvantage with this type of idealized representation is that the viewer if hurried or if not versed in photographic lighting effects will fail to appraise correctly the antique character of the object, and from inexperience misunderstand what he is seeing and voice a shallow judgment.

To show more truly the condition with aged wrinkles, folded bulges, tears and swollen or stretched areas, the light was directional from the north sky upon the Manuscript lying on the floor. In this case the natural distortions and cracking of the old paper made the ancient character convincingly realistic, and a truer picture of the fragile state was seen.

For a more exaggerated view of surface topography the guiding of the light was narrowed to a low grazing angle, and then the surface distortions became dramatically enhanced.

The disadvantages of a naturalistic illumination lie in the difficulties of coping photographically with the varying paper reflectances and colors from age, stains, or various faults.

The infinitely variable character of the incident light in the illumination of works of art on paper makes possible a deeper understanding of their character and history, and even some of the facets of their interpretation.

The faithful preservation of this single fair Manuscript by photo-facsimile for future purposes in its venerable authenticity, without cosmetic tampering as "restoration", has been a continuing concern here for the sake of historical truth.   —·—·—

Cartouche for the Fry-Jefferson Map of Virginia & Maryland drawn by Thomas Jefferson's father in 1751 (publ. 1755) on map paper in 4 parts as also later with Jefferson's "Original Draught" in its 4 Quads

The Carolina Charter in the tradition of English royal documents: A portrait of Charles II at the masthead with oval figures suggesting the design of Jefferson's "Original Draught"

Why the Declaration should appear on Map-paper - in 4 Quads and why it was decorated with a Portraiture

———— ✦ ————

Thomas Jefferson's ancestors had lived in Virginia for several generations when in 1708 Peter Jefferson was born, and he would become the father of Thomas. He had settled in Fine Creek near Tuckahoe. Owing to the need for surveying large areas of land, Peter Jefferson as a young man formed a partnership with Joshua Fry, an English immigrant. In 1737 they began surveyings of the very large Fairfax Estate which was said to exceed 50 000 acres.

Peter Jefferson through his maternal grandmother was related to a land-owning Randolph family, and by 1741 Peter had purchased Shadwell from William Randolph, having married Jane Randolph earlier. In 1743 Thomas Jefferson was born, his father then moving to Shadwell to manage the Randolph estate, where Thomas was also to live, at least until his ninth year.

Peter Jefferson with Joshua Fry had by this time embarked on a large and difficult surveying project - through unsettled wilderness areas - to determine the boundaries of a huge tract, and after this project had been successfully completed, Jefferson and Fry with an assisting party undertook to survey a more immense territory, which was completed in 1751, yielding "a map of the most inhabited parts of Virginia", with adjacent parts of Pennsylvania, New Jersey and North Carolina. The map was published in 1755 as the Fry-Jefferson map of Virginia.

After Fry was placed in command of the Virginia forces under Braddock against the French, with George Washington as his Lieutenant Colonel, he became ill and died, - leaving to Peter Jefferson his surveying instruments, books and mapping supplies. In the following year Peter Jefferson published their map, but two years later he died, and Thomas Jefferson inherited a complete surveyor's inventory of instruments with maps, map-paper, and surely a pantograph as a very important instrument in the drawing and combining parts of large maps. He also inherited 5000 acres of land including the promontory which he would call Monticello.

Jefferson's "Notes on Virginia" show his exact knowledge of maps including boundaries of the state of Virginia: "This state is therefore one-third larger than the islands of Great Britain & Ireland ... reckoned at 88357 square miles."- His view is clear: An inspection of a map of Virginia will give a better idea of the geography than any description in writing".

In his view, England was too small to rule a distant continent.

※ —✦— ※

*Manuscript's first Quad superimposed on 1797 Map of the
New World showing identical sizes of the two papers, 28"x 21«"*

Jefferson kept his large supply of paper of various sizes and types by the trunkful, and he would surely have considered small sheets of rough laid paper as unsuitable for the Declaration except for writing the early drafts. With a copy of the Fry-Jefferson map in his possession, his attention must have been drawn to map-paper for a major Document, considering Magna Charta, colonial charters and military maps, all in large formats.

As the Declaration was to be studied and debated by Congress a sharp focus on map-paper was inevitable, and the large sizes of such paper would have seemed ideal for an enlarged text easily read by the members of Congress standing near it; but Jefferson's creative visual perspective would also have desired a framing, - and here was an opportunity to create decorative borders as then frequently found on charters and old maps; and it would have been natural for Jefferson to select Francis Hopkinson as the one practicing artist in Congress equipped to do what he himself could not do alone by free-hand drawing such as portraiture. The form and design of the Document could thus emerge with decorative borders, and with the artist a plan for full portraiture was inevitable as this would substantiate authentication far beyond signatures alone. A few signatures may be copied but when combined with corresponding portraits they are more definitive, as in the modern driver's license.

Hopkinson's study in England of designs of charters and heraldic symbols would have led to the impressive decorations at the masthead. The form of the 1663 charter of South Carolina indicates oval figures along the sides with a display at the head as analog to the Manuscript's design.

Even before the invention of wove paper, map-papers were far superior in surface smoothness to plain writing paper, with advantages essential for decoration. Map drawings require precise delineation of embellishments, with figures and symbols from distant countries of differing peoples -showing remote places with examples of the inhabitants. Thus the style of the document could fit the character of the men founding the government. Collections of maps of the 18th century also show that maps were often drawn on 2 or 4 sheets abutted & overlapping from behind, and some old maps have unit dimensions close to those of the Quads of the Manuscript. *According to Records of the Map division of the New York Public Library*, the original Fry-Jefferson Map may no longer exist, and its exact size is unknown (presumably nearly Elephant Folio). But the earliest copies are from *four plates* called "the English plates", from which fact the form of the map was in *4 parts* exactly as with the *4 Quads of the Original Manuscript of the Declaration of Independence*.

Jefferson's Telescope

Surveyor in Action

In a study of thicknesses of different kinds of paper it was noted that old writing paper ranged from 0.08 to 0.14 mm, but that map papers were two to three times these thicknesses. One particular copy of the Fry-Jefferson map was measured as 0.19 to 0.20 mm thick at borders & 21 x 28 inches in area - a size approaching the old *Elephant folio size*.

A special feature of the paper of the Manuscript is its thickness. This has been measured with micrometers as 0.40 to 0.48 mm on typical areas near borders where not underlaid by linen. The paper cross-section shows a double-layer structure.

Each of the separate sheets are about double the thickness of ordinary old writing papers, or twice 0.08 to 0.14 mm. Thus the thickness of the Manuscript exclusive of linen equals two sheets of double thickness, glued together, or 2x 0.24 = 0.48 mm, equaling, in total, four times an ordinary sheet's thickness.

The Quads are not identical, the first being larger. The four are abutted together, retaining strength in joints by backing quads of differing sizes. As glued, each inner margin of a Quad is overlapped behind, & thus signatures appear on a single strong composite sheet.

Mapping was the key used in designing the settlements and connecting trade routes in North America and was practiced not only by Jefferson but by some other leaders in the Colonies. Mapping in the wilderness was a dangerous and time-consuming occupation - and a valuable training for the young men of the times. It was a necessary asset in Washington's career, and an honorable profession requiring basic knowledge of mathematics, geometry, astronomy, mechanics, and clear expository writings

———

Ownership of land was of high importance in the Colonies and surveying provided the basis under law. Land ownership largely determined the distribution of voting privileges, - a needed criterion for distinguishing between industrious and thrifty people who contribute to the tax support, and those who make no contributions to the land or the common good, and without enterprise are often a burden on a Colony. Mankind has always been festooned with *Parasites* of which the worst are a human species who frequent cities to prosper by *trading voting support* to politicians for increasing handouts, - an evil not accepted in the Colonies, but one now serving to perpetuate rascals in office for the moral degradation & ruin of the entire nation. By promoting indolent parasitic mobs of people, politicians are ravaging the manners and spirit of America unto Death: -- For "It is *the manners and spirit* of a people which preserve a republic in vigour," as Jefferson wrote, -- so feelingly - and prophetically.   ———

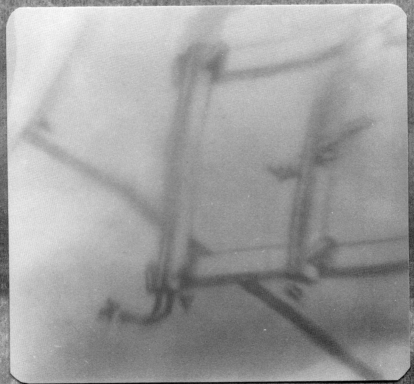

On a Geometric Thing in Space

A Thought not yet unveiled as real from sleep
Flickered below full consciousness, and seemed
To hover behind some curtain vaguely dreamed,
Fast held within its shape, a vision to keep.

Elusive as it was, it vanished once
Or twice, then reappeared to tempt the eye;
One reached for it, then lost it with a sigh
As though forgotten it had been for nonce.

It formed a geometric thing in space,
A strangely fashioned object, drawn, defined: -
Came abstract waves, - thin, nebulous, of mind,
Surrounding concepts intricate as lace.

It may not yet be fathomed how 'tis wrought --
The Mystery of substance made from Thought.

* * ⁂ * *
*   *
*

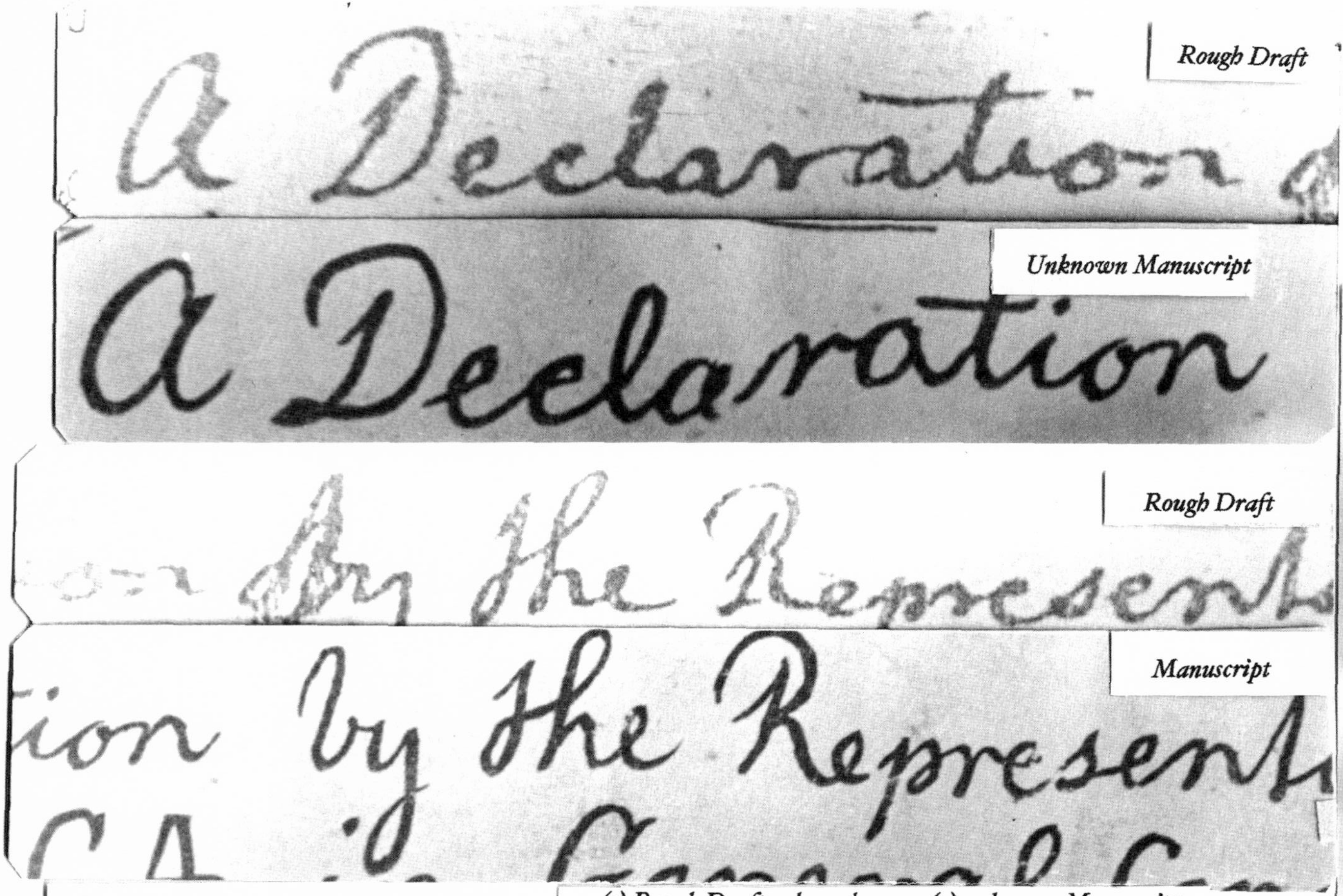

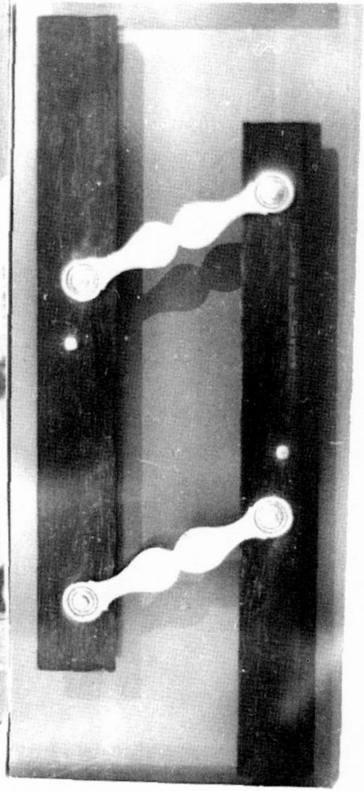

Comparison of handwritings in Headline: (1) Rough Draft enlarged versus (2) unknown Manuscript

Rough Draft

Unknown Manuscript

Rough Draft

Manuscript

How Superposed Handwritings can provide
Exact Authentication

For more than a century the four-page Rough Draft, with the crowded text confined in width to six-inch columns, has inspired academic studies of the Declaration, as seemingly the closest to an unknown original source. That it is overloaded with cramped lines of writing, tapering to illegibility, has not diminished a stream of the interpretations concerning it from flowing into history books. Without a title, but capped by the unspecifying provisional headline -- *A Declaration by the Representatives...* , its exact relation to a later abridged text on Parchment has left unanswered the questions of how 48 Congressman gathered around a table could have shaped this pocket-sized memo into form adequate for a printer, without the use of hand lenses to clarify obscure interpolations and to find space for the missing title as of its published July 4th date.

Inevitably, the Rough Draft had to be compared precisely with the unknown Manuscript. Although smaller, at a scale of only 3 : 8, the wording of its text was found identical to the Manuscript's, and also its corrections and alterations. Where overwriting or deletions by crossings out had been inserted in the Rough Draft, there were similar ones in the Manuscript, - and all of the details corresponded precisely in these parallel cases.

While comparisons were being made, an arresting geometric resemblance of shapes between the two separate texts began to form in one's visual memory. There were seen to be some startling similarities between the small headline of the Rough Draft and the large one of the Manuscript. The opening words in each case appeared to rise slightly as though on an invisible wave of the paper. Both headlines were tapered and also narrowed to the right.

Pursuing this geometric similarity in a midnight hour when imagined patterns of a relationship were too persistent to pass, a negative of the Rough Draft's top line was projected optically as an enlarged image onto a positive photoprint of the Manuscript's corresponding line. The sizes of the images were equalized by relative enlargement of the smaller one, and then they were superimposed, - the white light from transparent lines through the negative falling upon the opaque black shadow lines on the positive print. With precise adjustment of magnification & alignment of images, the duplicate headlines - *"A Declaration by..."* - became *coincident:* - by superimposition, the twin images had coalesced as one. and thus the composite image of the texts formed a reinforced or quasi three-dimensional relief, against darkness.

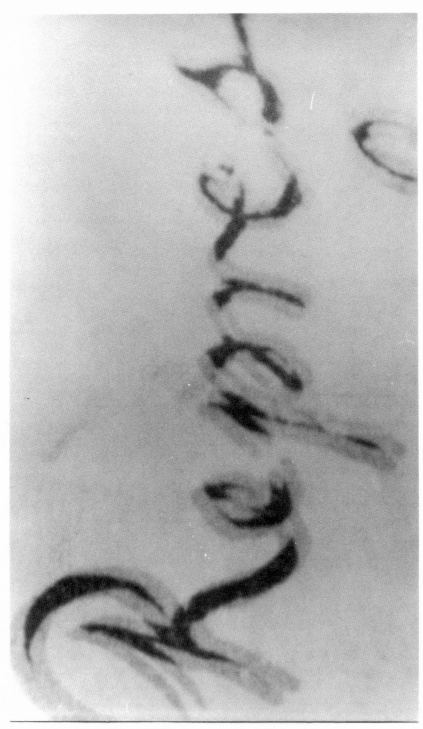

Superimposition of "Representatives" in headlines:
Unknown Manuscript on enlarged Rough Draft
near-coincidence throughout: Exact in dark areas.

Since the separate lines of the two texts had thus been fused together optically, it was interpreted that they had originated from a single source. The similarity of patterns with only minute deviations from exactness pointed unmistakedly to one as having evolved from the other by a duplicating *mechanical writing device*, thereby separating their relative importance into large and small, - primary and secondary - *original and copy*.

The strange relief-image lingering in mind was explainable as the known effect in optics which occurs when two similar images are superimposed, with one minutely displaced from the other in parts and providing thus a shadowing effect to be seen as though in third dimension, --- dramatically apparent, for example --- in interference microscopy. But here the effect with the manuscript images also confirmed that, although closely similar, they were distinctly less precise than photographic copies: -- i.e., they were more primitive and approximate than would have resulted from a precise photo translation. In fact, neither manuscript could have been a photo-copy or photographic derivative of the other, - proven by numerous small misfits in further superimpositions.

... Amongst the antique objects in the little chest out of the past, two things had possessed special fascination; - the riddle of the parallelogram, and the message within the secret drawer.

It was especially that curious worn device that had impinged upon subconscious thought in recollection: - two flat strips of ebony, hinged together by silver S's attached with pins so that when pushed in opposition the separating edges remained parallel, comprising thus a flexible parallelogram. Although not showing its secret plainly, it was recalled through lure of suggestion, tempting that it might at last speak. --

The parallelogram has the feature of following laws of shape and proportion, as a variable rectilinear field showing systematic changes of area when squeezed, and it provides by extension a geometrical method for guiding triangles, small and large but similar, upon a common base to create similarities at different scales. Thus from the uncommon powers of the parallelogram, a device based upon it may be anticipated which could have been used by Jefferson as scientist to create mechanical copies from a manuscript to form a copy-draft as a facsimile, but at reduced scale without photography.

This duplicating effect is directly identified with the parallelogram mechanism called the *Pantograph*, or Stork's beak, - familiar to artists, architects & draftsmen since the 17th century but not always familiar to laymen, or even to many historians.

Inspice et fac secundum exemplar

Wherein Writings authenticate by duplicating Shape -
ᘐ ——— ᘐ

The Pantograph was described seemingly for the first time by the German astronomer Christopher Scheiner, in his book written in Latin and published in 1631 in Italy. He had actually invented and named the instrument while he was living in the town of Dillingen, Swabia, in 1603 or before. It then had the special endowment of having been born in a dream, as is often the case in the graphic thoughts of those who are gifted with powers of visualizing geometric fantasy, wherein semblances of solid creations of one's mysterious psyche are vividly fabricated, even purposefully, arranged as on a kind of retinal video-screen of the mind, showing a moving series of abstract designs, until they coalesce into a hitherto unknown device.

It was not that Scheiner had set out on a journey of sleep to find such a creation but that a painter had one day come to him, saying *he had a Thing for the copying of an object, for use in Art*, but would not tell anything of it. And so Scheiner, in puzzlement, searched in his thoughts for many days to solve his curiosity, until it chanced that out of the *mysteries of sleep* his subconscious intimations did fashion a device in space, written upon the black of night.

While this mental invention of his was to prove in reality profoundly unprecedented in concept, and of high value in both the arts and sciences, Scheiner's far-sight progressed after this even so far that he would be, with Galileo, the first to discover and to speculate upon those celestial extravagances which became known as sun-spots. Yet one must here note that despite his fantastic achievements of mind he has not been adequately remembered, nor has his invention of the *Pantograph* been recognized as widely as its ingenuity and use warrant.

After Scheiner described his imagined invention to the painter he was told it was not the Thing secreted by the painter nor similar, and that would remain the secret of the painter. Yet we may suppose that it could have been a modificatio of the *camera obscura*, known to Leonardo da Vinci from earlier time, - and equipped with a mechanism to provide a tracing as a copy, effectively by following the details of an image already projected upon a darkened screen by the antique instrument. Such a device would have represented the painter's words, but it was not the pantograph. -- Yet Leonardo anticipated one, when he wrote in 1490, *"If a Thing is placed near another, superposing it, and there is no excess between them, they will be equal to one another."*   — ᘏ— ᘏ —

48

*Christopher Scheiner
and his Pantograph*

The design principle of Scheiner's pantograph is based upon the geometric characteristics of a large flexible triangle which contains a parallelogram coinciding along two of its sides, and bears reference points along its hypotenuse, one at each end, and the third where it intersects an arm of the parallelogram. The alternate sides of the parallelogram remaining parallel when the figure is squeezed or extended by moving the point O or T, the large triangle and the small one enclosed within it remain similar at all times. The details need now to be followed closely:

In reference to the figure, reproduced here from Scheiner, we infer as follows: - On the front (left) there is a pivot Q-X whereby the entire mechanism can be revolved and also elongated in either direction about this pivot as a center. The two principle arms of the parallelogram E-F and F-G joined at the pivot K-Y at the point F are extended considerably beyond the secondary arms at E and G, reaching N and P, so that now an imaginary straight line can be drawn between two adjustable points N and P on these extremities passing through the pen placed vertically at O on one of the shorter arms, E-H. It is seen that this line has completed and has become the base for two similar triangles formed upon it.

One of these triangles N-E-O has an apex O on the left secondary arm E-H, while the large triangle N-F-P has an apex at P on the right arm F-P. When the pointer P-T is moved, to scan a figure drawn on the paper b-c-d, the entire mechanism swivels about the pivot at Q-X which holds to a fixed point. By the theorems of similar triangles, the pen mounted at O describes the same path of travel on its smaller paper at a reduced scale as that being followed at T of the large figure.

The fixed laws of the parallelogram require the triangles to remain similar in all positions. The radii of curvature for the pen and point respectively remain in a precisely fixed proportion, so their travel patterns are exactly similar, - i.e. they duplicate geometrical shapes when moved. When the triangles are rotated round a common pivot, the apex of one will duplicate the other's pattern in all intricacies:- axiomatically, a Thing... placed near another, superposing it, and no excess between, they will be equal.

Later an engineer designed a pantograph for the King of France, described in Diderot's *Encyclopédie*, - in the volume published in 1763, with large illustrations. Fine examples appeared in Europe, especially in Germany, proving it to be an instrument indispensable in art, architecture and science.

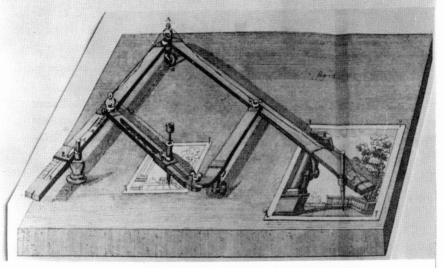

French Pantograph from "La Encyclopédie"

German "Storchschnabel" (Stork's beak)
Courtesy Deutsches Museum, Muenchen

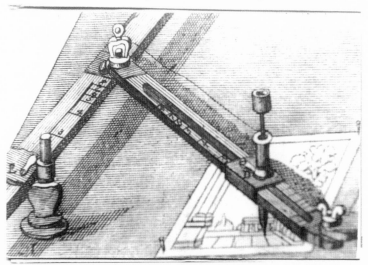

Detail of
French Pantograph

In proceeding now from Scheiner's essential geometric drawing, as representing the underlying principle, we find direct application in the French instrument shown in *La Encyclopédie*. The actual performance is as follows: The arms glide on ivory wheels or rollers, and pivot points. The four principal corners are designed to swivel. A writing pen with integral reservoir is shown vertically at the front in the lower left arm, retractable by means of threads when the intention is to interrupt the writing. The tracing point is at the right front where it is resting on a large architectural figure, copied at a reduced scale by pen.

Great attention is paid to the pivots to avoid excess motion. With a well made instrument, handwriting can be copied with only minor errors produced by slight clearances in the various pivots and by the elasticity of the main members. The fidelity of the copy is excellent to a casual glance but when studied closely the discrepancies are inescapable.

Francis Hopkinson was familiar with *La Encyclopédie* and had corresponded with Thomas Jefferson concerning information in it. Both would have been familiar with the pantograph from its large illustrations shown there, from their work as artist and architect. After later correspondence Jefferson exchanged pantographs with John Trumbull in connection with work on the painting of the *Signing of the Declaration... of July 4 1776*.

The Pantograph gave Jefferson a means for exact duplication of original manuscripts at any scale, assuring him of the precise form of his handwriting in a small copy as a desk-memo for editing of a text during its evolution. The duplication of his handwriting guaranteed unquestioned authenticity. Other methods of duplication were unknown in 1776: - the polygraph was not yet invented and could not make reduced-scale copies. The possible use of the pantograph in transcribing partially but incompletely the small interim copies of the Declaration may be a key for the fact that they are peculiarly similar, and a clue to the frequent ingenious exchanging of *and* with *&*, to equalize spacing.

The Rough Draft has authenticity proven through inheritance. Thence from the discovery that it had been copied directly from the unknown Manuscript by pantographic transfer at a reduced scale, the Manuscript as *the Fair Copy,* with 56 original signatures and its original contemporary portraiture, is evidently the unknown lost *Original Draught of the Declaration of Independence*; and Jefferson's grandson had termed the Rough Draft, "a Copy of the Original Draught of the Declaration ". (Ch-17)

Original Draught without errors

Copy errors enlarged from Rough Draft

Rough Draft

Original Draught

When a writing-Pen wavers it shows Transfer Error

The Pantograph joints during operation have a small play in the pivots whenever the angles of the arms change, allowing the arms to show a lateral discrepancy in the path of a circle when drawn, an error resulting from a lapse in the pivot when the copying arm reverses direction. The result is that such letters, as *a, b, e, l, o,* show narrower loops in a copy than in the original, with distortion added from arm elasticity.

In the Rough Draft the copying process resulted in complete closure of some loops of the vowels which are narrow but open in the Original Draught - consistent with the effects described above for the pantograph joints. Thus some mechanically made errors as loop-closures are seen in the Rough Draft.

Further pantographic peculiarities are to be found in the Rough Draft, as in the opening title - *A Declaration by...* where the third word is garbled and has been interpreted as *'of' & 'by'*. Such a transfer error would result if the copy-pen were not fully lifted during transfer and slid downward, creating a confusing shape, as would be expected if Jefferson had not become well-practiced in his manuscript-copying by instrument.

Other copy faults in the Rough Draft include multiple crossings of pen and vibration smudges, with instances where the pen failed to write at the start of a word, so missing ink-lines had to be added to complete single letters, -- effects not found in the Original Draught.

In the Rough Draft where the writing is nearly too small to be fully legible, it is evident that an enlarged copy could not have been created by a *reversed* transfer-- e.g., from the small text to a large one -- because in copying, the source must be fully legible. The loss of fidelity is always in the direction of the transfer.

Jefferson's use of a pantograph would have ornamented his architecture, since from books the instrument opened direct access to classical forms for simple transfer into drawings of new structures. Use of the mechanism may thus have assisted his classical designing related to masterworks of Antiquity. When designing he wrote, *"Palladio* is my constant companion".

As an old art, pencil tracing preceded pantography but was limited to copying at the original scale. In the *camera obscura* images could be projected by a lens and traced over glass, thus copying at variable scales as with a pantograph. Early drawings of the Scheiner mechanism illustrate its uses in combination with optical devices, producing copies of three-dimensional objects.

he has forbidden his governors to
unless suspended in their op
and when so suspended, he ha
he has refused to pass other laws
unless those people would re
inestimable to them & form
he has called together legislative bodi
the depository of their public recor
with his measures,
he has dissolved Representative ho
manly firmness his invasio
he has refused for
whereby the legislative powers
the people at large for their
exposed to all the dangers of
he has endeavored to prevent the
obstructing the laws for natura
to encourage

THOS. NELSON. JR.

SAM'L ADAMS

M. HUNTINGTON

line 41 - adjacent to Samuel Adams on Manuscript:
"he has called together legislative bodies at places unusual"

...the celebrated Boston Tea-Party for his Patriot friends

Why an Error in the Rough Draft was hidden by a Collage

The discovery that the Rough Draft text is *geometrically similar* to the Declaration's full original text was the initial basis for the perception that the Draft had been pantographed at a reduced scale from the Original Draught, and suggests why it had been mistaken for its prototype. It has been valued uniquely as an essential copy text during committee editing, & as a primary reference, - although appearing in form too small to be read easily by a full Congress, & written without title or signature, with ordinary ink on cheap paper.

In the Rough Draft two new paragraphs as alterations are nearly indecipherable, having been inserted during editing by Jefferson from Committee suggestions, but this illegibility is simply the result of their having been transferred at a reduced scale from additions of text in the Original Draught already squeezed in with smaller handwriting. The Pantograph could not reproduce legibly through a double reduction of size. A few lines were partly garbled. Jefferson by not anticipating numerous changes had not allowed space in the design for suggested alterations as additional text.

The third alteration of the Declaration was added on page-1 of the Rough Draft, and has interest from its proximity in the Original Draught to the portrait of Samuel Adams, - viewing it as alluding to one of his Colony's grievances. The text from line 41 referring to king George III reads:

> *he has called together legislative bodies at places*
> *unusual, uncomfortable and distant from*
> *the depository of their public records, for the sole*
> *purpose of fatiguing them into compliance*
> *with his measures.*

This repression was instituted under Governor Hutchinson in Massachusetts Bay as a public punishment, making meetings of the legislature difficult, which was the ugly design behind it, - requiring long rides on horseback by the towns people to the country, even in foul weather, to conduct essential business.

This addition as an alteration may have been suggested by Samuel Adams who had become an object of British criticism in the midst of New England turmoil. He had escaped the Tower in the previous year and was increasingly known for his resolute resistance, - especially at Lexington and Concord on April 19, 1775 when he escaped capture after Paul Revere's warning, and also at Boston harbor where he had entertained on the water at an evening tea party with his patriot friends.

... a collage on Rough Draft, 3 lines pasted on

Crude modern Pantograph copying photos of Rough Draft from Original

Attention is now drawn to a curious little collage on the 2nd page of the Rough Draft where Jefferson wrote 3 lines of text on a strip of paper and pasted these on top of lines 43-45 already written normally, but in an incorrect sequence, lines 40-42 having been skipped. In the Original Draught these lines are shown in correct order without crowding, but in the Rough Draft the superposed lines, attached as by a hinge on one side, covered the original ones. Later the end of the strip was also pasted and so when lifted, part of the strip including some text was lost.

This improvised patchwork of Jefferson's may be understood by presuming the Rough Draft had been transferred by pantograph from the Original Draught before assembly of the four large Quad sheets into a single one, & during transfer a copy error occurred through proportioned differences in the unlike formats.

The proportion of height/width as for a square or rectangle is known as the aspect ratio, and because the Original Draught is single-spaced and the Rough Draft double-spaced, the aspect ratios are different. Thus although the texts are identical, line by line, their numbered lines do not coincide at the ending of each page or quad. The Rough Draft's first page ends three lines ahead of the Original Draught's first Quad, and this line difference is the amount of the error leading to a collage. The skipped lines are evidently the result of a *copying omission* during transfer of text to the Rough Draft, from the Original Draught as the initially correct source.

Since it is established that the Rough Draft duplicates the textual content of the Original Draught, allowing for misplaced sentences of the collage after line 40, a notable feature of the later engraved copy is that it shows the collage lines of the text not as appended but in the order of the Original Draught (Ch-17). This correction substantiates that the collage was a result of a copy omission, with the missing lines pasted in,, but to show the lines in correct order on the plate to be engraved, new space had to be allowed. This extension is shown on page-2 of the fac-simile (*T.J. Randolph, Memoir... 1830).*

In order for the interlinear spacing to be adjusted during copying, a re-alignment was necessary from the start of each line of the Rough Draft, leading to a difference in starting positions laterally between the two separate texts, line by line. For a proper adjustment the paper for the small text could have been shifted slightly to bring each line closer to correspondence.. Actually some minute differences in corresponding starting positions appear in the two texts for each pair of corresponding lines.

Rough Draft with slanting lines & miniature notations

At this point it is to be noticed that along the left-hand margin on page-1 of the Rough Draft are three slanting lines drawn apparently from a point opposite line 12 of the text, and not quite even, as though attached from a separate paper strip for measuring; and also some miniature marginal notations had been added - *hand (writing)* - but not written completely in this copy. These lines are not shown in some published copies.

The texts in the case of the original and the copy require proportioning of their spatial arrangements so that they fill the areas of the two sizes of sheet, with one text single-spaced & the other text double-spaced. The slanting lines on the margin may comprise a proportioning scale for use with the mechanical instrument in laying out the format of the copy.

The geometric relationship between the Original Draught and the small Rough Draft may be expressed by measuring similar lines horizontally in the two cases and interlinear spacing vertically. Unfortunately, printed facsimiles of manuscripts may be without size-scales, such as are necessary for geometric analysis.

The format for the Original Draught's quads results in the width of the text block as nearly equal to the height. With portraiture and decorations the space of the text was limited almost to a square. The text block of the Rough Draft without portraiture & designed for a double-spaced format resulted in more space between lines. Thus in the small text, space remained for changes, while in the Original Draught the lesser interlinear space limited insertions to a small size, with slight overlapping, but larger than in the copy.

While the ratio of the line-length of the Original Draught to that of the Rough Draft is 8 : 3, the ratio of the interlinear spacings is obviously different, with a result that to the eye the text of the Rough Draft has been *opened* to a double spacing, for purposes of editing. It is found that the ratio of the two texts vertically on the line spacing is 1.8 : 1. The aspect ratios are thus different, which accounts for the inexact geometric similarity to the eye.

For readers hesitant to accept the notion of pantographic methods for hand copying of 18th century manuscripts, it should be noted that 20th-century copying processes in typography have included pantographic transfer methods from large drawings, yielding accurate dies and punches for micro-scale precision, - the same in principle as the transfer of handwriting with a like instrument. To reduce large handwritten text to a smaller size by pantographic transfer mechanically in the 18th century was then as practical as photo-copying is today by image transfer through a lens.

A DECLARATION

BY THE REPRESENTATIVES OF THE

UNITED STATES OF AMERICA,

IN GENERAL CONGRESS ASSEMBLED.

WHEN in the Courfe of human Events, it becomes neceffary for one People " to diffolve the Political Bands which have connected them with another," and to affume among the Powers of the Earth, the feparate and equal Station " to which the Laws of Nature and of Nature's God entitle them," a decent Refpect to the Opinions of Mankind requires " that they fhould declare the caufes which impel them to the Separation.

We hold thefe Truths to be felf-evident, " that all Men are created equal," " that they are endowed by their Creator with certain unalienable Rights," that among thefe are Life, Liberty, and the Purfuit of Happinefs—-That to fecure thefe Rights, Governments are inftituted among Men, " deriving their juft Powers from the Confent of the Governed," that whenever any Form of Government becomes deftructive of thefe Ends, " it is the Right of the People to alter or to abolifh it, and to inftitute a new Government," laying its Foundation on fuch Principles, and organizing its Powers in fuch Form, as to them fhall feem moft likely to effect their Safety and Happinefs." Prudence, indeed, will dictate that Governments long eftablifhed fhould not be changed for light and tranfient Caufes; and accordingly all Experience hath fhewn, that Mankind are more difpofed to fuffer, while Evils are fufferable, than to right themfelves by abolifhing the Forms to which they are accuftomed. But when a long Train of Abufes and Ufurpations, purfuing invariably the fame Object, evinces a Defign to reduce them under abfolute Defpotifm, it is their Right, to throw off fuch Government, and to provide new Guards for their future Security." Such has been the patient Sufferance of thefe Colonies; and fuch is now the Neceffity which conftrains them to alter their former Syftems of Government. The Hiftory of the prefent King of Great-Britain is a Hiftory of repeated Injuries and Ufurpations, all having in direct Object the Eftablifhment of an abfolute Tyranny over thefe States. To prove this, let Facts be fubmitted to a candid World.

The declaration on the Broadside

The unknown Manuscript as the Original Draught
- and as the Fair Copy

The writing of history becomes an illusive thing after starting with a single account of what was seen or told and then altering this through later designs. Modified versions   may appear from each of several successive generations, each having their own historical views, rewritten inventively. With alternatives from prejudice or even from   *revenge*, historical accounts multiply inaccuracies,   promoted for novelty or *political advantage*.

In the 20th century some writers have looked away from some 18th century facts as myth, with their sharp denials of Jefferson's account of the signing of the Declaration, necessarily on July 4, 1776. A few perceptive writers have foreseen a missing element, or even *a veil of mystery* overlying two centuries. Professor Carl Becker has raised justifiable questions concerning some historical denials:

" *The Declaration as finally adopted is... in the Journals of Congress; but that fair copy which Jefferson speaks of as the report of the Committee of Five has not been preserved; while the original Rough Draft... seems to have been used by Jefferson as a memorandum upon which to note later changes.*
" *It is possible that Jefferson was mistaken in thinking that he made a fair copy for the committee... if there was no fair copy, we must suppose that the corrected Rough Draft was itself the report of the Committee...*
" *I find it difficult to suppose that Jefferson would have presented, as the formal report of the Committee, a paper so filled... with interlineations that in certain parts no one but the author could have read it without a reading glass. On the whole the reasons for supposing that Jefferson made a fair copy, which was used as the report of the Committee & afterward lost, seemed to me more convincing than the reasons for supposing the Rough Draft itself was used as the report.*" Carl L.Becker.Declaration of Independence..aStudy of.History of Political Ideas. 1942

The unknown Manuscript, identified as the Original Draught with the text in a large hand and the form suitable for final revisions and signing, is evidently *the Fair Copy & the Committee Report*, cited by Carl Becker.

This Manuscript corresponds also to the prototype cited by Julian Boyd as "*The Lost Original*" with its close matching of the features anticipated by him, and now found in this one Manuscript, - wherein *The Lost Original* should be: 1) very large, 2) signed by Hancock, 3) marked with elocution symbols for a reader, 4) marked by Jefferson's title, & (5) headlined, "*A Declaration by the Representatives...*"
- All of these attributes are to be found only in this one Manuscript.

Jefferson would have known that manuscripts in printing shops were often cut up for efficiency in typesetting and also that damage could occur in Congress where editing was going on during severe controversy. Original work under debate for acceptance is at risk if exposed to mischief before revisions are settled.

When Jefferson presented the Fair Copy as framed from the Committee he was prepared with its duplicate as the Rough Draft, pantographed into the small format, and presumably to be used in Congress for recording amendments and deletions during debate. This duplication enabled him to protect the Original Draught or Fair Copy, folded in after hours or in a case, awaiting accepted additions or deletions upon it before presentation for signatures. Either manuscript could have been corrected and changed as agreements were reached, with the Draught receiving the agreed changes by Jefferson in his handwriting as penman. There were thus two identical texts with only one drawn in a large single-line format having reserved space for at least four dozen signatures.

The two manuscripts show the same changes, deletions and amendments, at the same positions, and mostly the same codings referring to the names of Franklin and Adams; but only the Rough Draft shows the reference to *a different phraseology inserted,* at the line in the Declaration where in published versions the wording of the Lee resolution was substituted for Jefferson's wording, which remained unchanged in the two manuscript texts.

The transfer between these two texts for the changes made in Congress suggest a simple copying by hand from one text to the other without instruments, which would be the case if the Rough Draft had been used as a memo of the adopted changes, with these being engrossed on the Fair Copy after approval. Since the changes by Congress were mainly deletions, simple bracketting was mainly used as the indication for deletion.

Jefferson's Autobiography shows only a short summary of what passed in Congress at the time and why a few members were then absent and who they were. His brief summary was evidently based on his *seven unpublished pages* of his notes made on July 4th, to which he referred explicitly in a letter to Samuel Adams's grandson, Mr. Wells. Discovery of a lost manuscript naturally invites questions or experienced opinion in authentication, but this Manuscript is unique in design, size, paper, ink, decoration, portraiture and signatures, and no other document has appeared - adequate for comparison. The Rough Draft standing as the shadow image of the Original Draught is also confirmation itself; - and other authentications will appear.   ℒ — ▣ — ℒ

Jefferson's Philippic against slavery as bracketted by Congress

"*...the Sentiments of Men are known
not only by what they receive...*"

———————————   ✑ —   ———————————

In a letter by Thomas Jefferson to William Fleming on July 1st 1776, written just before the final debating on the Declaration by Congress, Jefferson unburdened his concerns. Upon receiving word from Fleming that his own re-election as a delegate to Congress was confirmed by only a narrow margin, he thought that the Virginia Convention seemed to have doubted his reliability to vote for independence, whereas he had already written the Declaration in Committee for that, and it was being debated in secret session, just as his letter was being written.

Jefferson had expected his Declaration to be adopted at once, as the very discerning Committee with four or five of the most perceptive minds in Congress had fully approved it. He had held the letter open until July hoping to secure and then to reveal its adoption, but discussion was being prolonged to July 4th.

He also wrote regretfully of both Harrison's and Braxton's defeats for the next Congress, - and revealed from his own close re-election his sense of alarm: -

"*...I cannot be easy. If any doubt has arisen as to me, my country will have my political creed in the form of a Declaration which I was lately directed to draw. This will give decisive proof that my own sentiment concurred with the vote they instructed me to give.*"

Jefferson had not anticipated numerous corrections and additions injected by the Committee, as shown by the necessity of his having to crowd changes throughout the text for lack of space to the point where an alternate paragraph needed as an addendum had to be attached separately. He was also troubled with anxiety over losses of his text, by bracketting, which amounted to a quarter of the total content, including his phillipic against slavery. This ruinous deletion crushed his hopes of stopping the importation of tropical people who were being considered incompatible with European colonists.

Considerately he had written that *the sentiments of men are known not only by what they receive but what they reject.* In the Declaration he had bracketted expressions censored in Congress - but he had retained them as the original words *still visible.* Thus his text as edited still showed the censures of slavery *marked as for deletion.*

Avoidance of slavery issues in the Declaration may not have been necessary for final unanimity of the Colonies nor even crucial to gain independence, but it was believed to be so. Probably French support alone was vital for independence, but abolition of slavery was certainly imperative for the *Future* of the States.   -⌛

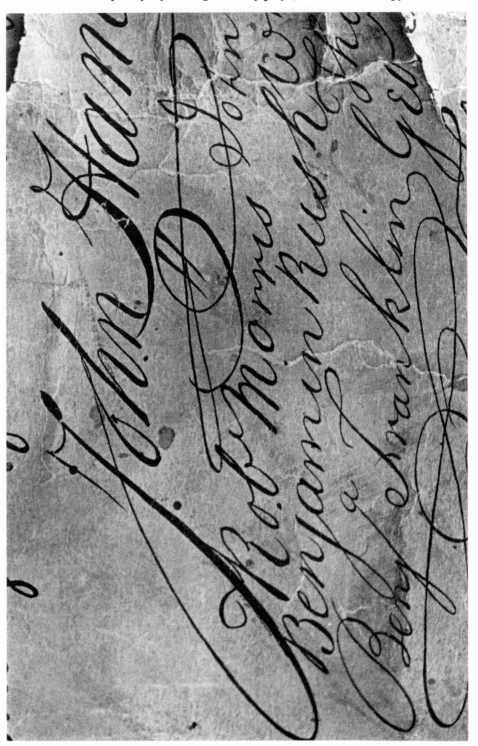

Wherein 41 Signatures graced the Fair Copy
...on the evening of July 4th 1776
——— ᘓ ———

" The debates" - wrote Thomas Jefferson in his Autobiography,-
"having taken up the greater parts of the 2nd, 3rd, & 4th days of July
were on the evening of the last closed; the Declaration was
reported by the Committee, agreed to by the House, & signed by
every member present, except Mr. Dickinson."

Before the signing, according to one account, John Hancock was
thought to have said, "We must be unanimous; there must be no
pulling different ways; we must all hang together..."

"We will all Hang together," said Franklin, "– or most assuredly
we shall all Hang separately."

The signatures on the Original Draught or Fair Copy were
written with a fervent intensity, nearly four dozen at first, without
order by Colony but in an unknown sequence.

The signatures without guide lines seem to fall within seven or
eight columns containing seven or eight imaginary horizontal bands
providing spaces flexibly for forty nine or more signatures. Nor was
Hancock to be confined in any space. Angered by ill-treatment in
the Customs episode of Boston harbor over his confiscated ship, by
his   near-capture in the night before the bloodshed at Lexington,
and surely from having been capped with a British bounty on his
head, he observed as he firmly drew his stately signature that it is,
"- large enough for King George to read without his spectacles."

The signatures may have been launched by the President at the
table, where he and the Committee could sign in key places along
borders to define boundaries: initially, John Hancock leading at the
top, left, then Benjamin Franklin as "the most famous man of his
world ", middle left. As both signed too expansively for the allotted
space, others were limited, and overlapping of signatures resulted
during the feverish decision making.

Jefferson as penman of the Committee probably signed early, at
the top right, and John Adams then known as the *Atlas of American
Independence,* at middle right.   Four key signatures may thus have
been balanced at the sides of the reserved space. With inducements
and pressure still necessary to force the divisive issue,   added
impetus would have resulted if the committee had passed the quill
initially to each of their immediate associates in their respective
Colonies.   More than three dozen signatures were yet to be
crowded on the reserved area, to add decisive accents to a possibly
Empire-splitting Document.

Clustering of Signatures of Representatives
as Colleagues of the Committee by Colony

+Mass+		Virg		Virg *Virg*
				Virg
				Mass
				Conn
*Penn *				
Penn				
		Conn		Mass
				Mass
Penn Penn		Mass Conn		

The positions of the Committee members' signatures are shown with stars.

The signatures of the Fair Copy show several variations in spelling: --
   Rodney wrote his first name as 'Casar' - not as Caesar.
   Rutlidge spelled his name with an 'i', - here & on the ParchmentCopy.
   In the 18th century, spelling variations of names were more frequent and
   incidental than later, and are to be expected.

The hand-lettered names under the Committee Portraits show a reversal:
Livingston and Sherman. This may be regarded as a natural error in the
heat of the times but such errors could not be corrected in an original hand-
drawn work.

In this imagined sequence Franklin's colleagues, Morton and Wilson may then have signed, near the lower left margin, - and below Adams, - Paine and Gerry near the lower right margin. The fourth Committee member, Livingston and his delegation, had absented themselves from voting *for lack of Instructions* and accordingly only Livingston's portrait later marked his part, and not his signature; - and this withdrawal explains the absence of New York's representation for the initial signing on July 4th.

The fifth Committee member, Roger Sherman in his natural modesty could have sensed uncertainty of position after the others and simply chose to sign below John Adams, either before or after the latter's nearby colleagues. In any case he appears as a rather silent enigma in published descriptions of the Committee's work on the writing of the Declaration. -

A perceptive man of natural honesty and evident strength of character, Sherman later proved of conciliatory value in the creation of the United States Constitution. It would be unfair to assume he had not a voice behind the writing of the Declaration, as it is to be remembered that the Committee met several times to discuss the points to be presented before the first text was drafted. It could be supposed that Sherman had assisted in shaping some of the ideas and principles in the first stages, although reference has not been found for his having written any parts of the text.

Soon after Sherman subscribed his name the form of the general signature would seem to have been fixed, and this hypothetical incomplete state is represented in the signature diagram, based on the assumed sequence as described here.

This signing sequence shows the necessary feature that the Pennsylvania support of three members comprised their actual but not unanimous majority, until July 19, when six late delegates had to find signature spaces where open, i.e.- Rush, Ross, Taylor, Clymer, Smith, - and Morris of unknown date. New York had delayed until July 15, when adjacent space for four was no longer consecutively available for Floyd, Ph. Livingston, Fr. Lewis, and Ls. Morris, - to be seated then for New York, with instructions. Robert Livingston was said to be away on defense business.

Although complete details of the signings are unknown, the positions of the signatures on the Fair Copy may suggest that the four Committee members signed while still at the table, then urged their nearest colleagues by Colony to come forward and sign alongside, thereby securing affirmation promptly and accounting for a clustering of the early signatures.

GEO. WAL

STEP. HOPKINS.

In estimates of signing dates, allowance must be made for changes of delegates from Pennsylvania and withdrawals from New York. In a total of fifteen or sixteen late signers, four of New York did not sign until July 15 and eleven others later in July, leaving forty or forty-one who signed on July 4th as in Jefferson's account that it was "signed by every member present except Mr Dickinson". In sum, four from New York were *absent* until July 15th, probably one from Maryland until July 18th, six from Pennsylvania until July 19th and four or five from Virginia, New Hampshire, and Connecticut, ---fifteen or sixteen in all:- thus 40 or 41 signing initially. Lists of those present on July 2nd–3rd were found in Hazleton - The History of the Declaration of Independence 1906).

The dating of signings by the members is difficult because of changes in July 1776, in secrecy.   Some were being replaced by their Legislatures because it was the admirable practice in the Colonies *to replace representatives who did not represent the voters*. The colonial legislatures were vigilant to make sure that instructions were followed in accord with citizens' sentiments.

All was chaos from British landings of 20000 men, - mostly Hessians, *bought* by George III as an enslavement - for the purpose of punishing the rebels in British America by murderous means.

The closing lines of the July 4th printed Broadside affirm that the Declaration was signed by order, by Congress, as verified by John Hancock. The Broadside indicates this in print - enigmatically, but evidently validating publication.

The contention that John Hancock signed for the Congress is naive. Congress consisted of delegates of independent Colonies, and these did not comprise a confederation or nation. John Hancock could not sign for more than his Colony. Publication of the Declaration on July 4th would not have been legal without signatures for each Colony, written on the Fair Copy to support the Declaration. A confederation had not yet been formed and representation required verification. - Thus the Fair Copy provided July signatures for each Colony. Assumptions that the printed words of the Broadside suffice for authentication are specious and point indelibly to a long-missing signed Manuscript.

The largest signature in the Fair Copy is John Hancock's, of seven-inch length. The most unusual is that of Step Hopkins, whose signature wobbles from a hand-tremor, apparent in his signatures written in his late years, and an important feature in authentication.

My hand trembles, but my heart does not, said Hopkins as he signed the Declaration, next to Jefferson.

Original Draught, Quad I
Vertical printer's ink-stain with surrounding oil-spread

Whether two Beaters stained the Fair Copy
- - with Globules of Printer's Ink

❦

After the close of the debates on July 4th and execution of the extensive signing as described by Jefferson, the next step for the Committee was to superintend the press by which the first printed copy called the Broadside would be produced. The Original Draught (Fair Copy) would have seemed too large and complex for the printer to read directly. Its many changes and crowded sequences would normally have required copying, but there was little time for this. *"We were in haste!"* John Hancock had exclaimed.

The speedy remedy in this emergency would have been a dictation of the tightly corrected text with its amendments, directly from the Fair Copy to the compositor at the press in the printing shop. Thus the Manuscript which had served as the Fair Copy or Committee report, and as the text critically debated in Congress, could also serve as the Printer's Copy for the initial printed Broadside as official text. This role of Printer's Copy had been suggested in 1922 by the eminent historian Prof. Carl Becker. In reflecting upon the missing Original or Fair Copy, he wrote: -

" The Declaration, as finally adopted, is to be found in the Journals of Congress; but that fair copy which Jefferson speaks of as the report of Committee of Five has... not been preserved... If there was such a copy, it was undoubtedly that copy as amended by Congress that was used by Dunlap for printing the text... and it is at least conceivable that it was inadvertently left with the printer, and so lost." (The Declaration of Independence:Studyofhistory of Political Ideas.1922)

The Manuscript was much too large and important to be lost. It must have been hidden. To the reflective mind it may suggest more than the words in it, as - look upon me to find unwritten tales...

An incident in the printing shop could here be imagined... It can be seen that the black streaks on the left edge of the first Quad show an incongruity, as being different in character from the writing-ink of the text. Each of these blotches shows a phantom stain in the shape of the initial splotch, diffusing outwardly from it in the paper.

These stains unlike writing-ink show the character of an oil, as linseed oil for instance, - an essential ingredient of old printer's ink. One may not suppose these disfigurements had come from writing quills. They rather suggest resemblances to crude tell-tale signs of a printing workshop, indicating the Fair Copy to have been also the *Printer's Copy* as presumed by Professor Becker.

Old Printing shop

Beaters beside Gutenberg Press
Photo by permission, Deutsches Museum, Muenchen

How this damage occurred may be imagined from contemporary events... Some signers were leaving to join an ill-equipped fledgling army of no experience, while others gripped the problem of equipping a force without material to do it, - for the revolting aim of killing brethren. Even worse was the bristling fact that the colonists were not unanimous. - The strong Colony of New York had not approved nor signed the Declaration, - stalling unanimity, - which could not prevail easily while loyalists and patriots were in bitter disagreement over independence.

In addition, the colonists were almost at each others throats over slavery - the *illegitimate* practice obnoxious to those of rational mind in Congress but profitable to plantation owners, and covertly to some shipping merchants. Jefferson's unyielding aims to abolish slavery were blocked, and his tough and dramatically justified philippic against it were treacherously deleted from the Declaration for reasons hidden under bitter controversy.

The Committee to superintend the press may have arrived at the printing shop in the evening strengthened with excitement from adoption of the Declaration for its first publication, but with grave doubt of consequences, overhanging and menacing like Domesday.

To imagine the workshop scene one is reminded that in 18th Century printing, the typefaces set by the compositor must be inked skillfully for the press by the journeyman, who holds two mushroom-shaped tools termed *Beaters*. These are covered with leather cloaks drenched in thick printer's ink to be spread upon the typefaces for transfer of the letter shapes to paper under pressure. The compositor must first study the manuscript's design.

If now the journeyman were to come forward to be at his clients' service with his pair of beaters, as illustrated, he would have been confronted by the largest manuscript he had ever seen. Then, astounded by the message, and touching down an outer margin to straighten it for scrutiny with wet beaters still in hand, he may forget the craftsman's discipline. In consequence the edges of his inked discs (beaters) could have touched upon the paper or splattered several blotches along the paper margins, downward from the wet edge of his rubbing tools. The damage having been done, there could be no remedy for its removal. In the tension of creative endeavor accidents in the graphic arts often happen, especially in critical situations, and correction may be almost impossible.

That printing ink was dropped upon the Fair Copy in the printing shop of 1776 is certainly not proven, but the strange presence of the special non-wetting ink is an indelible clue that this Original Draught was also the *Printer's Copy*, as inferred also by Julian Boyd.

Inking the plates with the beaters

Of Paper for Drafts, Manuscripts, and Printing

Having Knowledge and Art as an acquisition is a Privilege, not to be dispensed lightly by a free trade, - free, that is, of any repayment or compensation for the *toil* of Invention; - for this is the demand of the Barbarians, who lack both Attributes, as not having either the will or imagination to endure the efforts for attainment by Invention, and in idleness think the fruits of a man's thinking are freely for all.

Having Knowledge and Art for paper-making in earlier centuries was such a privilege, gained privately from long trial and endeavor, by experimentation, chemical and mechanical. This precious and most useful Art was protected by Secrecy in the houses of the paper makers, and zealously guarded for generations. Thus in Europe appeared paper from *industrious* countries, in many forms, sizes and qualities for different purposes, but by methods hidden and diverse.

In colonial times printers in the principal towns usually kept stationary stores with their shops, and they stocked papers of unusual kinds and sizes. Franklin with interests in ink, paper and type-faces, frequently visited these shops wherever traveling, and knew precisely as a printer the papers best married to inked-type in printing, and thus could advise for the suitable paper for Broadsides.

Francis Hopkinson was singularly the member in Congress most concerned with the Manuscript Declaration which was to originate in a *decorated* form with authentication enhanced by portraiture, such as he would have observed in the royal Documents of England. With his artist's discernment in papers, he would have favored a heavy, smooth map- or drawing- paper type for the Fair Copy, where fine surface finish was essential in rendering portraits, decorations and flags, but unnecessary for printed Broadsides.

Following authorization of the approved text of the Fair Copy for printing of the Broadside, and with the Committee ordered to superintend the Press, Franklin was on hand to advise on paper, type, ink, and format; and John Dunlap, of Philadelphia, recognized as a skilled craftsman, was chosen to print the Broadside on the night of July 4th, 1776. As the paper for the Broadside was not critical, common laid-paper was chosen for the first printings as it had also been for the Rough Draft and for the small interim copies sent privately to Virginia's statesmen by Jefferson. Only the Fair Copy had warranted a special drawing- or map- paper. (Ch-26--31) The selection of the papers for the drafts, Manuscript, and its Printing, were thus made by selection of papers, through Knowledge *&* Art; and locked within their compositions and structures were the secrets of their unique and appropriate characters.

In the Rough Draft, enlarged

In the Fair Copy, at a reduced scale
Jefferson's Diacritical Marks as emphasis

On the Elocution Marks in the Fair Copy
‘ “ ”’ “ ‘

Jefferson and Adams having collaborated in the editing of the Fair Copy were the two best qualified to make the translation for the compositor, which would have been done preferably by Adams. His texts in regard to capitals, punctuation and literary details were better written and laid out for direct printing than Jefferson's texts, which at times omitted capital letters and had variable punctuation.

The resultant printing yielded a balanced first-proof copy which however showed a new anomaly, - a number of unexpected marks, in the nature of quotation marks but without quotations.

To understand these marks it is recalled that Jefferson was not gifted in public speaking, preferring to write his ideas, and he had devised a kind of shorthand to be used when his writings were to be read. His signs were akin to those used in music for accent or loudness, and were called *elocution or diacritical marks*. Jefferson's sign for emphasis was a single apostrophe or comma over a word, or for greater accent a double or triple one. A reader could thus anticipate the spoken dynamics.

The final text of the Declaration required formal reading in Congress for debate and confirmation of accuracy. For this Jefferson would have entered his elocution marks in the Rough Draft and in the Fair Copy to assist the speaker, Harrison, possibly with critical notations in pencil for erasure after use.

Jefferson's elocution marks in the 1st Quad were evidently misinterpreted by the compositor as quotation marks, leading to insertions in the first quarter of the Broadside galley by mistake. When the proof sheet required removal of the typepiece for one of them, there resulted a misalignment found later in the first part of copies of the limited edition printed in the night of July 4th.

The Fair Copy shows a number of such elocution marks, not in the first Quad but in the controversial third Quad where sentiment was most agitated and the need for marks greatest. They were anticipated by Julian Boyd as one of the features to be sought in the lost Original.

Julian Boyd's prediction is confirmed in the Fair Copy which shows eight double and five single marks in the 3rd Quad. The Rough Draft shows five double and four single marks on the 3rd page, mostly corresponding to those in the Fair Copy in their relative positions but not entirely. There are also small differences in the shapes of the marks, but the Fair Copy shows no trace of pencil marks nor of any ink erasures.

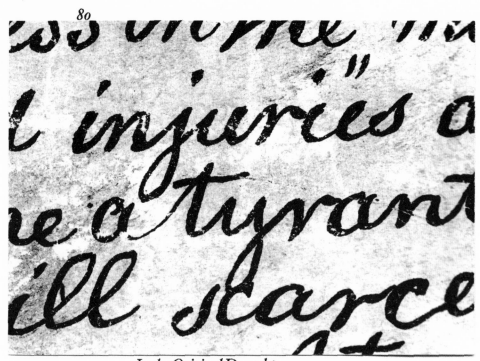

In the Original Draught
the word 'injuries'
with elocution mark over the letter "e"

In the Rough Draft
the word 'injuries'

Unlike the Broadside proof sheet, the Fair Copy does not show elocution marks in the first Quad, nor does the Rough Draft on its first page. It seems possible that Jefferson had made his elocution marks in pencil for formal reading but neglected to erase them until after the printing of the proof sheet.

In documentary writing, erasure of text is prohibited but the pencil marks as only temporary were not part of the text, and in the turbulent night it could have been forgotten to remove some before printing. When the proof sheet showed the marks the removal of their type pieces left misalignments in spacing.

It was unnecessary to erase those marks in the third Quad because they are within the expunged sections not to be printed and it is probable that Jefferson intended to keep some of the marks as essential to his composition, as do musicians in their notation with accent marks, considered as punctuation.

In the same paragraph which shows the marks of Quad-3, from line 110 (*In every stage of these oppressions...*) there occurs the line. "our repeated petitions have been answered only by repeated injuries". Historians have cited the last word as originally *injury* (singular), - and that the plural, *injuries*, is to be found only in Jefferson's *Autobiography* and in the Rough Draft, where the word is claimed to have been singular originally but to have been erased and corrected by Jefferson after the first printing.

This notion of ink erasure is in error. The form in the Fair Copy is plural, *injuries*, as is also the form in the Rough Draft, which shows no hint of a claimed erasure but only of a slight pen wobble. Jefferson would not have *erased* text anywhere for any reason. One of the admirable features of the Declaration is that it is responsibly and plainly straight-forward, - devoid of all political trickery.

The error of *injury*, as in the Broadside, could have entered as a compositor's mistake, as also, *unalienable*, line 9. Neither form is in the Fair Copy. They may have come from a presumed Adams dictation and then passed from Broadside to Parchment Copy.

In the Broadside and later in the Parchment Copy several peculiarities have been criticized by writers, including over-use of capital letters, but these are found in the Adams copy as taken from the initial paper. The extensive use of capitals followed 18th century usages which are more Germanic, and the practice was also much used in old English literature, for emphasis. Various origins of anomaly cited here account largely for the singularities in the first printed Broadsides.

A Declaration by the Representatives of the UNITED STATES
OF AMERICA, in General Congress assembled.

When in the course of human events it becomes necessary for one people to
dissolve the political bands which have connected them with another, and to ~~advance from that subordination in which they have hitherto remained, &to~~ assume among the powers of the earth the ~~equal &independant~~ station to
which the laws of nature & of nature's god entitle them, a decent respect
to the opinions of mankind requires that they should declare the causes
which impel them to the separation.

We hold these truths to be self-evident ~~sacred & undeniable~~; that all men are
created equal ~~&independant~~; that ~~from that equal creation they derive~~ they are endowed by their creator with equal
~~rights some of which are~~ ~~inherent~~ & inalienable; among which are these ~~the preservation of~~
life & liberty, & the pursuit of happiness; that to secure these ends, go-
-vernments are instituted among men, deriving their just powers from
the consent of the governed; that whenever any form of government
~~shall~~ becomes destructive of these ends, it is the right of the people to alter
or to abolish it, & to institute new government. laying it's foundation on
such principles & organising it's powers in such form, as to them shall
seem most likely to effect their safety & happiness. prudence indeed
will dictate that governments long established should not be changed for
light & transient causes: and accordingly all experience hath shewn that
mankind are more disposed to suffer while evils are sufferable, than to
right themselves by abolishing the forms to which they are accustomed. but
when a long train of abuses & usurpations [begun at a distinguished period,
& pursuing invariably the same object, evinces a design to ~~subject~~ reduce
them to under absolute Despotism ~~arbitrary power~~, it is their right, it is their duty, to throw off such
government & to provide new guards for their future security. such has
been the patient sufferance of these colonies; & such is now the necessity
which constrains them to [expunge] alter their former systems of government.
the history of the present king of Great Britain ~~majesty~~ is a history of [unremitting] injuries and repeated
usurpations, [among which appears no solitary fact ~~to contradict~~ to contra-
dict the uniform tenor of the rest [all of which] have in direct object the
but all have
establishment of an absolute tyranny over these states. to prove this let facts be
submitted to a candid world. [for the truth of which we pledge a faith
yet unsullied by falsehood]

Jefferson's Memoir copy as a Legacy --
the 1829 engraved Fac-simile of the Rough Draft

Some selected writings of Jefferson's were published in 1830 as *Memoirs...** by his grandson, T. J. Randolph, the executor *&* legatee of the manuscript papers; and bound in Volume-1 is an engraving as a *Fac-simile* Rough Draft. (* *Memoirs, Correspondence, Miscell., & Papers of Thomas Jefferson*)

Randolph's publishing of Jefferson's writings was a valuable work, especially the steel-engraved print of the Rough Draft, drawn in 1829 before Jefferson's papers were given to the government. It is termed by Randolph a copy or *Fac-simile of the Original Draught & Rough Draught.* As an engraving of the Rough Draft, it is fully authenticated by the grandson through inheritance and publication. The engraved print is in fact a duplicate traced from the Rough Draft while that draft was still held in the family, - then without the title *Rough Draft*, but identical to and in reality the same as the copy now in the Library of Congress and termed Rough Draft.

The 1829 Fac-simile is a printing from so precisely accurate an engraving of the Rough Draft as to show transferred traces even of its strange artifacts, and it shows the exact size of the text (Ch-10). This text averages nearly 11 x 6 inches per page, and it shows the corrections, marginal notations, and other features of the Rough Draft but with more clarity of the crowded corrections.

As the Rough Draft is found to be a mechanical tracing at a scale of 3 : 8 by pantograph of the text of the *Original Draught of the Declaration of Independence* (or *Fair Copy*), the Memoir engraving is thus not only a direct *fac-simile* of the Rough Draft but is also a reduced fac-simile of the Fair Copy's text *&* corrections but without decorations, portraiture, or signatures.

It is established that the Rough Draft duplicates the exact text of the Fair Copy, allowing for the collage; -- and thus an important feature of the fac-simile print is the misplaced paragraph, -- not as a collage but in consecutive order as in the Fair Copy. This confirms that the collage corrected an omission in copying: -- and to enter it in sequence on an engraved plate required extra space, making the second printed page longer than the others, because of the space in extension for words in the collage. Jefferson's manuscript secrets & identifications may not have been fully revealed to his entire family,. and the Fair Copy was probably hidden.

The *Memoirs* of 1830 is a rare authentic source for early texts of the Declaration, and a permanent record of the evolution of the Committee text including revisions.

Comparison, Page 4, of the Memoir Copy and Rough Draft with
Jefferson's marginal notation: "a different Phraseology inserted"

The engraving is thus a substantiation at reduced scale for the full text of the Fair Copy as well as of the Rough Draft, but has not drawn attention, while the Rough Draft shows damage by overuse. The Memoir copy without the smudge-damage of an impermanent ink, has been found additionally to comprise an exact facsimile of the photographic print of the Rough Draft published by Julian Boyd and the Library of Congress in 1943, and it appears to be clearer in the crowded alterations.

A special feature in the fac-simile and in the Rough Draft is to be found on the margins, page-4, in Jefferson's hand, beside the 3rd line of the last paragraph, - *with the kings of Great Britain.* Jefferson annotated: - *a different phraseology inserted*, - as a direct reference to the origin of the split-paragraph as printed in his Autobiography and in *Memoirs*. (Ch-18)

The appended terms *Rough Draft* and *Independance declaration* are written on page-4 of the Rough Draft, vertically on the margin, but not convincingly in Jefferson's hand. The engraved print of 1829 shows no trace of these terms, -- indicating that they were not written on the Draft before 1830, as not Jefferson's annotations.

Jefferson had surely preserved in his family's security not only his initial paper with its committee corrections, and the Rough Draft, but almost certainly and secretly his Fair Copy... This would account for its *disappearance* in 1776, and also for the fact that it could never be found in the Archives and was apparently never published.

The fac-simile shows that Jefferson kept his manuscripts in his possession throughout his lifetime, - *as did Washington, Adams and Madison*, - securing continuity to posterity through a grandson or granddaughter to avoid the perils of transfer to covetous hands; and it is a peerless reference, proving that under Jefferson's foresight his manuscripts were preserved for a distant future and posterity.

The manuscripts & printings of the Declaration comprise a series:
1) The initial lost paper, read by Franklin, copied by Adams, annotated repeatedly by the Committee, and copied fair as
2) The Fair Copy (Original Draught) with corrections, alterations and the *intended* excisions of Congress, bracketed for deletion;
3) The Rough Draft reduced in size directly from the Fair Copy;
4) The first Broadsides printed from the Fair Copy, July 4, 1776;
5) Interim 4-page copies of the text as framed in Committee, and sent to Lee, Wythe, Pendleton, Mazzei... July 8 & later.

IN CONGRESS, JULY 4, 1776.

A DECLARATION

BY THE REPRESENTATIVES OF THE

UNITED STATES OF AMERICA,

IN GENERAL CONGRESS ASSEMBLED.

WHEN in the Course of human Events, it becomes necessary for one People to dissolve the Political Bands which have connected them with another, and to assume among the Powers of the Earth, the separate and equal Station to which the Laws of Nature and of Nature's God entitle them, a decent Respect to the Opinions of Mankind requires that they should declare the causes which impel them to the Separation.

We hold these Truths to be self-evident, that all Men are created equal, that they are endowed by their Creator with certain unalienable Rights, that among these are Life, Liberty, and the Pursuit of Happiness—That to secure these Rights, Governments are instituted among Men, deriving their just Powers from the Consent of the Governed, that whenever any Form of Government becomes destructive of these Ends, it is the Right of the People to alter or to abolish it, and to institute new Government, laying its Foundation on such Principles, and organizing its Powers in such Form, as to them shall seem most likely to effect their Safety and Happiness. Prudence, indeed, will dictate that Governments long established should not be changed for light and transient Causes; and accordingly all Experience hath shewn, that Mankind are more disposed to suffer, while Evils are sufferable, than to right themselves by abolishing the Forms to which they are accustomed. But when a long Train of Abuses and Usurpations, pursuing invariably the same Object, evinces a Design to reduce them under absolute Despotism, it is their Right, it is their Duty, to throw off such Government, and to provide new Guards for their future Security. Such has been the patient Sufferance of these Colonies; and such is now the Necessity which constrains them to alter their former Systems of Government. The History of the present King of Great-Britain is a History of repeated Injuries and Usurpations, all having in direct Object the Establishment of an absolute Tyranny over these States. To prove this, let Facts be submitted to a candid World.

He has refused his Assent to Laws, the most wholesome and necessary for the public Good.

He has forbidden his Governors to pass Laws of immediate and pressing Importance, unless suspended in their Operation till his Assent should be obtained; and when so suspended, he has utterly neglected to attend to them.

He has refused to pass other Laws for the Accommodation of large Districts of People, unless those People would relinquish the Right of Representation in the Legislature, a Right inestimable to them, and formidable to Tyrants only.

He has called together Legislative Bodies at Places unusual, uncomfortable, and distant from the Depository of their public Records, for the sole Purpose of fatiguing them into Compliance with his Measures.

He has dissolved Representative Houses repeatedly, for opposing with manly Firmness his Invasions on the Rights of the People.

He has refused for a long Time, after such Dissolutions, to cause others to be elected; whereby the Legislative Powers, incapable of Annihilation, have returned to the People at large for their exercise; the State remaining in the mean time exposed to all the Dangers of Invasion from without, and Convulsions within.

He has endeavoured to prevent the Population of these States; for that Purpose obstructing the Laws for Naturalization of Foreigners; refusing to pass others to encourage their Migrations hither, and raising the Conditions of new Appropriations of Lands.

He has obstructed the Administration of Justice, by refusing his Assent to Laws for establishing Judiciary Powers.

He has made Judges dependent on his Will alone, for the Tenure of their Offices, and the Amount and Payment of their Salaries.

He has erected a Multitude of new Offices, and sent hither Swarms of Officers to harrass our People, and eat out their Substance.

He has kept among us, in Times of Peace, Standing Armies, without the consent of our Legislatures.

He has affected to render the Military independent of and superior to the Civil Power.

He has combined with others to subject us to a Jurisdiction foreign to our Constitution, and unacknowledged by our Laws; giving his Assent to their Acts of pretended Legislation:

For quartering large Bodies of Armed Troops among us:

For protecting them, by a mock Trial, from Punishment for any Murders which they should commit on the Inhabitants of these States:

For cutting off our Trade with all Parts of the World:

For imposing Taxes on us without our Consent:

For depriving us, in many Cases, of the Benefits of Trial by Jury:

For transporting us beyond Seas to be tried for pretended Offences:

For abolishing the free System of English Laws in a neighbouring Province, establishing therein an arbitrary Government, and enlarging its Boundaries, so as to render it at once an Example and fit Instrument for introducing the same absolute Rule into these Colonies:

For taking away our Charters, abolishing our most valuable Laws, and altering fundamentally the Forms of our Governments:

For suspending our own Legislatures, and declaring themselves invested with Power to legislate for us in all Cases whatsoever.

He has abdicated Government here, by declaring us out of his Protection and waging War against us.

He has plundered our Seas, ravaged our Coasts, burnt our Towns, and destroyed the Lives of our People.

He is, at this Time, transporting large Armies of foreign Mercenaries to compleat the Works of Death, Desolation, and Tyranny, already begun with circumstances of Cruelty and Perfidy, scarcely paralleled in the most barbarous Ages, and totally unworthy the Head of a civilized Nation.

He has constrained our fellow Citizens taken Captive on the high Seas to bear Arms against their Country, to become the Executioners of their Friends and Brethren, or to fall themselves by their Hands.

He has excited domestic Insurrections amongst us, and has endeavoured to bring on the Inhabitants of our Frontiers, the merciless Indian Savages, whose known Rule of Warfare, is an undistinguished Destruction, of all Ages, Sexes and Conditions.

In every stage of these Oppressions we have Petitioned for Redress in the most humble Terms: Our repeated Petitions have been answered only by repeated Injury. A Prince, whose Character is thus marked by every act which may define a Tyrant, is unfit to be the Ruler of a free People.

Nor have we been wanting in Attentions to our British Brethren. We have warned them from Time to Time of Attempts by their Legislature to extend an unwarrantable Jurisdiction over us. We have reminded them of the Circumstances of our Emigration and Settlement here. We have appealed to their native Justice and Magnanimity, and we have conjured them by the Ties of our common Kindred to disavow these Usurpations, which, would inevitably interrupt our Connections and Correspondence. They too have been deaf to the Voice of Justice and of Consanguinity. We must, therefore, acquiesce in the Necessity, which denounces our Separation, and hold them, as we hold the rest of Mankind, Enemies in War, in Peace, Friends.

We, therefore, the Representatives of the UNITED STATES OF AMERICA, in GENERAL CONGRESS, Assembled, appealing to the Supreme Judge of the World for the Rectitude of our Intentions, do, in the Name, and by Authority of the good People of these Colonies, solemnly Publish and Declare, That these United Colonies are, and of Right ought to be, FREE AND INDEPENDENT STATES; that they are absolved from all Allegiance to the British Crown, and that all political Connection between them and the State of Great-Britain, is and ought to be totally dissolved; and that as FREE AND INDEPENDENT STATES, they have full Power to levy War, conclude Peace, contract Alliances, establish Commerce, and to do all other Acts and Things which INDEPENDENT STATES may of right do. And for the support of this Declaration, with a firm Reliance on the Protection of divine Providence, we mutually pledge to each other our Lives, our Fortunes, and our sacred Honor.

Signed by ORDER and in BEHALF of the CONGRESS,

JOHN HANCOCK, PRESIDENT.

ATTEST.
CHARLES THOMSON, SECRETARY.

PHILADELPHIA: PRINTED BY JOHN DUNLAP.

X. The First Official Text of the Declaration of Independence, as inserted in the Rough Journal of Con

On Jefferson's *a different phraseology inserted* --
as found in the Rough Draft

-- --- --- -- --

At the close of the Broadside appears an enigma, a reference to a signed witnessed paper, cryptic in uncertainty: -

Signed by Order and in Behalf of the Congress,
-- John Hancock, President

Did Hancock alone sign by Order and in Behalf, or did Congress-, the President attesting this? With the signed Original Draught (Fair Copy) traced to the printing shop as the lost Printer's Copy, the Broadside's reference to signatures of Hancock and Thomson queries, " What were they written upon ?" - No record is known, but clues lie in the Rough Draft and in Jefferson's *Autobiography*. -

The Fair Copy required space for re-wording of its last paragraph - but no space remained. Needed for this was an *authenticated attached addendum*. Such a paper is indicated in Jefferson's Autobiography by two endings of the Declaration as split-paragraphs, differing in their phrasing and word order, as shown below: --- one version, as in the Fair Copy and Rough Draft, left column; - and the different phrasings as in the Broadside, right column, after line-146: -

"We, therefore, the Representatives of the united
States of America ... do in the name, and by the
authority of the good people of these Colonies, (line-146)

(Fair Copy & Rough Draft)	(Broadside & Parchment Copy)
1 (We)..reject & renounce all allegiances & subjection to the Kings of Great Britain / & hereafter	2 (declare)... they (Colonies) are absolved from all allegiance to the British crown
2 we utterly dissolve all political connection which may heretofore have subsisted between us & the people, & Parliament of Great Britain	3 ..and that all political connection between them & the state of Great Britain is, and ought to be, totally dissolved
3 we do assert and declare these colonies to be free and independent states	1 (We)... declare that these united Colonies are, and of right ought to be, free & independent states

The differently phrased paragraphs (right column) were not part of the Declaration as framed but were revisions for the texts of the Broadside and Parchment Copy as re-worded by Congress, adopting partially the wording of Lee in a resolution for independence.

... will have it; the road to happiness is open to us too; we will climb it in a separate state ... we must ... acquiesce in the necessity which denounces our ... and hold them as we hold the rest of mankind enemies in war, in peace friends.

We therefore the representatives of the United States of America in General Congress assembled do in the name & by authority of the good people of these [states] reject and renounce all allegiance & subjection to the kings of Great Britain & all others who may hereafter claim by, through, or under them; we utterly dissolve all political connection which may have heretofore subsisted between us & the people or parliament of Great Britain; and finally we do assert and declare these colonies to be free and independant states, and that as free & independant states they have power to levy war, conclude peace, contract alliances, establish commerce, & to do all other acts and things which independant states may of right do. And for the support of this declaration we mutually pledge to each other our lives, & our sacred honour.

An addendum to the Fair Copy was needed to clarify the final revision for the printer, with authorization, and is indicated by a notation in the Rough Draft, line 146: -

In Jefferson's hand a note reads, *a different phraseology inserted,* which could mean an insertion into the text by an addendum onto the Fair Copy to show the revision, -- requiring only Hancock's witnessed signature for validation.

The closing statement of the printed Broadside seems to refer to the Fair Copy as having been signed "by Order of the Congress and in Behalf of the Congress", - the President of the Congress certifying this with his signature on the Draught's addendum as the written adjunct for the close of the Broadside, as witnessed (attest. Chas. Thomson, Secretary).

The wording suggests an intentional enigma: - The Broadside is from a Document - signed by whom? - By Congress - although not showing names, - but attested by its President in truth?

The approved changes by Congress from line 146 replaced the wording of Jefferson's with phrasing from the Lee Resolution. Jefferson was logical and clear; but the revision after Lee is weak, - its text extracted from one written by Pendleton for the Virginia Legislature. Lee's arguments adopted for the Broadside were drawn in a contrary order and cast in a weak passive voice. Jefferson's stronger first-person prose was direct, emphatic, and superior: -

Lee: *the Colonies... are absolved of all allegiance...*
Jef: *We reject & renounce all allegiances and subjection*
       to the King...
Lee: *all political connection is, and ought to be,*
       totally dissolved.
Jef: *We utterly dissolve all political connection.*

Usage of a passive mode in the adopted paragraph of Lee was incongruous, suggesting that Congress was hiding from their own conclusion, as though endeavoring not to be discovered. This version has the same illogic that results if, quoting Fowler, " The point is sought to be evaded ".

Congress added in desperation an ingenuous coda, *appealing to the supreme judge of the world* - crying out as though to the *One only* who might hear a lamentation of unfeigned sorrow.

    < *Final paragraph of Fair Copy.*

As for the 40 or 41 real but secret signatures, folded paper sheets as an envelope covering them could have been overlaid; and it may be supposed that an addendum, signed by Hancock, also recorded *the different phraseology* quoted by Jefferson -- and was lost later.

Gate, Governor's Palace, Williamsburg with monarchial symbols

A Declaration by the Representatives of the
AMERICA in General Congress assembled.

When in the course of human events it becomes
...solve the political bands which have connected...
among the powers of the earth the separate and eq...
...nature and of nature's god entitle them a decent...
...requires that they should declare the causes which...

We hold these truths to be self-evident; the...

sustain un they are endowed by their Creator with inherent and...
alienable rights are life, liberty, and the pursuit of happiness; that...
are instituted among men, deriving their just pow...
that whenever any form of government becomes des...
right of the people ...to... abolish it, and to...
its foundation ...on such principles ...organising...
them shall seem most likely to effect their safety a...
will dictate that governments long established shou...
...fient causes. and accordingly all experience hath s...
...after *...pared to suffer, while evils are sufferable, than to right the...*
they are accustomed. but when a long train of abuses a...
left out. *...quished period & pursuing invariably the same object, ...*
absolute despotism, it is their right, it ...their duty, to...
...vide new guards for their future security. such ha...
etc. *...colonies & such is now the necessity which constrain...*

One of six or seven copies: - Lee copy, damaged in storage

In British America of 1776 there was no central government and the 13 colonies under British rule were administered by the King's appointed governors. The Committees of Correspondence were already assembling a loosely organized confederation by carrying on secret exchanges of information on plans for independence in the shadows of widespread loyalist vigilance and threats.

In this climate the Continental Congress carried forward their designs, which were aimed at the securing of independence under the collaboration of the separate colonial legislatures, and these were already advising to form their own independent constitutions.

During the crucial weeks of debating on the revolutionary matter of independence, authority over the distribution of papers or declarations especially for the Continental Congress was probably so loose as to be almost non-existent. What had been written was pushed into hiding under clamps of secrecy.

The foregoing matters resulted in numerous written documents some of which were to be concealed from public knowledge for many years and these included especially Jefferson's copies of the Declaration, which was under burning discussion. Without official restrictions and with the need for disclosures to key patriots within the governments, Jefferson penned a number of covert copies in his own handwriting which disappeared from public knowledge, - not to reappear for several generations.

The private retention of these copies and related writings by others resulted in hidden sources of valuable documents, which could not be known by historians for a very long time. Some of what has been pieced together in these present pages concerning the Colonial hidden papers and manuscripts may not be found in history books. In particular Chapters 5 and 17 to 21 have required disentangling of errors and misnomers which have been applied arbitrarily for a long time to manuscripts after their confusing reappearances in the hands of collectors or of institutions a century or more after disappearance.

It may not be widely realized that Jefferson created 6 or 7 covert copies of his original text, mostly hidden in the heat of the American war for Independence. It is possible that an institution upon acquisition of sheets of text in Jefferson's handwriting might claim to hold the Original Declaration, but small interim copies now in Libraries were not signed and have no claim to being the Original. They were intended mostly for key statesmen in the Colonial Legislature of Virginia to show Jefferson's committee text as framed before changes and major abridgment.

A 19th-century *Souvenir Declaration* with 56 forged signatures and an official attestation that they are indistinguishable from the Original, although obviously contrived. The text was mutilated with 19th century accents and fanciwork, and showed a portrait of Washington who was not a member of the second continental congress of July 4, 1776.

After writing -and, with the Committee, editing the initial sheets of the Declaration, with its numerous additions, alterations, and corrections, -Jefferson drew what he called the Original Draught or Fair Copy. He also made for desk-copy use a facsimile, as the Rough Draft, at a scale of 3 : 8, double-spaced for notations; and he may then have considered the necessity to make a secret signatured Reserve Copy accurately by pantograph - in case the Original were lost.

When disputes began in Congress over censures written in the Declaration against slavery, the likelihood of the Fair Copy being abridged led Jefferson to write several copies to preserve the full text as framed. He wrote six or seven *duplicates* of the Committee text here termed *interim copies*, with the later deletions by Congress indicated in two of these and readable. The recipient of one such copy may not have known about others, and the entire series disappeared with completion of the Parchment Copy on August 2nd.

The terms *Original Draught* or *Fair Copy* apply only to the large Manuscript that vanished on the night of July 4, with portraits not finished, and it is not known who saw the decorated work. Since the existence of the Fair Copy was unknown outside of Congress, the term *original* may have been applied in error later to any small copy.

In view of secrecy rules, Jefferson also safeguarded against exposure of the Declaration by omitting from his interim copies the date, signature and title, writing only *"A Declaration by..."* The small copies thus did not show their origin.

After 1800, identification of the manuscripts became complex, with the federal government publishing facsimile signatures traced from the Parchment Copy, and also allowing calligraphers to trace signatures from it for producing *souvenir copies.*

Early in the 19th century copies appeared with authentic looking faked signatures and formats decorated with pictures or portraits on the borders unrelated to the Declaration. These cheap counterfeits with odd writing styles obscured impressions in the public eye as to the character of the Declaration in Jefferson's handwriting. As a result, false impressions of authenticity multiplied, & if an unknown Declaration appeared it drew little attention.

In 1876 during the Centennial of the July 4th signing of the Declaration, an unknown copy was published in Harpers Magazine's Supplement, and seemed not to attract interest; but re-examination suggests that it deserves an exact analysis for comparison with the known handwritings of the times, and that its provenance might be illuminating if discoverable.

DECLARATION OF INDEPENDENCE.

In Congress 4th July, 1776.

Unlike known copies of the Declaration, the Harpers facsimile has a three-column horizontal format, of total width greater than height, but showing the complete text. Its striking feature is a brace of signatures which has appeared on no other document except at a larger scale on the Fair Copy, the two having precisely similar handwritings. However, after a study by photo-enlargements of the Harpers facsimile as published from its unknown source, it was seen that the pen lines show copy errors and are too coarse and imprecise for acceptance as original hand-written work. It appears that its source had been transferred by pantograph from the Fair Copy, at two different scales for text & signatures, probably in 1776.

A distinctive feature of this Harpers copy may be seen in about the center of the text where a word *unacknoleged* shows Jefferson's frequent spelling error, omitting *w* before *l*, and *d* before *g*. The same error occurs in the interim copies, - and in the Fair Copy also, where it had been corrected with a very small *w* and *d* written neatly above the proper location, and in similar ink. These errors had been fully corrected later in the Broadside and Parchment Copy, but not in the Harpers copy, where the loop of the *g* is missing from *acknowledged* (*-ledaed* instead of *-ledged*). Absence of the loop is evidently another pantographic copy error of omission.

The Harpers copy in a script closely similar to the Original, - with signatures, but more compact & without decorations, - would seem to represent a secret Reserve Copy. In Colonial times a second manuscript comprised a back-up copy in case an original were lost.

In making a Reserve Copy, a reduction of the original text of two columns with signatures would have shown an awkward format. For Jefferson as architect, a compact modification would have been so simple with his instruments that he could have deftly formed a plan with new proportions simply through rapid estimations by eye.

To design a suitable reduced format Jefferson may have started with a sheet half the quad-sized paper, or 22 x 14 inches, for the entire document at 1/3 scale. This size would have enabled him to use about the same reduction of text as in the Rough Draft, or a scale of 3 : 8 of the letter sizes in the Fair Copy. Unlike that Draft he did not need to double-space this text as it was not intended to be edited. Thus the Reserve Copy, if equal in scale to the Rough Draft, may have the same line-length, composed in three columns as a text block of 20-inch total width. It is to be remembered that in that distant period fine paper was uncommon and valuable, and standard sizes were usual, without cutting. This reduced scale copy would have had the advantages of portability, with convincing authenticity for reference or presentation.

all have it: the road to ~~glory~~ & to glory & happiness is open to us too; we will ~~tread~~ ~~it~~ de- ~~part~~ it in ~~apart from them~~ ~~we must~~ ~~they~~ we must ~~then~~ and acquiesce in the necessity which ~~pronounces our~~ denounces our ~~eternal~~ separation and hold them as we hold the rest of mankind enemies in war, in peace friends

We therefore the representatives of the United States of America in General Congress assembled do in the name & by authority of the good people of these [states] reject and renounce all allegiance & subjection to the kings of Great Britain & all others who may hereafter claim by, through, or under them; we utterly ~~have~~ dissolve all political connection which may ~~have~~ heretofore sub- sisted between us & the people or parliament of Great Britain; and finally we do assert and declare these colonies to be free and independant states and that as free & independant states they have full power to levy war, conclude peace, contract alliances, establish commerce & to do all other acts and things which independant states may of right do. And for the support of this declaration we mutually pledge to each other our lives, & our fortunes, & our sacred honour.

Measurements concerning the size ratio between the Rough Draft & the Fair Copy indicate a value between 1 : 3 (0.333) and 3 : 8 (0.375), as an *approximate* setting for the copying pantograph. The Rough Draft has been reproduced in print in various size-scales but usually without an indicated size specification. In the Memoir writings of Jefferson, edited by his grandson, the *1829 facsimile* of the Rough Draft as an engraving is intrinsically accurate, and is used here as a standard at a scale of one-to-one for determining the size-reduction by pantograph in copies from the Fair Copy. As a primary reference, the Library of Congress in 1943 published very accurate & finely sensitive photographs of the Rough Draft at a scale of 1 : 1, as confirmed here by superimpositions with the Memoirs Copy.

From the sizes of text in the Rough Draft and in the Fair Copy the ratio of line-lengths is apparently little more than 1 : 3. The true ratio may be found by measuring lengths between identical points within a line of words, for the large and the small cases. Using dividers in the first few lines of text, the measurements showed a proportion approximating 3 : 8 in copying, - meaning that the word sizes in the Rough Draft are actually 3 : 8 of their corresponding size in the Original. Old pantograph scales were often set in round numbers as proportions.

The form of the Reserve Copy in three columns suggests that it had been copied as a compact small scale duplicate of the signed Fair Copy, without portraiture or flags and in the text scale of the Rough Draft; but unlike the Draft, this Reserve Copy has the single-line spacing found in the Fair Copy, also showing a complete reproduction signature at a scale -presumed as about 5 : 8 to the Original, but estimates of its true size are uncertain.

It was an astonishing feat for one man, under the pressure of the revolutionary crisis, not only to compose a state paper of the great breadth and permanent stature of the Declaration, but also to copy the text about ten times in a few days for its necessary and diverse usages, with precision of style and content, -- while also carrying the Original through a divided Congress, --- safeguarding its preservation, securing designs of embellishments and portraiture, -- and all this while suffering forebodings of future misinterpretations from adversaries' attacks, intensified by the blind arrogance behind the failure of Congress *to secure then the abolition of slavery* through Jefferson's axiom of man as equal & *i*ndependent before the law.

Accounts of the lost Original's history suggest that in legislative matters Majority opinion -and Rule from it- may be in fatal error; and consequences are disastrous after bludgeoning by Majority opinion. Superior minds are often in the minor proportion, & lose in voting.

Resolved ~~that the...~~

That these United Colonies are, and of right ought to be, free and independent States, that they are absolved from all allegiance to the British Crown, and that all political connection between them and the State of Great Britain is, and ought to be, totally dissolved.

That it is expedient forthwith to take the most effectual measures for forming foreign alliances.

That a plan of confederation be prepared and transmitted to the respective Colonies for their consideration and approbation.

Richard Henry Lee's Resolution of July 2, 1776

Richard Henry Lee Portrait from Fair Copy

Richard Henry Lee having written and proposed the Resolution for Independence might have been chosen to write the Declaration but was not present at the crucial time. However his devotion to liberty and independence made it certain that he would receive an early copy, confirmed by Jefferson's letter to him dated July 8, 1776:-

> *"I enclose you a copy of the Declaration of Independence, as agreed to by the House, & also as originally framed..."*

Did Jefferson mean a copy as framed and a copy as approved, or only one copy showing both states? -- It seems probable that Jefferson sent a Broadside, as approved, but also a full copy showing *what men receive as well as what they reject* - thereby another interim copy of the text before excisions in Congress.

Letters in the 19th century in reference to the Lee copies have been confusing by misinterpretations. The Lees did possess one interim copy and probably a Broadside; but a covert third copy was implied when Lee's grandson reported that Jefferson had made *two fair copies*, and that since his primary Fair Copy as the true Original had disappeared, Lee's copy in its place could be called the Original.

Confusion increased when young Lee gave a hand-written copy of a Declaration to the American Philosophical Society. That unknown copy was probably the interim copy transmitted on July 8, 1776, as referred to above, but the secretary of the Society claimed it to be the Original based on young Lee's word that his grandfather's duplicate copy had *replaced* Jefferson's lost Fair Copy as the Original.

The value of a covert Lee copy would lie essentially in its indisputable provenance. As R. H. Lee was known as a respected statesman in Virginia, a Lee Document has unquestioned validity. Lee's commentary on a second fair copy suggests that the Harpers copy may be the presumed hidden Reserve Copy.

After 1876 the Reserve Copy seemed to have disappeared until the Bicentennial, in 1976, when a picture of it emerged in a book published by Dover on the American Revolution, with pictures from Harpers as published a century before. The Prang Company in Boston had made lithographs from the copy according to a microfilm reference of a Harpers facsimile. In 1776 lithography was unknown and a litho-text non-existent then. The enigma of a secret Reserve Copy is unsolved, but points to the existence of a second secret document, -- hidden for 100 years, but having been copied initially like the Rough Draft from Jefferson's lost Original, -- thus further authenticating that by unique similarities.

JOURNALS

OF

CONGRESS:

CONTAINING THEIR

PROCEEDINGS

FROM JANUARY 1, 1776, TO DECEMBER 31, 1776.

PUBLISHED BY AUTHORITY.

VOLUME II.

FROM FOLWELL'S PRESS.

PHILADELPHIA.

1800.

Thursday, July 4, 1776.

Resolved, That application be made to the committee of safety of Pennsylvania for a supply of flints for the troops at New-York: and that Delaware government and Maryland, be requested to embody their militia for the flying-camp, with all possible expedition, and to march them, without delay, to the city of Philadelphia.

Agreeable to the order of the day, the Congress resolved itself into a committee of the whole, to take into their farther consideration, the declaration; and, after some time, the president resumed the chair, and Mr. Harrison reported, that the committee have agreed to a declaration, which they desired him to report.

The declaration being read, was agreed to as follows:

A DECLARATION by the Representatives of the UNITED STATES of AMERICA, in Congress assembled.

WHEN, in the course of human events, it becomes necessary for one people to dissolve the political bands which have connected them with another, and to assume, among the powers of the earth, the separate and equal station to which the laws of nature, and, of nature's God, entitle them, a decent respect to the opinions of mankind, requires, that they should declare the causes which impel them to the separation.

We hold these truths to be self-evident, that all men are created equal; that they are endowed, by their Creator, with certain unalienable rights; that among these, are life, liberty, and the pursuit of happiness. That, to secure these rights, governments are instituted among men, deriving their just powers from the consent of the governed; that, whenever any form of government becomes destructive of these ends, it is the right of the people to alter or to abolish it, and to institute new government, laying its foundation on such principles, and organizing its powers in such form, as to them shall seem most likely to effect their safety and happiness. Prudence, indeed, will dictate, that governments long established, should not be changed for light and transient causes; and, accordingly, all experience hath shewn, that mankind are more disposed to suffer, while evils are sufferable, than to right themselves by abolishing the forms to which they are accustomed. But, when a long train of abuses and usurpations, pursuing invariably the same object, evinces a design to reduce them under absolute despotism, it is their right, it is their duty, to throw off such government, and to provide new guards for their future security. Such has been the patient sufferance of these colonies; and such is now the necessity which constrains them to alter their former systems of government. The history of the present king of Great-Britain is a history of repeated injuries and usurpations, all having, in direct object, the establishment of an absolute tyranny over these states. To prove this, let facts be submitted to a candid world.

He has refused his assent to laws the most wholesome and necessary for the public good.

He has forbidden his governors to pass laws of immediate and pressing importance, unless suspended in their operation till his assent should be obtained; and, when so suspended, he has utterly neglected to attend to them.

He has refused to pass other laws for the accommodation of large districts of people, unless those people would relinquish the right of representation in the legislature: a right inestimable to them, and formidable to tyrants only.

He has called together legislative bodies at places unusual, uncomfortable, and distant from the depository of their public records, for the sole purpose of fatiguing them into compliance with his measures.

He has dissolved representative houses repeatedly, for opposing, with manly firmness, his invasions on the rights of the people.

He has refused, for a long time, after such dissolutions, to cause others to be elected; whereby the legislative powers, incapable of annihilation, have returned to the people at large for their exercise; the state remaining, in the mean time, exposed to all the dangers of invasion from without, and convulsions within.

He has endeavoured to prevent the population of these states; for that purpose, obstructing the laws for naturalization of foreigners; refusing to pass others to encourage their migrations hither, and raising the conditions of new appropriations of lands.

He has obstructed the administration of justice, by refusing his assent to laws for establishing judiciary powers.

He has made judges dependent on his will alone, for the tenure of their offices, and the amount and payment of their salaries.

He has erected a multitude of new offices, and sent hither swarms of officers to harrass our people, and eat out their substance.

He has kept among us, in time of peace, standing armies, without the consent of our legislatures.

He has affected to render the military independent of, and superior to, the civil power.

He has combined, with others, to subject us to a jurisdiction foreign to our constitution, and unacknowledged by our laws; giving his assent to their acts of pretended legislation:

For quartering large bodies of armed troops among us:

For protecting them, by a mock-trial, from punishment, for any murders which they should commit on the inhabitants of these states:

For cutting off our trade with all parts of the world:

For imposing taxes on us without our consent:

For depriving us, in many cases, of the benefits of trial by jury:

For transporting us beyond seas to be tried for pretended offences:

For abolishing the free system of English laws in a neighbouring province, establishing therein an arbitrary government, and enlarging its boundaries, so as to render it, at once, an example and fit instrument for introducing the same absolute rule into these colonies:

For taking away our charters, abolishing our most valuable laws, and altering, fundamentally, the forms of our governments:

For suspending our own legislatures, and declaring themselves invested with power to legislate for us in all cases whatsoever.

He has abdicated government here, by declaring us out of his protection, and waging war against us.

He has plundered our seas, ravaged our coasts, burnt our towns, and destroyed the lives of our people.

He is, at this time, transporting large armies of foreign merce-

naries to complete the works of death, desolation, and tyranny, already begun with circumstances of cruelty, and perfidy, scarcely paralleled in the most barbarous ages, and totally unworthy the head of a civilized nation.

He has constrained our fellow-citizens, taken captive on the high seas, to bear arms against their country, to become the executioners of their friends and brethren, or to fall themselves by their hands.

He has excited domestic insurrections amongst us, and has endeavoured to bring on the inhabitants of our frontiers, the merciless Indian savages, whose known rule of warfare is an undistinguished destruction, of all ages, sexes, and conditions.

In every stage of these oppressions, we have petitioned for redress, in the most humble terms: Our repeated petitions, have been answered only by repeated injury. A prince, whose character is thus marked by every act which may define a tyrant, is unfit to be the ruler of a free people.

Nor have we been wanting in attentions to our British brethren. We have warned them, from time to time, of attempts, by their legislature, to extend an unwarrantable jurisdiction over us. We have reminded them of the circumstances of our emigration and settlement here. We have appealed to their native justice and magnanimity, and we have conjured them, by the ties of our common kindred, to disavow these usurpations, which would inevitably interrupt our connexions and correspondence. They, too, have been deaf to the voice of justice and of consanguinity. We must, therefore, acquiesce in the necessity, which denounces our separation, and hold them, as we hold the rest of mankind, enemies in war, in peace friends.

We, therefore, the representatives of the UNITED STATES OF AMERICA, in GENERAL CONGRESS assembled, appealing to the supreme Judge of the World for the rectitude of our intentions, do, in the name, and by authority of the good people of these colonies, solemnly publish and declare, That these United Colonies are, and of right, ought to be, FREE AND INDEPENDENT STATES; that they are absolved from all allegiance to the British crown, and that all political connexion between them and the state of Great-Britain, is, and ought to be, totally dissolved; and that, as FREE AND INDEPENDENT STATES, they have full power to levy war, conclude peace, contract alliances, establish commerce, and to do all other acts and things which INDEPENDENT STATES may of right do. And, for the support of this declaration, with a firm reliance on the protection of DIVINE PROVIDENCE, we mutually pledge to each other, our lives, our fortunes, and our sacred honour.

The foregoing declaration was, by order of Congress, engrossed, and signed by the following members:

JOHN HANCOCK.

103

New-Hampshire.	Josiah Bartlett, William Whipple, Matthew Thornton.
Massachusetts-Bay.	Samuel Adams, John Adams, Robert Treat Paine, Elbridge Gerry.
Rhode-Island.	Stephen Hopkins, William Ellery.
Connecticut.	Roger Sherman, Samuel Huntington, William Williams, Oliver Wolcott.
New-York.	William Floyd, Philip Livingston, Francis Lewis, Lewis Morris.
New-Jersey.	Richard Stockton, John Witherspoon, Francis Hopkinson, John Hart, Abraham Clark.
Pennsylvania.	Robert Morris, Benjamin Rush, Benjamin Franklin, John Morton, George Clymer, James Smith, George Taylor, James Wilson, George Ross.
Delaware.	Cæsar Rodney, George Read.
Maryland.	Samuel Chase, William Paca, Thomas Stone, Charles Carroll, of Carrollton.
Virginia.	George Wythe, Richard Henry Lee, Thomas Jefferson, Benjamin Harrison, Thomas Nelson, jun. Francis Lightfoot Lee, Carter Braxton.
North-Carolina.	William Hooper, Joseph Hewes, John Penn.

Signatures of July signings as printed in the Journals

South-Carolina.	Edward Rutledge, Thomas Heyward, jun. Thomas Lynch, jun. Arthur Middleton.
Georgia.	Button Gwinnett, Lyman Hall, George Walton.

Resolved, That copies of the declaration be sent to the several assemblies, conventions and committees, or councils of safety, and to the several commanding officers of the continental troops; that it be proclaimed in each of the United States, and at the head of the army.

'UNANIMOUS', in the Original Parchment Copy's title,
August 2, 1776
as (inadvertently) published in 1906

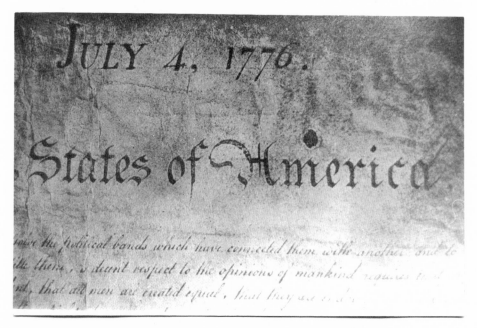

Original Parchment Copy as misdated on August 2, 1776

The wealthy slave-traders and plantation owners were acutely sensitive to Jefferson's censures of slavery, and their approval of the Declaration as first presented could not be had simply by bracketting proposed deletions or even by partial expunging, as Jefferson had done. Censures of slavery still visible were sure to be rejected by some colonists, thus causing failed unanimity.

Originally it had not been planned to make a new version of the Declaration, but on July 19, 1776 this was proposed and approved, specifying that the Declaration should have a new title and be rewritten on parchment for permanence. But parchment was not advantageous under the circumstances; - although tougher than paper it is subject to cracking when dried, and ink upon it has less penetration and is easily lost. The history of the later Parchment Copy shows that the change for permanence was a failure.

Congress had intended with a new title to show unanimity, to convince Loyalists but also apparently, as an excuse, *to abridge Jefferson's Fair Copy and to replace it secretly* with a clean censored text devoid of all visible bracketted opposition to slavery, - thus avoiding reference to bitter controversy. By this stratagem the message of full Independence and Liberty was apparently to be obscured from public view by being permanently hidden, *&* replaced on parchment by a shortened text, falsely antedated to July 4th.

It is now plain that the scuttling of the intended title and the suppression of the Fair Copy were a subterfuge of some obstructive representatives to hide from scrutiny their brutal offenses listed in the full original text. But a stratagem to refuse approval and its consequent unanimity, - until the Declaration would be debilitated by drastic abridgment would maliciously prefigure Blackmail.

John Adams wrote reflectively, "I have long wondered that the Original (Draught) was not published. I suppose the reason was *the vehement Philippic against slavery* -- one of its best parts.

Jefferson himself was not deceived. His opposition to slavery had been uncompromising and sincere. He regarded the Declaration as a primary opportunity to outlaw slavery forever, while viewing its continuation as the root of ultimate disaster. He was not comforted by a diverting tale of *The Hatter,* told to him by Franklin, to ease his deep foreboding, - a trivial tale of how group pressure can muddle well-reasoned goals with trivia. Jefferson had acutely foreseen increasing hostilities between peoples so dissonant and also so incompatible in backgrounds, traditions, philosophy and natures as to incite perpetual conflict, leading inevitably to civil wars.

One of many printed exemplifications of the Parchment Copy
- after its ruinous wet-transfer onto paper, in 1823.

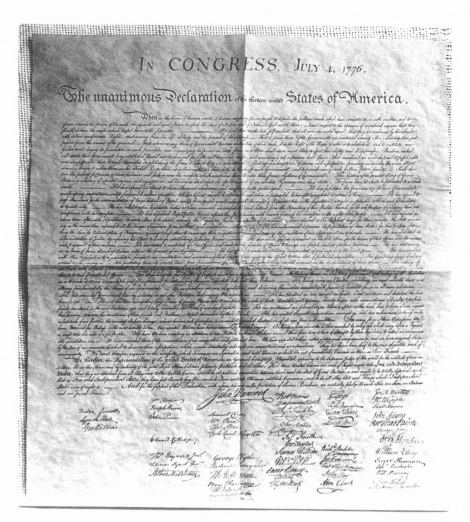

The crucial point which shows the source
of each manuscript is its Title or Headline. -
This was changed on July 19, 1776 to 'UNANIMOUS'

The uncertainties & confusion over the signing of the two great historical documents -- proven as completed on July 4th on paper, and on August 2nd on parchment -- are resolved in the Journals of Congress for 1776,- and these occur in several forms: -

a) The Rough Journals -- Charles Thomson's handwritten daily records of those transactions in the Congress which were not too secret to be on such a record.

b) The corrected Journals of Congress - with written accounts of various transactions modified for accuracy.

c) *The Secret Journals of Congress* -- referred to by Jefferson and others: 1st published some years after the transactions.

d) Printed Journals -- the published printings of the manuscript Journals, with minor corrections.

The *crucial point* in the Journals, distinguishing the Source of each of the various Declarations in manuscript form, is the *Title* or *Headline* recorded in the Journals -- because these were changed on July 19th and a different title was permanently adopted.

If the published Declaration shows the title, *"The Unanimous Declaration of the 13 united States of America"*, it must have been taken from the Parchment Copy, not completed until August 2nd. That title was unknown on July 4th, and the Parchment Copy could not have been signed before its completion.

Without a modified title as *"Unanimous..."* but with the headline reading, *"A Declaration by the Representatives..."* the first printed Declaration - the *Broadside* - must have been taken from the Committee's Fair Copy as the text edited in Congress from July 2 and completed on July 4th. That this Manuscript was signed is indelibly proven from the *Journals of Congress of 1776* for the foregoing date as first published in 1777 and in its exact reprint of 1800.

The Fair Copy is certified in the July entry as signed on July 4th, the Broadside attests to this, and the Journal's *July entries* list 55 who signed as part of that Document. Assertions to the contrary are false as shown in the Journal as final authority.

The Parchment Copy as the official document replaced the Fair Copy, having its abridged text copied by a scribe apparently from the Broadside text, -- and this Copy was signed from August 2nd cumulatively at intervals to November 5th 1776.

These two separate signed documents correspond exactly to the two referred to by Jefferson as those compared at the table on August 2nd, but a controversy over this has a curious cover-up, long veiled by the second Continental Congress. --

That the Fair Copy written on paper was to be replaced by the Parchment Copy, in secrecy, is proven by the fact that the above published Journal of Congress makes no reference to a Parchment Copy as of July 19, nor of August 2nd, nor to a new *unanimous* title. Those references lie snugly in the security of the *Secret domestic Journals of Congress*.

As quoted by Prof. Carl Becker, the Secret domestic Journal for July 19 stated:- *"Resolved, that the Declaration passed on the 4th be* fairly *engrossed,"* - and, - *"engrossed on parchment with the title and style of 'The Unanimous Declaration of the 13 united States of America' "* . -- On August 2nd another entry reads, -- " *The Declaration of Independence being engrossed and compared at the table was signed by the members".*

- It is thus indisputably clear that the Declaration printed in the Journals for July 4th, and signed by 55 representatives, is not the Parchment Copy - not yet written. The July Original was correctly called, *"The Declaration of Independence"*, *&* after its text was abridged and engrossed on parchment, that became the Parchment Copy with the *unanimous* title, and that was compared at the table with the *paper Original,* on August 2nd, and then signed. One of Jefferson's accounts of the signings of August 2, written in 1822, states: --

"I received the new publication of the secret Journals of Congress, wherein is stated a Resolution, July 19 1776, that the Declaration passed on the 4th be fairly engrossed on parchment, and when engrossed, be signed by every member; and another of August 2nd that being engrossed and compared at the table, was signed by the members. That is to say the copy engrossed on parchment was signed by the members after being compared at the table with the original one, signed on paper as before stated. I add this *P.S.* to the copy of my letter to Mr. Wells, to prevent confounding the signature of the original with that of the copy engrossed on parchment."

A reference to the July 4th signing is also given by Benjamin Franklin, in a letter to Mrs. Mecum, exactly on an anniversary of July 4th 1776. He refers explicitly to the signing on that date, wherein were *"pledged our lives, our fortunes, and our sacred honour..."*

John Adams referred to the decisively anti-slavery Original as still unpublished and unknown publicly after many years.

The absolute rejections of slavery by Jefferson, John Adams, and Franklin were intrinsically inherited in principles of their close English & Scottish ancestry, traceable without compromise to the Tudor dynasty, notably to Queen Elizabeth in 1562 and later. (Ch-39)

✳   ✳   ✳

Will uns der Ehre Kertze blenden,
und von dem wahren Licht abwenden,
das nie verlieret Glantz und Schein:
So muß ein Schirm der blöden Augen,
damit sie scharff zu sehen taugen,
die Sterblichkeits-Betrachtung seyn.

The Parchment Maker

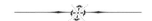

Praise to him
    Who oft times looks on the Reckoning Skin --

If Honour blinds when we have much to answer for
    And diverts us from that true ceaseless Light -
        That never loses Brilliance in our Sight, -
    The thinking Eye must then be shaded more
    And rendered fit to perceive with Recognition,
So in the end we turn to seek in Contemplation.

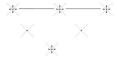

How a Scribe's august Declaration
antedated itself to July 4th

The copy of the Declaration to be engrossed on parchment was not authorized to be written until July 19th nor completed until August 2nd, & it is odd to find it antedated to July 4th. The new text was an abridgment of the Manuscript, expurgated to secure unanimity & predated four weeks, Congress with nearly two dozen lawyers agreeing on acts shadowed with shenanigans.

The changed headline of the Declaration announced the new July 19th unanimity, its text showing only final provisions and sentiments indicated after full excision of bracketted or crossed-out sections. The absence of *Independence* from the new title inexplicably passed without objection. Those sensitive to the implications of the greatly weakened Declaration must have regarded a retention of *Independence* as clashing with its intended meaning after the total deletion of the censures of slavery.

And was this copy with new title and predate a 2nd edition? or was it valid, as *unanimous* and falsely dated *July 4th* when its text had not then been approved by all of the 13 Colonies?

Congress found itself mired in its own confusion of contradictions, essentially derived from the differences in ways of life in the northern Colonies vs. the southern ones, or the individual farmers or merchants vs. wealthy plantation owners with slaves. To hide a rift in principle, Congress chose to hide the whole controversy by total excisions from the Original Draught where it blazed unreservedly for *Liberty* - in its entirety.

Having published a July 4th Broadside *signed by order*, a signed manuscript was legally required as evidence, and upon suppression of the Fair Copy the substitute became necessary.

A possible artifice may have been to inscribe similar duplicate signatures on the Parchment Copy so that after comparison at the table it could masquerade convincingly in replacement while showing only a clean abridged text, - the remainder gone.

As abridged from the Fair Copy, and as a validated signed Document, re-titled, and mis-dated July 4th, it could have been supposed that only this Parchment Copy need be shown as the official document and as the only visible legal form: - but could replacement signatures on parchment seem authoritative if approval on July 4th was by only 11 Colonies, contrary to the new title & date ?- Or was the replacement validated by a political twist? -- As the parchment skin was too small for comparable signature space, the duplicate signatures had to be written at half the original size.

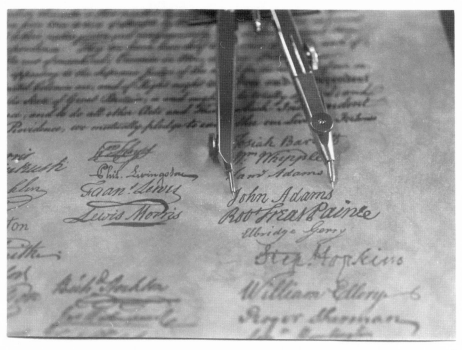

Setting for the reproduction of
signatures to a smaller scale

The new signatures thus had to be smaller but similar, - yet it is not in the common ability of 48 penmen to write one set of signatures, and four weeks later to write a similar set at a fixed size-reduction of one-half, as was done. Signature copying suggests that a device had been used for mechanical reduction, or for marking reserved space during duplication, - e.g., with proportional dividers.

In recollection of the pantograph used previously for the Rough Draft, it has been questioned whether this was used to outline signature positions and even to sketch them in pencil by transfer from the Fair Copy, but this procedure seemingly would have been refused as too contrived, and in addition Jefferson may have preferred not to emphasize his private use of the instrument which would naturally have been extended to architectural plans, as painters have obscured its use in the copying of portraits for duplication of their paintings from one original.

Proportional dividers reproducing similarities.

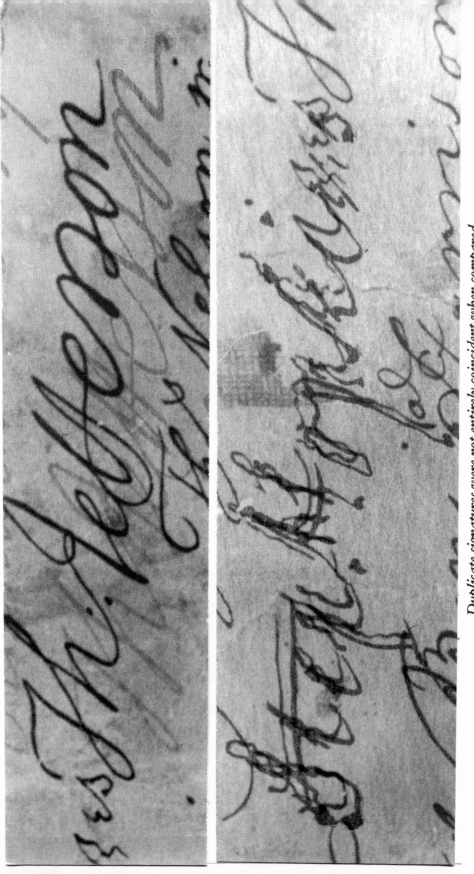

Duplicate signatures were not entirely coincident when compared at the same scale. There had been two separate signings.

In pursuit of this matter, the signature of Jefferson on the Fair Copy, and also its twin on a facsimile of the engraved Parchment Copy, were enlarged photographically and equalized in size, then superimposed. While the two signatures had been written in the proportion of 2 : 1, they were not entirely coincident when brought to the same scale. The measured slopes of the last few letters in the Parchment Copy version became increasingly more slanted and narrower. Although these signatures seemed at first glance to be duplicates, they differed partially in their letter-slopes, as seen when enlarged. That they had been written independently seems certain, but probably with use of a spacing control.

In signing with a duplicating set of signatures of fixed sizes, proportional to the initial ones, a problem originates in the overlapping of the written lines, which occurred during the heat of their original July creation. Their entanglements were very great: - John Penn hung his signature by its loops upon the horizontal underline of John Hancock; Oliver Wolcott's fancy work produced a cloud of swirls which hung upon the sweeping tail of Williams' ample W; George Clymer swept William Ellery's signature into his province; Robert Morris barged directly through Hancock's J -- with his initial R.

To reproduce the original order of the July signatures would have invited the complications of overlapping, and this would have created in duplication an artificial appearance. Simply by isolation of the individual signatures as applied to a facsimile, in their order by Colony, as in the Parchment Copy, overlappings were avoided, - but the passion had died.

THOS. M. KEAN.

He made a valuable contribution ...
but in recollection - he had the wrong date,
the wrong document and the wrong weather.

How two muddy Boots betrayed a flickering Memory

Beginning on August 2, the signers of the Original Draught affixed their names on the Parchment Copy. Urgency had wilted after signings on July 4th (with a few late additions on July 15 *&* 19). Although compared at the table, writers have avoided saying with what were the comparisons, - but all was clarified by Jefferson to Samuel Adams's grandson, Mr. Wells, as - signatures on paper, July 4th, and on parchment, August 2.

Nearly a year later one signer, Thomas McKean, found that his name was missing from the Parchment Copy and he wrote of his displeasure over the omission, asserting that he had voted for Independence, - and he was permitted to sign in 1777. He further charged that no member of Congress had signed on July 4 and none before August 2, except John Hancock for the Broadside.

This curious dispute led to long-lasting skepticism and denials of any July signings by some later historians, continuing even to the present day.

Owing to secrecy which shrouded discussion in Congress, the members were not authorized to say or write anything of what they were deciding in the Statehouse. It was prohibited to make reference to signings or to discussions. The objective was to prevent the British from identifying supporters of the Declaration - so as to avoid lethal vengeance or capture.

The controversy aroused by McKean's claim is illuminated by his fanciful recollections of the events of mid-1776. According to his letters written a quarter century after the events, he claimed that on the morning of July 4th he met Casar Rodney in his muddy boots at the Statehouse door, after a posthaste ride from Delaware to break the tie vote of his Colony, then in balance.

McKean in attaching Rodney's arrival in muddy boots to his assertion that *nobody signed on that day*, had forgotten that the dramatic ride in a thunderstorm was made on the night of July 1.

Rodney had been summoned without reference to the Declaration as not yet under discussion, and McKean was correct in saying that nobody signed on that day (July 2): - but that was the day of the vote only on Lee's Resolution, written on a scrap of paper too small for 48 signatures, and that paper was simply endorsed by John Hancock who had recorded each Colony's simple majority vote by a check mark.

Philada July the 4th 1776

Sir — I have inclosed you a Summons directed to
the Sheriff to Summon the Members for our Coun
ty to meet in Assembly at Newcastle on the 22d day
of this Instant. which I hope you will have
put into his hands as soon as possible after it
comes to yours — I arrived in Congress / tho detain
ed by thunder and Rain / time Enough to give my
Voice in the matter of Independence — It is now
determined. by the thirteen United Colonies with
out even one dissenting Colony — We have now
Got through with the Whole of the declaration, and
Ordered it to be printed. so that You will soon have
the pleasure of seeing it — Hand-bills of it will
be printed. and Sent to the armies. Cities, County
Towns &c. — To be published or rather proclaimed
in form — — Don't neglect to attend Closely and
Carefully to my Harvest and You'll obli[g]
                          Yours &c —
                          Caesar Rodney

Caesar Rodney's letter of July 4, 1776
confirming his arrival on July 2, in a thunderstorm,
to vote on the resolution (not the Declaration)

Thomas McKean made a valuable contribution in sending for Rodney to rush to Philadelphia and break a tie vote, but his memory after 25 years, was confused over the dates of the Resolution with voting by colony alone, and the date of Congress' voting on the Declaration including its signing by 40+ members present. The first date was not July 4th noted as a sunny day by Jefferson who bought a thermometer on his walk to the Statehouse, - but was July 2 after the thunderstorm, marked by a rain-soaked rider in muddy boots. McKean absently had the wrong date, the wrong document and the wrong weather.

Nor does the story end with that explanation of McKean's error. As it was repeatedly and forcefully rewritten by him in the early 19th century, several historians picked it up later like a banner of iniquity, waving it vainly in trying to discover a non-existent memory failure in *Jefferson's* recollections.

The initial confusion in the dispute began simply because the original Manuscript seemed to have disappeared on the night of July 4, although it would have surfaced secretly on August 2 before invisibility suggested its non-existence. Then in 1823, inquiry was made of the State Department whether Jefferson's Original Manuscript was in the archives with the Journals of Congress, but in a search it could not be found.

When Jefferson was asked where it was, he wrote that, *It should be with the records of Congress*, --- but not that it would be.

This mysterious absence of the Original Manuscript passed with little concern until 1873 when the historian, Chamberlain, found a Journal of Congress stating that the Declaration was signed by the members on July 4, 1776. After reading this truly archival source he asserted that it proved the Journals of Congress may not be relied upon for accuracy because *he knew* that it had not been signed in July (- before he was born).

Still later, in 1906, the distinguished historian Hazleton cast much doubt on there having been any signature on July 4th, and he expressed skepticism on whether there had been any July signing of the Declaration. Finally the late Professor Dumas Malone reviewed the matter & concluded that Jefferson probably had not written the Document that he claimed was signed as the Fair Copy and that he may have simply made up the story in old age.

These twisted conclusions have advanced over a 200-year span. They defy the testimony of Franklin, Adams, Hancock and others, all outweighed by McKean's befogged assertions, and later supported inexplicably by mistaken writers of history.

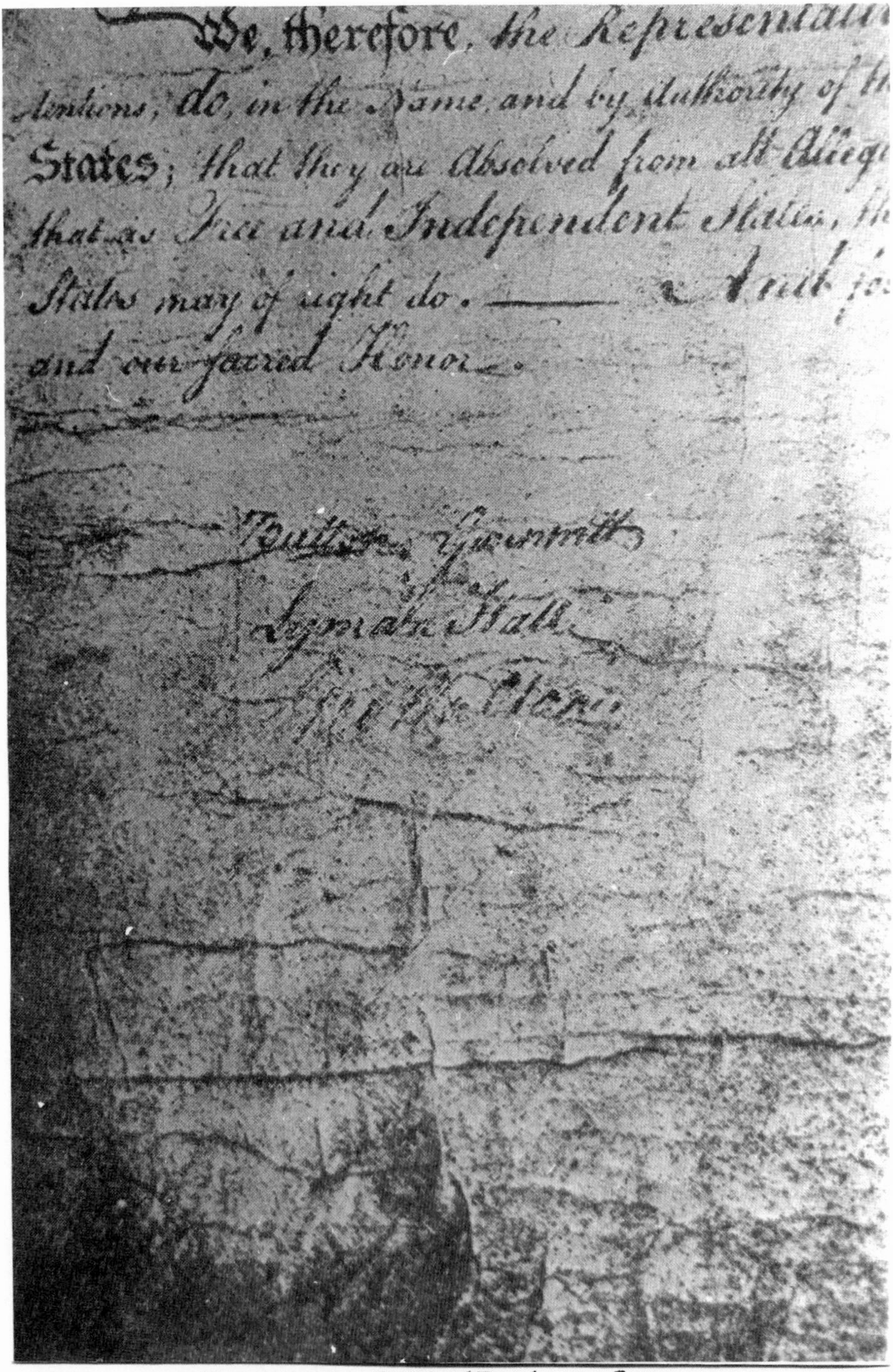

We, therefore, the Representatives...

...tentions; do, in the Name, and by Authority of t...

States; that they are Absolved from all Allegi...

...that as Free and Independent States, th...

States may of right do. ———— And fo...

and our sacred Honor.

Button Gwinnett

Lyman Hall

Geo Walton

*Lower section, Original Parchment Copy,
mutilated in a wet-copying transfer (1823)*

Wherein certain Signatures were withdrawn
- as though by Aerial Spirits

× × — × × — × ×

The initial *Parchment Copy* of August 2nd 1776 was written by a scribe onto parchment, from the Broadside text, and it is rarely seen. It is not an original manuscript but is a copy-text and is represented by a facsimile, also called the Parchment Copy, but known to be not a true likeness of the initial Parchment Copy of the actual date, August 2, 1776.

The material of the initial Parchment Copy was one animal skin scraped smooth, too small to encompass the large lettered text & signatures of the Fair Copy of July 4th in its original size. The drastically new format comprised a single block of text instead of two compact paragraphed columns, and it had a line-length across the page of more than 190 characters (letters), or nearly three times the number as in one line of the Fair Copy.

The new text coursed in mixed styles - a scribe's *script* slowed with heavy Gothic boldface lettering. These contrary or diverse styles coupled with very long lines of small letters tended to obstruct readability, and excessive punctuation with many dashes hindered clarity because divisions of thought became obscured.

With a new title devoid of *Independence* and bracketed sections of the Fair Copy excluded from the new text, the initial Parchment Copy was adopted as the official Document. It was moved like a fugitive during the Revolution as the British harassed Congress. Later it remained in the care of the Confederation, and was held as a Charter when the *United States of America* were founded in 1789.

The Original Manuscript (Fair Copy), with bracketed deletions, vanished in 1776, - its whereabouts unknown then, and afterward...

The Parchment Copy was kept rolled up, and was repeatedly unrolled for visitors, especially calligraphers seeking tracings of the fragile signatures for making *souvenir copies*, - a destructive practice as the ink did not penetrate the parchment skin and flaked easily.

By 1820 copies of the Parchment Copy had been printed at least twice as souvenir facsimiles with traced signatures. Editions published in 1818 and in 1819 showed signatures contrived more accurately than later engraved ones, but the copies were disfigured by pictures on the borders not relevant to the Declaration. In form the Souvenirs were pretentious and spurious. One sent to John Adams was returned directly with his orders to send no more.

In later time the Parchment Copy was frequently referred to as *The Declaration of Independence,* - a title which it never bore.

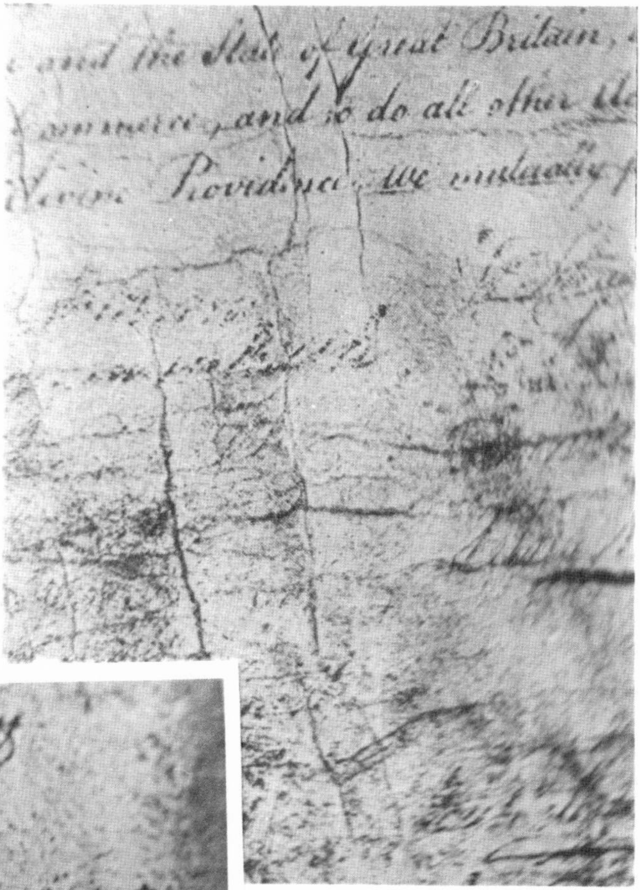

Damaged
Parchment
Signatures

Damage to the Parchment Copy progressed so rapidly that in 1823 the Government undertook to make a copper-plate engraving for making multiple copies -- to provide for public distribution.

The result of this engraving effort was a disaster. - The application of wet paper for transferring ink directly to a copper plate for engraving resulted in major losses of ink from the Parchment Copy's signatures. Restoration was attempted but the copper plate was engraved with faulty patterns. In consequence the duplicated signatures could not show real sensitivity of quill, but a rather contrived appearance. Hancock's signature was distorted, with the 'H' flattened at the base to a static shape, not as a pen-stroke but as though *carved* in metal.

The resultant plate yielded impressions of signatures not wholly authentic in character, although accepted and cherished as symbolic. Much of the sensitive calligraphy was destroyed, and the facsimile 'parchments' cannot be standards for exact comparisons.

After 1823 the Parchment Copy was hung on a Government office wall for some years, in direct sunlight. This exposure dried and embrittled the skin causing shrinkage, fading, and losses of signatures - almost as if by occult design.

By the twentieth century the Parchment Copy came to be revered mostly through the memory of its message, while its appearance had become so damaged as to be an embarrassment. It has been exhibited by facsimile, from a distance and behind glass, without opportunity for close study. But the myth of its sole original status has persisted. When it required moving to a secure sanctuary within the portals of a handsome new and scientifically designed Archive, staffed with numerous experts in manuscript preservation, it was born thither in an *army tank* with a small armed military legion carrying on to protect it.

The true state of the Parchment Copy has remained obscure ever since the disastrous attempt to create an exact facsimile of it over 175 years ago. However early in the twentieth century the Government Printing Office published a book intended for public sale, describing the evolution of the Declaration and also including a printed photographic facsimile of the present state of the actual 1776 Parchment Copy in goodly detail, revealing the devastation of its signatures, little of which is apparent in the initially engraved prints. This archival work comprised a valuable contribution to manuscript scholarship, and a lesson in preservation, as an authentic record of the Parchment through its long and complex history.

Ruined Hancock signature, Parchment of August 2, 1776

This fascinating photo-reproduction of the Parchment Copy itself showed devastation to most of the signatures in the lower quarter and obliteration of much of the Hancock signature.

A water transfer of inked images attempted without pre-testing was unscientific. Non-destructive methods should have been developed before the signatures were attacked. The failure was compounded by the disaster being hidden from the public, with concealment persisting to 1906. It was also disturbing that after the author of the book had published his work on the facsimile,- surely for the public domain and deserving to be public knowledge,-- he was reproved by Congress, according to the Superintendent of Documents, who attempted unsuccessfully to recall the books, as if by censorship.

Concerning authentication of the Declaration, the President of the United States in 1823 asserted that the engraved signatures on the prints of the Parchment Copy were *indistinguishable* from the parchment source, a judgment inexplicable. It follows that expert authentication by eye without measurement may become guesswork.

Such has been the unfortunate life of the Parchment Copy:- refused the title - *Declaration of Independence*, desecrated by the water-plate transfer of 1823 and followed by its century-long cover-up, - yet greatly admired by its loyal countrymen who yearn for that beauty of unquenchable spirit, humane compassion and intrinsic honesty which its initial message held for Mankind.

Notwithstanding such a traumatic history, the Parchment Copy has been enshrined as an Official charter and text of the *Unanimous Declaration of the 13 united States of America* and it commands great veneration and respect. The form of its signatures as originally intended remains familiar through printed copies from one engraving. It is perfectly protected in the National Archives and apparently fulfills its destiny.

The Rough Draft as the unabridged small-scale manuscript Declaration shows in detail the intense struggle in clarifying the principles which were evolved & shaped according to ideas of Liberty, which were in the hearts of the Committee, but not fully understood generally in the 2nd Continental Congress.

The Original Draught as *The Declaration of Independence* is the definitive forerunner of all the Declarations and was penned 13 years before there was a United States of America. It is the prototype of all the copies, but officially superseded by the abridged text from it, on parchment, known as the Parchment Copy, and re-titled --

The Unanimous Declaration of the 13 united States of America

Genealogy of the Copies of the Declaration

L i s t i n g

Ten Jefferson Manuscripts, June - July 1776: -

1) *Initial lost paper* (fragments claimed to exist)
2) *Original Draught* or *Fair Copy* (post-Bicentenial discovery)
3) *Rough Draft* (in Library of Congress) Ch- 5, 8-11, 17-19
4) *Reserve Copy* (published anon. but still hidden) Ch-19
5) *Copy* for Geo. Wythe (in New York Public Library) pg-013
6) *Copy* for R.H.Lee (in American Philosophical Soc.) pg-013
7) *Copy* for E.Pendleton ? (in Massachusetts Hist. Soc.) pg-013
8) *Copy* for Phil. Mazzei (given to a deLafayette)
9) *Copy from Notes* (used for the Autobiography)*
10) *The Copy for the Autobiography* * (Ch-18)
11) *The Madison Copy, 1783* *

Derivative Copies

12) Adams copy, June 1776 (Ch -5,)
13) Initial Printed Broadsides, July 4/5 1776 (Ch-15)
14) Official Parchment Copy, Aug. 2 1776, misdated July 4, (Ch-21 -23)
15) Engraving of the Parchment Copy, 1823 (Ch-23)
16) Printed Facsimiles from the Engraving, 1823 + (Ch-23)
17) Memoir Copy (Rough Draft Engraving), 1829 (Ch-17)
18) Memoir Fac-similes, from the Engraving, 1830 (Ch-17)

----

* The Madison Copy and the Copy for the *Notes* appearing in Jefferson's Autobiography do not have the format derived directly from the other Jefferson manuscripts, but they do show the split paragraph or alternate version for the final paragraph of the Declaration as described in Jefferson's Autobiography. Neither the Fair Copy nor the Rough Draft shows both written forms, but the Rough Draft indicates in Jefferson's hand along one margin from line 146 - *"an alternate phraseology inserted "*. (Ch-18) A copy for John Page has been claimed to exist but is unknown, and may be the one credited here as the Pendleton copy. The rare or little-known copy in the *Memoirs...* of 1830, was published by Jefferson's grandson T. J. Randolph (Ch-17) directly from its engraving of 1829. It is of definitively high importance.

Genealogy of the Manuscript-copies of the Declaration
and the printed derivatives

———————

A genealogy of the manuscript-copies of the declaration was not possible until the recent discovery of the lost Original as well as of the re-appearing small interim copies. A new composite diagram indicates a probable sequence of eighteen known copies. This diagram beginning at the left margin shows the text sheets based on the Committee's notes and termed by Jefferson his *initial paper*. From these sheets at an early stage, before or even after Franklin's first reading, John Adams made his copy (Ch-5), and the initial sheets or their derivatives were passed between Franklin and Adams several more times for their *corrections*, each said to be interlined in his own handwriting. Three *alterations* evidently as short paragraphs were suggested to Jefferson verbally by the Committee, and were inserted into the evolving text. (Ch-5,)

From the resulting *amended paper* Jefferson carefully drew his large Fair Copy showing the text of the Committee throughout its cumulative stages and as approved, before it was laid *unaltered on the table*, for Congress then to modify and sign. (Ch-12, -14) A small duplicate of the Fair Copy text as the Rough Draft was also drawn by Jefferson, for noting changes during the editing of the Fair Copy. This duplicate text was evidently made by pantographic transfer (Ch-9), & is shown directly below the Fair Copy as four small pages.

According to Jefferson, Adams, and Franklin, the initial signing of the Fair Copy occurred on the evening of July 4th (Ch-14), after which the committee were instructed to attend the press, when the first Broadsides were printed in the night for selected distribution to each of the Colonies. (Ch-15) These are shown directly to the right of the Fair Copy.

After drastic deletions by Congress, Jefferson evidently wrote six or seven small interim copies showing the approved Committee text before abridgment, as his version, and sent these to colleagues in Virginia. The copy for Richard Henry Lee was sent on July 8th and the others probably close to that time. (Ch-19) They are shown as emanating with similar texts from the Rough Draft but without the detailed changes. They are the small copies exhibited in Libraries (Pg-13), but the Mazzei copy may be lost.

Not until August 2nd was the Parchment Copy ready for its signing, and it then displaced the *vanishing Fair Copy* to become an official document. (Ch-21) It was not reproduced until 1823. (Ch-23)

———

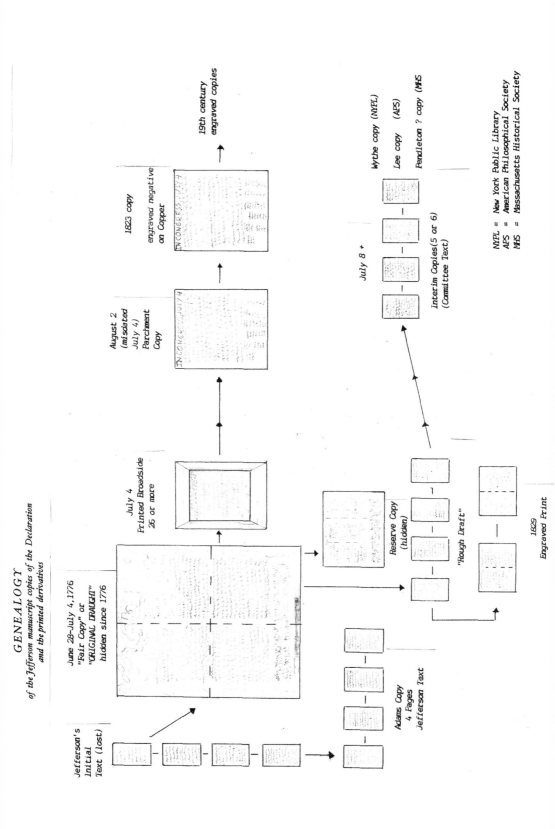

GENEALOGY
of the Jefferson manuscript copies of the Declaration and the printed derivatives

Jefferson's Initial Text (lost)

June 28–July 4, 1776 "Fair Copy" or "ORIGINAL DRAUGHT" hidden since 1776

Adams Copy 4 Pages Jefferson Text

July 4 Printed Broadside 26 or more

Reserve Copy (hidden)

"Rough Draft"

1829 Engraved Print

August 2 (misdated July 4) Parchment Copy

1823 copy engraved negative on Copper

19th century engraved copies

July 8 +

Interim Copies (5 or 6) (Committee Text)

Wythe copy (NYPL)
Lee copy (APS)
Pendleton ? copy (MHS)

NYPL = New York Public Library
APS = American Philosophical Society
MHS = Massachusetts Historical Society

PART IV

Of Manuscript Paper

Contents

▨▢▨

Papermaking representations photographed in
"The Deutsche Museum", Munich, Germany, with special permission.
The approx. 3" high wood carved figures are shown
with their handmade tools in their traditional settings.

A Paper Maker sitting on a vat ('Fass') with his tools:
4. a rack or sieve, ('Rechen') in his left, 5. a stirring staff, ('Ruehrstecken') in
his right hand, 7. the mold ('form') on the floor leaning against the vat.
   His products: 1. A pointed paper bag ('Duede') on his head,
2. A legal, ('Kantzley') paper, and 3. A letter paper ('Post Papier') sheet on
his right arm. Reams of paper under his feet.

The Vatman lifting a mold containing pulp from the vat

Lumpensammler nach einer Zeichnung von Ludw.g Richter

Rag collector

*Paper
Fibers
Mostly
Flax
are
extracted
from
RAGS*

*Rags
sorted*

*Rags
weighed
and
stored*

Rags beaten

Vatman, Coucher and assistant for press

*Molds
for making
laid paper
& hangers
for drying*

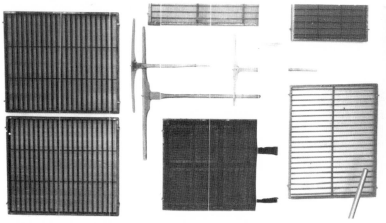

lifting a sheet of paper from a press

Why the Papers of the Manuscripts are different
◦ ☐ ◻ ▢ ⬧

The Rough Draft having watermarks of Holland manufacture has an 18th century *laid pattern of fine grooves* on the surface, a ladder-like appearance within the surface from the form of the mould used in manufacture, with the typical roughness of common old papers; but the paper of the Fair Copy shows smoothness *without laid-lines,* and is too thick for watermarks to appear if present.

These differences suggested that the dissimilar papers were chosen for separate uses: - a cheap ordinary paper for successive drafts during revision and a large drawing- or map- paper of clarity and permanence for a final fully-signed official Document. It was evident that the laid paper is of the thin type for simple writing but that the paper of the Fair Copy is of a type for display and delineation of artwork when large sheets are needed - having such smoothness that a pen may glide evenly and sensitively over the surface for portraiture, decoration, signatures, and a large (*fair*) text.

The paper-making process in England and Europe in the 18th century consisted in making single sheets by hand from pulps of beaten linen rags pressed flat, dried, bonded with a glue-gel as sizing, *&* re-dried as paper. The details will relate to the Fair Copy.

The flax as the basic cellulosic 'stuff' was extracted from cleaned, meticulously selected linen rags (rarely cotton) - white for best quality. The fibres from these were broken down by machinery *&* dispersed in water as a pulp, then drained of excess liquid. For this critical step a shallow sieve was dipped into a vat containing a slurry of the pulp. The sieve when lifted from the watery suspension, and drained, left fibres in quasi-horizontal directions upon the screen bottom, which impressed its irregular form into the pulp. This mass of fibres formed a limp sheet and was then pressed against felt to squeeze out water, repeatedly, until the firm sheet could be pressed and dried to raw paper, which was finally to be soaked in glue-size, pressed again, and dried slowly to the finished product.

The imprint of the bottom of the sieve formed of wires was permanently implanted in the soft rag pulp and resulted in the laid-lines *as micro-grooves*. Both the laid-lines of the paper itself and the special water-marks if present are best seen by holding the paper toward light, since they are patterns of thinner light areas - visible from their transparency compared with the more opaque paper mat. Since the lines are mould impressions showing in transmitted light, especially shaped wire patterns came into use to imprint symbols as a maker's identifications - the imprints now called *water-marks*.

Mold with sheet of paper and "Deckel" for holding paper

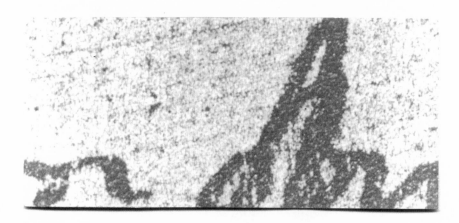

greatly enlarged laid paper in Rough Draft

early "wove paper", ca. 1760

In earlier times vellum (or fine parchment) was in use as a more ideally smooth writing surface for manuscripts, but was expensive since vellum is an animal skin and requires scraping to be flat; and with the introduction of paper in 11th century Europe, economy and ink-retention of paper proved to be superior, although of rougher surface from unevenness of the moulds used in the wet processes.

Around 1757, the English fine-paper maker, James Whatman, had 'reduced to practice' his inventions for improving paper quality and smoothness by means of finer sieve or dip-mould structures, using special metallic gauzes, *loom-woven as linen*, to span the mould bottom -- its geometry perfected to avoid mould imprints and to control water-drainage.* Paper was thus created without showing grooves in transmitted light. It was called *wove-paper or velin* according to its similarity to vellum (parchment); but its ink retention was superior by deeper penetration of ink.

In the Fair Copy, the appearance of surface-finish corresponds to early wove-paper examples but this appearance is not an exact qualification; and although the Fair Copy shows no trace of laid lines, its kind of paper - whether wove-, map- or drawing-type - are the explicit categories which characterize it. One of the first three books printed by Baskerville on Whatman's new wove-paper was *Prolusions* in 1760, and examination of it has shown here that its macro- surface structure is visually similar to that of the Fair Copy.

It is possible that a smooth paper of a secret type was in use in other countries, especially in Italy, at a much earlier date than English wove-paper but this is uncertain. Some foreign map papers were of smooth drawing types though not called a wove type, and it could be that some of these were secret formulations equivalent to Whatman paper -but with their details hidden in manufacture.

About 20 years after Whatman's invention, new wove-paper was copied widely, appearing in other countries. It was familiar to Jefferson who imported it for a few of his architectural drawings, & Hopkinson probably had used some map- or drawing- papers.

These smooth 18th century drawing papers or wove types were permanently stable, as were other older papers made from linen rags with natural gel-size and alum; - and these have proven far superior to the later *scientific machine-made papers* of the 19th century employing wood pulp, acids and caustic chemicals saturated with fillers, and synthetic resins replacing gel-size in the formulations.

The Fair Copy is found to be of the of 17th- 18th century map- or drawing-types of the 1st Class. According to John Balston*, "The high quality papers of 250 years ago are as robust as ever they were then and proven to last". *J.N.Balston: The Whatmans & Wove Paper. vol-3. 1998.

Identification of fiber structure in old paper depends on a sophisticated research microscope

Cameras /
Spectroscope

Phototube

Binocular tube
Eyepieces

Analyzer /
Compensator Slot
Limb, adjustable
(supporting)

Vertical Illuminator
Epi Light source,
Polarizer / Filters,
Objective Lens
Mechanical Stage
Rotating Stage

Substage Condenser
Aperture Diaphragm

Substage Polarizer
Focusing Knobs
(adjustable to 0.2 µ)
Field Diaphragm
Illuminator

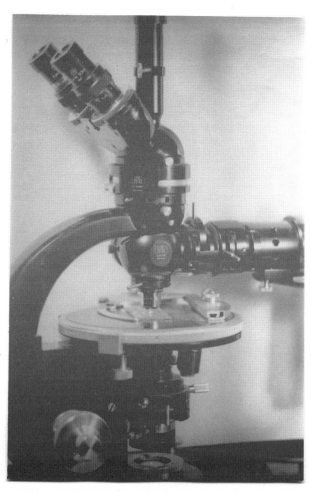

Carl Zeiss GFL Research Microscope

The Flax plant

The micrograph (200x) of the Manuscript paper shows flax fiber in a matrix of a translucent glue-like solid.

Chapter - 26
The Hidden Nature of Paper

The composition of paper is far more complex than appears to the unaided eye, and its type may not be judged by guesswork. The *experienced eye* cited by some as a qualification for final authority is surely a thing spun in the brain. Resemblances viewed and appraised by sight alone cannot yield exacting judgments.

European papers of the 18th century as stated are composed largely of cellulose fibres of flax taken from cleaned beaten linen rags, together with solidified gels from animal glues. Cotton fibres were added mainly after the invention of the cotton gin after 1790.

Only well into the 1800's did wood pulp invade the paper industry, together with inorganic fillers. Fibres of such paper although of a related cellulose are different from flax fibres in micro-structure. In addition, the processing of wood involved the use of acidic & caustic chemicals whose residues could cause insidious deterioration, and with addition of synthetic resin, fillers, and dyes, different basic structures emerge. Finally the primary new goal was to become an economic one, consequential from the industrial revolution,

It is thus crucially important to characterize papers, old & new.

Identification of the fibre and gel-size structure of old paper depends on a versatile research microscope with strain-free optics and precision focusing for transmitted, reflected & polarized light, in both brightfield and darkfield modes.

Old papers thus examined show the individual fibres and their fragments with distinguishing features and arrangement clarified in orientation and depth by the focusing system. The fibres do not unite themselves into flat sheets but are scattered only roughly in the plane of the paper and tilted at many angles.

This fibrous mat contains numerous small nests having shallow void spaces of varying depth and breadth. These nests are partially open, with fibres interlocked and somewhat fragmented, and show channels within the range of capillary dimensions, spreading randomly or interconnected to other nests by sub-capillaries. This network would comprise a kind of blotter into which a liquid would penetrate uncontrollably, - and must be permeated with *gel-size* to close the connecting capillaries and limit ink penetration. For this purpose a writing-paper had to be impregnated or coated with the gel-size. after formation.

'Glue-sizing' (agglutinant) consists of undried *gel-size*. (Ital. assi'dersi, Lat., Assidere, to sit down), - meaning by derivation *that which painters use to make the colours sit well*. The Artist knew the necessity of a *size* upon canvas.

Writing with ink on Gel alone

without light background

with reflecting background

The gel-size in old paper together with the dense highly reflecting fibrous mat were sufficient without additions to enhance reflected whiteness so that ink marks show with strong contrast. But when machine-made paper was introduced in later 19th century, replacements of the former gel-size and alum were effected through synthetic resins or rosin, and aluminum sulphate; but this was an error in several ways: - e.g., the rosin when dried and heated has the property of being only with difficulty wet with water and of becoming brittle; also, the newer papers were filled with cheap loading materials such as kaolin (up to 15%), which were intended to close the pores and to make the paper surface whiter and smoother. Later it was seen that the old gel-size provided superior strength & durability. The synthetics deteriorated & the new paper embrittled.

The gel for sizing of old paper was drawn from animal connective tissue by extraction with hot water from bones and also from scrap leather discards, and it was necessarily combined with alum. The gel itself or collagen, is familiar as a jelly-like translucent substance of many uses, but in paper it serves as a flexible *adhesive* in the fixing of the fibrous mat. It does not entirely fill the nests in the fibre structure & contrary to some notions it is hydrophilic, i.e., it is wet by water or ink. A membrane of the gel-size formed by drying a solution of gelatin powder can be written on with ink, as with paper, but alone it lacks reflectance, so writing may not stand out by contrast, unless the gel is laid on a reflecting background.

The use of the alum with gel-size is an ancient invention promoting the adhesion among the fibers by crosslinking the gel-size to the cellulose, lending strength to the mat & contributing to the writing surface. The alum acts as a mordant and is a preservative in the presence of the natural products - flax and animal gels.

The fibres of flax are elliptically tubular with lengths typically exceeding 30 to 60 μ (microns) and cross-sections up to 10 μ, and they are marked, bamboo-like, by nodes across their long axes, separated irregularly by a few μ of length. Cotton fibres are, in contrast, twisted into spiral forms, at once apparent. The nests or open spaces, fringed with fibres, extend up to 5 or 10 μ.

In the Fair Copy the fibres are mainly of flax having curved or rounded surfaces & distinguished by birefringence, while much of the fibre content is partly crushed & entangled. Since in old paper the fibre components are disarranged and tilted at random in the surface plane, & overlapping, with rough nests interspersed between them, it should be clear that the idea of a paper surface as a flat smooth white plane upon which pens may draw continuous even lines is a simplified illusion, - and that internal composition is vital.

Alum in Gel

*Darkfield micrograph of Alum Crystals: A natural double salt
of Potassium & Aluminum Sulfate, in regular Octahedra"*

Secrets of old Paper -- their animal Glues & alchemistic Alum
-- as found in the Fair Copy

It has been seen that the strength and durability of old papers depend on their animal glues as *colloidal solidified gels with alum* and that these gels limit ink penetration and provide strong adhesion within a fibre net, and also that they provide writing surface through their smoothness and hydrophilic nature (= affinity for water).

Alum is a natural double salt of potassium & aluminum sulfate, crystallizing in regular octahedra with associated water molecules at each crystal corner. Since ancient times alum has been used not only in the glue-size of paper but also in other secret concoctions. This crystal unit with associated water molecules proved essential to the paper's stability as included in the internal linkages of the glue to the fibres. Although the term, *alum* applies to several related substances, with other trivalent metal ions, including magnesium, that of aluminum is usually the most common. In the 17th-18th century its role may not have been completely understood scientifically but it was known to be indispensable, and its presence in old paper should be indicated as confirmation of age.

Original instructions are rare in the old paper-making art, as they were handed down not in writing, but are discussed perceptively in a work depicting the difficulties with glue size, translated here:

G.Chr. Keferstein. Paper-making *Instructions. 1766.*(G.Bayerl & K.Pichol. *Papier. Rowohlt.*1986)*

"In manufacture, animal *glue-sizing* was deposited from thin sizing brews quickly, to each sheet separately; but as this required long experience the boiling and glue-sizing were usually done necessarily by the master himself. The glue-size (or *gel-size*) was made from sheep and deer hooves, bones and discarded leather, and skins from tanners. Boiling glue-size was a foul smelly matter bringing many paper-mills into disrepute... Wetting or glue-sizing requires skill: - if fresh paper is to be sized, the sizing must be of the proper kind.

"Take 40 or 50 Schock (bushels) of sheep legs, let them soak daily in a barrel in clean water for a few days, wash them carefully, then let them boil in a large kettle or better in an iron pot. Skim the fat that swims above the brew and pass this size through a basket into barrels. Add to these sheep legs, some good kinds of glue leather and then drain the glue through a cloth into small barrels. "For this it is understood that you have to have 20 to 25 pounds of Alum... If your glue-size is clear and still milk warm, begin in God's name the wetting; however do not take handfuls of it that are too big -this would make bad paper. All this requires a practiced hand..."

Glue kitchen:
"Several sheets dipped into the sizing brew"

"This is without doubt one of the most difficult types of work and requires much experience and patience If you know everything well, you are smart (*so seyd ihr klug*).   However, if I can give you some advice, - *Do it Your self*.

"The wetting and passing through refers to the sizing procedure proper. Several sheets were held with a little block of wood at one end and dipped into the sizing brew; then the sheets were grasped on the other side and dipped again. Dexterity and correct use of the block assured an even distribution of the size over the entire sheet. After draining   the sheets were taken to the glue-size press, squeezed and hung up for drying again.

"The good quality of the glue-size depended not only on the ingredients and the boiling but to a certain extent on the weather Many are the references to the weather accorded necessary not to spoil the glue-size; viz., the amount of Alum in the glue-size brew should be increased, if the heat of the summer was great or stormy weather was expected. In general, winter and summer were the seasons that were unsuitable for sizing, and autumn also because of its weather fluctuations.   Paper millers not only had to observe and anticipate the weather for their work but they often had their own 'recipes' for boiling the size, which were kept secret and thus have rarely been transmitted in a written form. About half the kettle, in which the paper sheets were sized, held water; the other half waste with additions, and about 1/20 consisted of Alum.

"After sizing the paper had to be smoothened, at first by hand but later a water driven beating stamp was invented. In the 18th century, hand *&* water driven smoothening roller and beating stamps were added. Paper was pressed repeatedly when moist, and sheets were alternately layered."

According to John Balston,* "Sizing is an additive process that confers on the paper the ability to bear ink. The traditional practice of immersing the unsized sheet in a tub filled with a hot solution of gelatine to which potash alum had been added was observed in the 18th C. The function of the alum was to fix or cross-link the gelatine to the cellulose sub-strate. Excess gelatine was pressed out and the sheet dried once again in a loft under carefully controlled conditions, first cooling the paper to convert the size from the *sol* to the *gel-state;* and then either protecting it from exposure to excessive chilling or ensuring that the size did not revert to the sol state as it might have done in very hot weather. This was always a very tricky operation, 'Le collage du Papier manque souvent'".

*John Balston: *The Whatmans & Wove Paper, Its Invention* .... *1998. vol - 3*

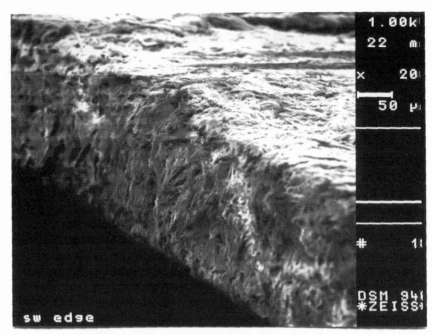

Micrograph of side of a chip of the Manuscript paper through a
Carl Zeiss Digital Scanning Electron Microscope - DSM 940.
Courtesy, Carl Zeiss, Oberkochen, Germany

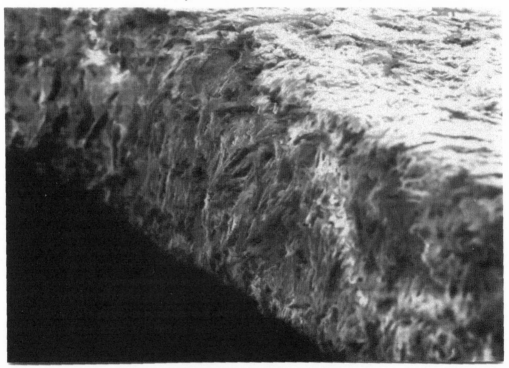

End-Section of above, enlarged by 50%

It would be naive to claim that water-marks are definitive in the appraisal of old documents. In the case of the Fair Copy the double layer of a double-thickness paper, combined with a glued interlayer and linen backing, rule this out completely. It is also questionable to determine age here by carbon dating, for although quantitative over long periods it would seem inappropriate for precision in time-spans of only two centuries for which the sensitivity is weak.

Fortunately for this research, the drastic shifts in the chemistry and mechanics of paper-making after the 18th century make micro-analysis of unique power in evaluations. Foremost of the available methods are chemical microscopy & the determination of elements by scanning micro -X-ray spectroscopy in the electron microscope, - methods which can be used on a minute non-destructive scale with unequivocal results where essential components and definitive structures can be directly identified or determined, and related to image sites on the paper.

Through the courtesy of the Electron Microscope Division of *Carl Zeiss*, Oberkochen, Germany, small samples of paper of the Fair Copy were examined under the scanning ray of an *Electron Microscope, Digital DSM 940,* having then the critically unique feature of simultaneously identifying individual elements, by micro-X-ray spectroscopy on selected surface areas 0.1 mm which were already in view at various magnifications from 1000 to 100 000 x.

It was easily confirmed first that the Fair Copy's paper is of double-layer thickness with a glued interface, and further that the writing surfaces had undergone a gradual *"leathering process"*, or embrittlement of the gel-size, with cracking as in leather, - a result of long-term aging in the surface, showing both the nature of the *size* and a centuries-old history.

When small areas of writing surface were scanned with this instrument to a depth of approximately 150 Å at 1 to 10 kilovolts, the sharply identified elements included Aluminum, Potassium, & Sulfur; and these are the essential constituents of Alum, the common double sulfate of Potassium & Aluminum which is already cited as the natural mineral used in making the glues for the handmade papers up to the 19th century.

Magnesium was present, probably as a component of a natural mineral, *Schoenite,* sometimes found with Alum, - a double sulfate - of potassium with magnesium in place of Aluminum. Traces of Sodium were ascribed to salt by handling. In addition were found Calcium and Sulfur which together with Oxygen may compose Gypsum, strongly suggesting contact with a plaster wall.

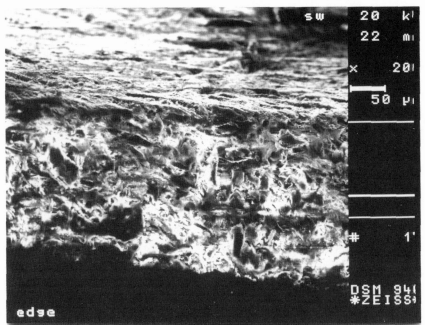

Micrograph of side of a chip of the Manuscript paper through a
Carl Zeiss Digital Scanning Electron Microscope - DSM940.
Courtesy, Carl Zeiss, Oberkochen, Germany

Also was found Silicon, which is the major constituent of very fine sand, frequently used in older writing as a dust, scattered on writing paper to absorb excess ink.   Although blotting paper was in use by the 15th century, absorption of wet ink on paper by fine sand continued nearly to the present.

The scanning method indicated that the paper was mostly organic material, which must rule out 19th century papers loaded with inorganic fillers such a kaolin, not present in old papers.

Thus it was found by electron-microscopic qualitative analysis *&* light-microscopic examinations that the paper of the Fair Copy has a structure and sizing corresponding to a high quality rag stock from flax, coated with protective gel-sizing, containing the essential alum of old paper, which with its affinity for water exerts attachment for ink. The basic flax consistency with sizing and lack of fibre directional orientation confirm manufacture before the use of machines, fillers and destructive chemicals in the 19th century. In optical nature the paper conforms to an old map type.

By the above micro-techniques the paper of the Fair Copy contains elements in common 18th-century usage for glue-size content, with the predominance of flax fibres corresponding to hand-made papers common before 1790; and the constituents of Alum as found are essential within the nature of hand-made paper of the period, while from the finish *&* unique optical properties it is decisively of the 18th century.

It was found valuable in this research to have at hand a practice with European optical devices including unique modern innovations in microscopy. It should be noted that historically the inventions and development of precision optical and electromagnetic systems from early rudimentary microscopes and the *invention of optical glass* to the creation of the *transmission- and scanning- electron microscopes,* with *electromagnetic lenses and spectroscopic derivatives* -- being the *essential bridge* as a basis to computer technology -- have nearly all been European, especially German, in their historical discovery, conception, and scientific development to perfection.

These achievements by imagination and precision of execution were by design a result of recognition and appreciation in classical pre-war European education of *real inequality of intrinsic intelligence & genius* among individuals, according to inborn genes and background- whereby students with gifted minds, and *will-power*, are separated early in schools so that as superior youth they can advance to creativity, responsibility, and leadership, unimpeded by meanderers.

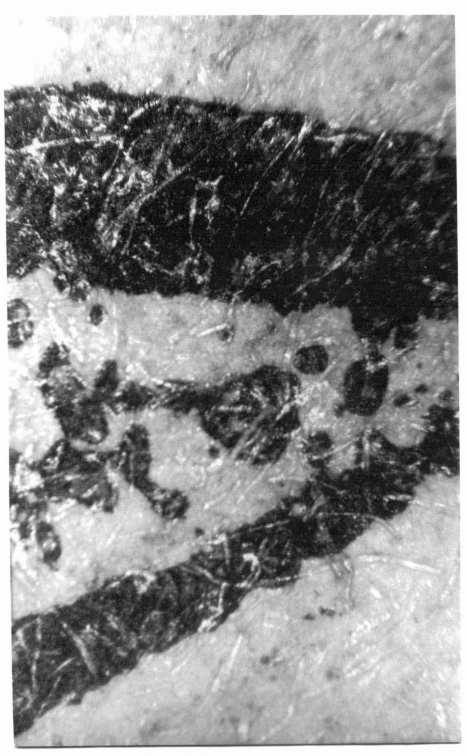

An enlarged detail of written letter of Manuscript

The Nature of Ink-lines in Micro-reality

Ink-lines on paper are not smoothly continuous dark streaks on a flat white plane, but comprise segmented stains of the ink-pigment, deposited and dried upon the uppermost fibres, and on solidified gel-size surfaces interspersed among the fibres or even coating them. A quill upon old paper deposits ink in forms defined partially by the contact geometry, with the boundaries of the lines irregular from incomplete wetting and flowing of ink, - thus delineating a curiously hand-made appearance. On fibre surfaces the ink may be retained only partially, with micro-discontinuities not resolvable by eye alone. A quill's ink-lines having irregular borders are identified easily in comparison with *printed* impressions.

The microscope reveals exactly how ink has flowed onto and into a paper surface, and shows conclusively whether the ink was deposited as from pressure printing by type, wetting from an engraved surface, wetting as by planographic printing, or flowing from a quill. The distinctive mode of ink-transfer may not be judged unequivocally by unaided guesswork without the use of lenses.

In relief printing, a typeface after coating with printer's ink impinges on the paper under force, creating measurably deep impressions into it and depositing ink directly on the bottom; but also, the typepiece may lap a narrow microscopic border around the edge of the impressions made into the paper, which become permanent, the depth varying with press and type-face geometry.

In an engraving process, the plate holding the design when pressed upon the paper leaves an impression of the engraved structure, sunk into the paper as with type or letter-press. However the ink is transmitted to the paper through wetting from ink-saturated cavities in the engraved plate.

In lithography, the paper is pressed with an inked pattern which has wetted the surface selectively upon thin layers in a process not relevant to manuscripts of 1776 as not yet invented. Marks made by this method are easily identified by their structure.

In the Fair Copy it is found that the written text and signatures were written by hand with quills, directly upon the paper. Where one signature crossed another the order is clear, the second lying atop the first. Wherever a line crossed another the 3-dimensional effect may be apparent. No trace of printing, engraving, or lithography has been found in the Manuscripts, signatures, text, or decorations. The entire work has the unmistakable characteristics in its microstructure of a unique hand-made creation.

Optics above stage

Optics below stage

Micro-examinations of the Fair Copy's paper are especially effective under darkfield illumination. In this method a vertical illuminating beam is bent inwardly toward the plane of the paper by refraction or by reflection from annular rings concentric about the front of the objective lens. This illumination is very oblique or grazing and with diaphragms in the beam produce shadows which enhance thickened tracks of ink. If one line intersected another the cross-over may be discernible from shadows under grazing light.

In darkfield, back-reflection from lens elements is avoided and thereby any haze resulting from normal incident-light is unseen, as directed to the fibres. Various details of the structure stand out in three dimensions: -where surface topography is flat, the background is black, comprising a darkfield. The effectiveness of the method with high contrast is based on ultra-microscope principles in which particles too small to be resolvable for the eye are shown by side-illumination as single diffraction discs about minutiae, - a type of visibility shown by floating dust specks in a darkened room illuminated by directional rays of sunlight.

With darkfield illumination the fibres of 18th century paper show the nodes in the cellulose structure of the flax, and also the twists without nodes in cotton if present, - modern papers having a different character in comparison. It is also revealed exactly where the ink has wetted the fibres or has spread and lodged upon gel-size. Variations between ink marks from a quill versus printing are seen as *hand-made* by the quill.

Under polarized light the optical character of the fibre may be discerned quantitatively, including its ellipticity or roundness as well as the local slopes over an entire surface, together with exact areas wet by ink. The shapes of ink-lines upon old paper are complex and the elusive topography can hardly be delineated in a single image; but by continuous focusing over a scanned surface a composite picture can be visualized in memory, disclosing how important is the smoothness of the surface for delineation of sharp ink lines and multiple dots.

Printer's ink which is partially similar to black *writing -ink* may have like permanence and insolubility in water, - and has additions of an agglutinate, including soap and an oil, - which serve to produce a more viscous fluid, - capable of adhering to the type face from which it is applied onto paper. Printer's ink is used especially for its convenience of application as well as opacity. But its oil may show itself as a tell-tale stain of unwanted printer's ink on manuscripts, as described. (Ch-15)

Dark field
Epi Plan
Objective

Illuminating lens system
below the stage

front condenser lens system
with polarizer

Diaphragm for the
illuminating beam

The optical nature of paper in transmitted light may be seen in a microscope with illumination from the condenser below the stage, passing light through the paper rather than reflecting it as incident light from above. Translucent fibres are then seen in depth with cell-walls darker on their sides.   In old paper, as stated, the sizing is the gel-medium holding as a gluing agent the fibre system. Without *gel-size*, fibres would not mat compactly, and like a wad of cotton or flax could not alone form a sheet. As noted, a gel-size provides cohesion within a micro- system   but also   as   a hydrophilic solid it serves in the writing surface, while the fibres reinforce the   structure, providing crucially important white background of *high reflectance* to give ink a strong contrast on paper.

Fibres of paper differ greatly in their morphology. The flattened twisted hollow cotton fibre is easily distinguished from the flax fibre with its nodes. In flax, cotton or other plant fibers, the main constituent is cellulose, the molecules of which consist of hundreds of B-glucose entities attached together. Both readily absorb water and are swollen by it. This absorption, producing swelling, occurs in the amorphous regions of the fibres because of their free-spaces.

A re-enforcing effect in paper of the glue-size with alum results from the crosslinking with the tough strings of fibrous cellulose, and owing to the sub-micron dimensions of the minute subdivisions of the glue-size it becomes very efficient both in strengthening internal adhesion, and blocking deep ink penetration. The role of the gel in contributing wetting surface for ink may be seen by forming a small leaf or sheet of solid gelatin and then writing on it with a pen. The written lines are visible but only weakly unless the background is made white, as by laying the leaf on paper.

The fibres in old paper are thus not the sole writing surface, but a re-enforcing network for the glue-size, also providing *reflecting surface* below & around the opaque dark ink, which flows over this composite surface, wetting it, but not penetrating deeply where it is blocked by solid gel, leaving a dark track only where deposited.

The paper of the Fair Copy thus shows a high-grade character of surface finish as the large sized-*canvas* for the *pen-and-ink artist* in portraiture and decoration, as well as for display of its author's ideas in sharp definition for the documentary record. This display is uncomplicated by the micro-grooves of a laid-paper texture or by the smudges and oxidation of impermanent ink, as found in the small drafts, and it is uniquely authenticated by the combination of sharp black signatures with *their* corresponding contemporary portraits, in permanent original form.

❁✦•✦•✦•✦❁

Gall formations on oak leaves, from Mount Defiance, New York

Sectioned gall from oakleaf

Why the Ink is black
❧

The usual colonial writing inks were made from galls, mixed with a vitriol or iron salt, in water. Galls are formations on leaves or bark, of insect origin, and contain larvae and also much tannin and gallic acid. The vitriol is ferrous sulfate, reacting to form in water with the gallic acid of the gall an ink containing iron sulfate particles which stain with a brown color. This liquid ink when spread on paper is oxidized by further reactions with the paper, turning to a darker ferric compound, more nearly blue-black, but as a writing ink it is not permanent and undergoes further slow oxidation, nor is it impervious to water. Plain cheap types of ink as made in colonial times evidently were not permanently stable and reacted with paper.

The ink of the Rough Draft is of this type, and its deterioration is evident in several instances, especially where letters or entire words have been smudged or lost, leaving watery stains, for example --in line 90.

It should not be imagined in view of their scientific knowledge that Jefferson with Hopkinson, as artists, and Franklin as a printer would have used this ordinary type of ink for the final Draught of a state Document. The claims of some writers, that the Rough Draft is the original manuscript of the Declaration, reflect an inadequate grasp of the requirements for such a Document, not only in terms of its paper but also of its ink.

Far back in the past a very different type of ink had been invented. As early as the 4th millennium B.C. the Egyptians, and also at an early date artists of China and scribes of India, devised inks which were non-fading and permanent in respect to their color and their insolubility. These were the carbon inks which were used in ancient records and drawings. The basic pigment of these inks which have come down in their essential invariable form is black carbon, crudely as a form of charcoal but more ideally from the soot of burning oil or other organic compounds. The soot here referred to originates in smoky flames as unoxidized carbon and is deposited on the chimneys of oil lamps, there occurring in a minute state of subdivision. Carbon deposits are prepared more copiously when flames from such lamps or other sources of burning oils impinge upon a cold metal surface, from which they may be wiped or scraped to gather the finely powdered black deposit. This occurs in a continuous process if the metal plate is rotated slowly above the flame while the deposit is steadily scraped off.

To make a carbon writing-ink, black carbon dust is suspended in water with surface-active media retaining the suspension which can flow in a stream through capillary space as in a quill. Free flow along such space requires a fine particle-size suspension to avoid clogging.

The finer the particle-size the blacker is the residue. The size may be reduced to one-tenth or even to one-hundredth micron (0.1 - 0.01 μ). Even without modern techniques the ultra-fine particle-size of carbon ink has always been unique.

In a microscope image, the carbon particles are complex, derived from the basic crystal systems of carbon (graphite or diamond) but may be mixtures of complex variations of these as heterogeneous aggregates. They decrease in size below the resolving power of the light microscope. While the largest of these black carbon particles have facets to reflect light which are only barely visible, the mass extend in size below the wavelength of light becoming totally non-reflecting, - i.e., black.

Graphite crystallites as a component in black carbon have a unique character - both for writing as pencil lead and as unseen components of black carbon pigment - through their affinity for water on a molecular basis. It was discovered many years ago (1940) by this Author, - that the slipperiness of graphite is not intrinsic in its plate-like crystal-structure alone as then universally supposed, but is due to adsorption films especially of water vapor, which *cover* the carbon atoms and ensure low cohesion of sliding surfaces. Without these films graphite is not slippery. This discovery suggests that these crystallites should improve the mobility of hard carbon in black ink. [*High-vacuum experimental apparatus* >—

Ink lines on paper from carbon ink have a unique smoothness with a jet-black finish and are capable of delineation of the finest and most precise lines. This is the ideal ink for the artist and archivist, producing patterns unchanging in time and unaffected by oxidation or water solubility. As in the formulations of India- or China-ink, they are essential to the cartographer or architect. As stated, the quill lines of the text on the Fair Copy lie upon the paper - a strong sized mat of flax fibers without wood pulp, with a distinct type of gel-size. The ink is not an ordinary colonial writing ink based on iron-gall and is without their components. It is opaque, jet-black, and shows minute characteristics of sub-microscopic crystallites of black carbon, - as in inks known in Egypt, China, and India for thousands of years, and favored for ease of application, richness, insolubility and above all for its undisputed permanence, - non-fading and chemically inert upon paper through time. ——————

The idea for this device came from insight of empty space above a surface, so the surface could be studied without impinging of gases or vapors upon it, - exploring questions of interactions at an interface when one object slides upon another. In pursuit of such inquiry, an electro-magnet was built (by the Author) to form magnetic linkages around an iron hoop having teeth laced by coils of wire sequentially, forming a series of magnetic fingers about the periphery & resulting in a rotating magnetic field outside of a glass bell jar which isolated the surface under study, - while the hoop induced a torque or twisting moment by inductive interaction with the caged structure within, causing rotation at 30 revolutions per second, in a vacuum when necessary. This magnetic propulsion through a glass wall created sliding action between the moving surface and stationary slider bearing on it, for observation of the nature of sliding friction & influences of electric current transfer, dependent on atmosphere. The driving action stemmed from magnetic fields produced by alternating electric current along each of 3 wire circuits; in phase sequence, the resultant being directional by successive induced reactions, as a motor. Atmospheric effects electrically may be understood as akin to those of a thunderstorm - in the micro-spaces.

Sliding contact apparatus for studies in graphite lubrication. See page 1.

High vacuum apparatus for Graphite experimentation,
by the Author, as published on the front cover of the
Journal of Applied Physics, Volume 19, January 1948

Liberty, & the Freedom of the Heavens

When the exploration of worldly space in the 18th Century turned to small things, scientific inquiries continued with study of micro-interfaces & crystals, but regarding environmental effects with & without air, these things were magnified with microscopes, and this led circuitously in the 20th Century to electrical & magnetic effects in the space of closed tubes, in vacuum, as a subject which could & did evolve toward an incandescent lamp, then a vacuum tube, the X-Ray tube, with its unconceived radio, and its visual derivative TV, even the Radar; - but not without knowledge of flux as fields of force, – invisible, unfelt, magnetic, but with electrical interactions, mathematical. Therefrom, with freedom of independent thinking, the unfettered mind could turn also to larger space & outer space and reduce apparent distances with lenses *as* telescopes, so the laws of immemorial time in space could gradually be perceived, fathomed, calculated with proximity; and later, although that great vastness of the heavens was by spells perceived to be immeasurably hot, deathly cold, seething, colliding with dusts, comets, planetoids, planets, suns, black-holes, quarks, galaxies in collision, these things could be explored with more than telescopes. Spaceships through the same freedom of ingenious thought -that made the smallest things almost visible & the largest inconceivable, -finally launched inquiries as a series of Pioneers, in courage, outward toward eternity...

One of the Author's inventions was necessarily on board for the voyage. -

Old friend Pioneer 10 checks in with NASA

Courtesy of NASA
An artist's rendition of Pioneer 10 passing Jupiter.

The Washington Post

NASA has made contact with an aging space probe that is hurtling toward oblivion.

Engineers at the NASA Jet Propulsion Laboratory's Deep Space Network in Goldstone, Calif., sent a signal March 1 to the Pioneer 10, which is about 7.5 billion miles from Earth. At 1:47 p.m. on March 2, the network's facility in Madrid heard Pioneer's response. It was the first time the probe's handlers had contacted the craft since July 9.

Pioneer was launched March 2, 1972, and became the first spacecraft to study Jupiter up close. In 1983, Pioneer became the first man-made object to leave the solar system. It has been speeding through space since its mission officially ended March 31, 1997.

It is headed toward the constellation Taurus, where it will pass the constellation's nearest star in about 2 million years.

Liberty, Free Inquiry & Space

⌛ — ⌛

Liberty is essential to Science, as it permits *Freedom of Inquiry,* and Science is essential to Man as his shield against Superstition, - which is an Evil from the errors of belief in oft-told tales as Semblances of the *Bliss of Futurity, &* also belief in *Dreams as real Life* fabricated *through sensual desire* into *Delusions of the Impossible.*

Science has no interest in Superstition. The history of science from ancient Grecian times has included the creative idea of observing, - finding strange things, but trying to understand them... testing strange appearances or happenings or effects-- rather than applying asserted belief to a thing and accepting it without questioning. Blind belief is ruled out by Science -- ruled in by Religion, wherein Faith is to believe as you are told, and *the Act of Faith* has been torture unto death if you question the Superstition.

Some of the most mysterious effects in nature were known to the Ancients:- for example Thales of Miletus, one of the seven Sages of Greece, around 600 BC was familiar with the behaviour of *amber* when rubbed as becoming attractive to various kinds of small particles; and this effect was known along with others which were familiar to philosophers for centuries, as mentioned by Pliny, but naught came of it. Only *mysteries* of electricity were apprehended.

After the ravages in Europe by Barbarians in the dark ages the scene was much changed. Only then were the first systematic inquiries on the strange attractivity of amber looked into. Sir William Gilbert in his great work "De Magnete" (1600) described unique inquiries on this and sequels to it as true inductive investigation in which he showed that the Earth is a huge magnet, - all this by free systematic logical inquiries and experiments to corner the mysteries and establish small principles to illustrate or arrive at hypotheses leading to natural law. Following, with the same kind of systematic reasoning and experimentation (later termed scientific), the whole subject of electricity & magnetism was opened up for the first time in the history of mankind; & it should be seen that none of this great intellectual treasure originated in Africa or Asia or South America where Tyranny and Superstitions were so entrenched that this essential freedom of inquiry and thought was not possible; and virtually no Originations were made from those alien peoples. Electrical Science was uniquely the achievement of the countries of Western Europe, Great Britain, & North America, with successive discoveries not only in Electricity & Magnetism but into the entire basis of what has become Modern Science.

NASA via Associated Press

The luminous mysteries of outer space
- across unimaginable distances

∞∞∞∞∞∞∞∞∞∞∞∞

∞∞ ∞∞ ∞∞

∞

∞

Of the Micro-world

The little rays we cannot see or face
Are of the Micro-world - within its Orb, -
Celestial in its governance and laws,
Transversing all our Earth and outer Space. -

Their undulations create Nature's colours
And travel with the speed of lightning flight; -
Their small dimensions lie below our sight,
Their energy does multiply our powers.

Unvarying are their radiant frequencies,
Illimitable through ageless sequences,
Inscrutable by awesome silences,
Insoluble in luminous mysteries...

Their World o'ersways with Laws above a Nation, -
They had their ancient Origin before Creation.

"If free inquiry be restrained now
the present Corruption will be protected"
and new ones encouraged   --- *Thomas Jefferson*

"Reason and free inquiry are the only effectual agents against error. Had not the Roman government permitted free inquiry, Christianity could never have been introduced.   Had not free inquiry been indulged at the era of the Reformation, the corruptions of Christianity could not have been purged away. If it (free inquiry) be restrained now, the present corruptions will be protected and new ones encouraged. Were the government to prescribe to us our medicine and diet, our bodies would be in such keeping as our souls are now... Government is just as infallible too, when it fixes systems in Physics. Galileo was sent to the inquisition for affirming that the earth was a sphere; the government had declared it to be as flat as a trencher, and Galileo was obliged to abjure his error. His error, however, at length prevailed.   The earth became a globe, and Descartes declared it was whirled round its axis by a vortex. The government in which he lived was wise enough to see that this was no question of civil jurisdiction, or we should all have been involved by authority in vortices. In fact, the vortices have been exploded, and the Newtonian principle of gravitation is now more firmly established on the   basis of reasons than it would be were the government to step in, and to make it an article of necessary faith. Reason and experiment have been indulged, and error has fled before them.   It is error alone which needs the support of government. Truth can stand by itself.   Subject opinion to coercion: whom will you make your inquisitors? Fallible men; men governed by bad passions, by private as well as public reasons. And why subject it to coercion?To produce uniformity. But is uniformity of opinion desirable? No more than of face & stature. Introduce the bed of Procreates, & as there is danger that the large man may beat the small, make us all of a size, by lopping the former & stretching the latter. Difference of opinion is advantageous in religion. Is uniformity attainable? *Millions of innocent men, women and children since the introduction of Christianity have been burnt, tortured, fined, imprisoned, yet we have not advanced one inch toward uniformity.* What has been the effect of coercion? To make one half the world fools and the other half hypocrites. Reason & persuasion are the only practicable instruments. To make way for these, free inquiry must be indulged; & how can we wish others to indulge it while we refuse it ourselves?   But every state, says an inquisitor, has established some religion. No two, say I, have established the same. Our sister states... have long subsisted without any establishment.They flourish infinitely. Religion is well supported; of various kinds, indeed, but all good enough.

The Fair Copy endorsed by Thirty Authentications

1   The Fair Copy (The Original Draught) was signed with fifty-six *Original Authenticating Signatures*, written with quill & black ink, all of high fidelity and sensitivity as found only in Originals. 54 of these names are listed as signers in the Journals of Congress, *July 1776*. (Ch-14)

The same July signers also signed the initial Parchment Copy on *August 2* and later, as recorded only in *The Secret Journals of Congress*. These later signatures were partially ruined in a failed transfer for engraving in 1823. The derived signatures in the printed facsimile Parchment Copy are partially similar in shape to those in the Fair Copy but only half their size and have curious deviations. (Ch-23)

2 The Fair Copy is framed along borders with finely drawn *Original Authenticating Portraits of 48 Signers* (& Livingston, who did not sign but was on the Committee of Five).   The number 48 corresponds   approximately to the voting membership in Congress, July 15-19, 1776, before increasing to reach 56 in November. (Ch-24)

3 *The Committee of Five* shown in the masthead of the Fair Copy is the only closely contemporary portraiture known, and appears to be the *source in outline* used by Trumbull for the Committee in his painting of the 1790's based on a Jefferson sketch given him.

4 None of the Original Portraits in the Fair Copy has been identified as a copy of a known contemporary portrait. In most cases, these Originals are the only portraits of seemingly appropriate ages for the subjects as of 1776. The discrepancy between the numbers of portraits and of signatures is owing to the smaller earlier July membership, & indicates completion of the *design of the portraiture* for the Fair Copy not later than July 4 - 18, 1776. (Ch-24)

5 The Fair Copy's Portraiture as to membership does not show the *errors* of the Trumbull painting made nearly two decades later, which included several non-signers & omitted several signers. The Fair Copy is correct in membership to July 20 1776, but not quite complete. (Ch-32)

6 The Fair Copy has the largest John Hancock signature of record at seven-inch length, - twice the size as in the Parchment Copy,- and with higher sensitivity and calligraphic perfection as written by a quill. Hancock had said at the time that it would be, *"large enough for King George to read without his spectacles."* (Ch-14)

7 The Portraiture was created in ink by the rare 18th century *Stipple drawing technique* brought to London from Italy at the time when Francis Hopkinson was studying art and portraiture there. It was noted during sessions of Congress in 1776 that he was occupied in *"Drawing Caricatures of the Members",* and he was the only artistically trained member capable of portraiture and design based on antique documents. Secrecy excluded outsiders. (Ch-24)

8 The Fair Copy's *Portrait of Thomas Jefferson* bears a close similarity in structural features to the later authentic Houdon bust of Jefferson in the New York Historical Society. (Ch-48)

9 In the Fair Copy, the *Portrait of John Adams (1776)* has a close profilostructural relation to the *physiognotrace of Adams* drawn accurately about 1800 with a complex tracing machine.

10 In a search of contemporary Colonial drawings examples were not found from which any of the 49 portraits had been copied.

11 The Fair Copy is the only Manuscript found with the *Original Title* quoted by Jefferson *&* by the Committee, and designated -
"(ORIGINA)L DRAUGHT of the
DECLARATION OF INDEPENDENCE"
This title appears on inked bands along the lower margin. No other known manuscript shows this original title. The usual headline at the top of various Jefferson copies is shown also on the Fair Copy: -
"A Declaration by the Representatives..." (Ch-48)

12 The *Fair Copy (& Rough Draft)* show the *Authentic Text* of the *DECLARATION OF INDEPENDENCE,* with this title only in the larger Manuscript; and this text was published in Thomas Jefferson's autobiography, including his version of the closing split-paragraphs. The text corresponds exactly in *content* to the *Broadside* of July 4 if allowances are made for the shiftings of certain paragraphs, and for deletions by bracketting as in the Fair Copy and Autobiography.

13 The Fair Copy shows the *Corrections & Alterations,* identically to those of the Rough Draft and of the *unknown Reserve Copy,* and also as explained in the Autobiography. (Ch -5, -19)

14 The Fair Copy displays *Six Contemporary Flags:* - four described in writings of 1775-1776, and two unknown. (Ch-45)

15 The Fair Copy contains *two forms* of *s,* and also of *and* or *&,* as well as some misspellings, viz., *unacknoleged,* also in the Rough Draft. These deviations are characteristic of Jefferson's usages.

16 In its text the Fair Copy shows clearly the precise geometry of Jefferson's handwriting as shown in the Rough Draft; and corresponds to it, word by word and line by line, at a scale of 3 : 1 (or 8 : 3) but with single rather than double line spacing. The Rough Draft by photographic analysis through enlargement and with superimposition, has not a photo-exact relation to the Fair Copy; but it has *geometric similarity with the exactitude of hand-tracing,* obscured only by its double line-spacing (interlined space for notation). As a nearly identical geometric copy at 1/3 scale, the *Rough Draft* of known authenticity from Jefferson's grandson, is thus indicated to be a *pantographic copy* of the Fair Copy, additionally validating the Fair Copy. (Ch -8, -9)

17 The Fair Copy is one of the largest Documents in all history, measuring 54" x 43" for the combined 4 Quads, and the letter-size of its text is at a scale of 3 : 1 (or 8+ : 3) compared precisely to the Rough Draft (and possibly to the still hidden Reserve copy). The large size offered close viewing by several members at one time, and required only *one collective set of signatures* on the unified sheet.

18 The form of the Fair Copy is a linen-backed Composite of four Quads, each a double layer comprised of 18th century *map- or wove-type paper* from rag stock of *Elephant folio size.* The *four-Quad format* on large map- or drawing- papers is akin to the Fry-Jefferson Map of Virginia, drawn by Thomas Jefferson's father and published in 1755 *from four plates,* & later inherited by young Thomas. (Ch-28)

19 The Fair Copy shows a series of *Stains* of unique character, near the left margin, - not writing ink but *printer's Ink,* containing (linseed) oil, which would diffuse in paper. The *Lost Original* was believed by Prof. Carl Becker to have been the *printer's copy,* suggesting the origin of the stain as from a printer's shop. (Ch-15)

20 The paper of the Fair Copy is similar in finish to some map paper and drawing paper types. These were characterized by very smooth surfaces without visible laid lines, and available in large thick sheets. In the Fair Copy each Quad is a double-layer of a double-thickness paper, abutted together and backed by fine Linen attached by a natural glue adhesive into a single sheet strongly bonded throughout.

The old linen with its strong adhesion has retained the massive quad structure in tact although from repeated folding the joints between quads have failed in many places, probably as anticipated.

21 The Fair Copy shows three *Alterations* as new Paragraphs, referred to by Jefferson and found also in the Rough Draft, but shows the correct order of paragraphing at the point where in the Rough Draft the order was mixed in copying and the error was corrected by Jefferson himself, with a *collage* pasted over several lines of the text. (Ch-5)

22 The Fair Copy shows 13 *diacritical or elocution marks* in the 3rd Quad which were symbols used by Jefferson to assist the reader in presentation by the speaker of the Congress (Harrison), reading for debate *&* approval. The Rough draft shows correspondingly most of the elocution marks on the 3rd page. (Ch-16)

23 While the Rough Draft shows indelibly, as many as *30 Technical Errors* attributable to *pantographic copying* faults and artifacts, the Fair Copy shows no such errors.

24 The Fair Copy with all of its alterations, corrections, deletions, elocution marks, and structural features is thus the exact prototype and source for the Rough Draft as its pantographed derivative, - which thus authenticates the Fair Copy through the Randolph inheritance and transfer of it with the Jefferson papers directly to the Library of Congress after 1829. (Ch-17)

25 The Fair Copy is also indicated to have been the source for pantographic copying of the unknown or unidentified Reserve copy with its duplicated *reduced* signatures, as appearing in Harpers in 1876, and in a book published by the Dover Press in 1976. The whereabouts of the presumed Reserve copy is unknown. (Ch-9, -19)

26 None of the signatures examined in the Fair Copy is found to show pantographic errors or precise geometrical identity to the signatures exhibited on the *engravings* of the Parchment Copy of 1823; and the initial Parchment Copy signatures can no longer be used for precise comparisons since their mutilation then. (Ch-9, -23)

27 Through macro-enlargement and microscopy the signatures on the Fair Copy are found to be positive lines on top of paper, criss-crossing themselves three-dimensionally, and are neither engravings, printings, nor lithographic reproductions. (Ch-29)

28 The ink of the Fair Copy is not a gall-derived ink common in Colonial times, but proven a *black carbon ink*, -in use for documents and drawings by architects *&* scribes, in Egypt, China, and India for thousands of years, known for *opacity*, *insolubility*, and above all for *permanence*. Franklin had experimented early with black ink.(Ch-30)

29   Professor Julian Boyd wrote that there had to have been a *Prototype* for the Declaration of Independence, " that it was *Signed* on the evening of July 4, 1776, and that it then *disappeared* from history." He outlined the characteristics or special features which should be found in it. His predictions are fulfilled in the Fair Copy:

The Fair Copy is *very large*, *signed,* and shows all the *corrections & insertions*, *alterations* (new paragraphs*), &* paragraph *shiftings* resultant in the Broadside and mostly indicated in the Rough Draft. It also shows *elocution* marks of Jefferson for the reading of the text to Congress before approval, and which appear in no other manuscript, except incompletely in the Rough draft. (Pg-013)

30   The Fair Copy authentications further include a number of findings resulting from *an extensive scientific study* of the paper *&* ink of the Fair Copy, including examinations by *light microscopy, scanning electron microscopy, and micro X-ray spectroscopy;* and also a study of 18th century paper-making techniques *&* compositions. (Ch -26, -31).

The advanced scientific techniques show that the paper of the Fair Copy contains chemical elements of *Alum*, a natural double sulfate of potassium *&* aluminum (or Mg for Al), essential in the making of 18th century and earlier papers; and that 19th century fillers and wood-pulp products are absent. *Linen fibers* as found in the Fair Copy are the common single reinforcing component for pre-19th century papers, and are basic for permanence.

PART V

Part - V

The Lost Original - Examined

———— ————

Contents

Part - V
Contents - continued

Left wing of Original Draught, Quad I

On the Portraiture of the Fair Copy -- as drawn in Life

Returning to the Fair Copy, - one's eyes are cast to the borders where appear numerous portraits drawn as from life: -faces reflecting pensively, concerned, restless, drawn together, yet relating to the text's message - and absorbing all attention. They linger in memory in haunting mysticism, re-echoed in Thomas Carlyle {1853} :-

Often I have found the portrait painter superior in real instruction to half a dozen written biographies, or rather, I have found the portrait was as a small lighted candle by which the biographies could for the first time be read, and some human interpretation be made of them.

This startling sentiment tells us that amid cargoes of facsimiles, copies of copies, even forgeries, - one good colonial portrait drawn in 18th century life is a rarity. Portraits for that period painted a century later as copies of lost pictures or of illustrious faces drawn after the Revolution show *imagined resemblances* as *of 1776*:- but to see now these unknown Originals is to sense *a presence incomprehensible.*

The portraiture gradually was seen to comprise designs of varying mirror symmetry enhanced by olive branches, too young to bear fruit, - the branches serving as a symbol of the *unity* amongst the members, evidently a kindred people, of one race, with but one single working language, aiming at a decisive action by means of a declared unification. --- *e pluribus unum*

The harmonious weaving of the branches amongst the portraits provided a continuous decorative border along the text. In the masthead the portraits spreading toward the middle formed two wing-shapes of four faces each, - capping the side columns of 18 each and flanking the distinguished Committee of Five, overlooking from the top center, -- thus 49 portraits in all.

The portraiture of the Fair Copy was found to include 48 signers, and Robert Livingston, who did not sign, leaving a discrepancy of 8 compared with 56 signers by the end of 1776. This difference seemed curious until it was seen that Congress increased in size rapidly in July 1776. Lists of those present on July 2nd & 3rd include about 41 members present & intending to sign, - a little less than the portrait spaces reserved but much less than the later total of 56 signers.

Increasing membership numbers in Congress in mid-1776 provide a basis for difference between numbers of portraits & signatures. The Patriots' aim was to unify feeling for *independence*. As some of the members were undecided and others in opposition, there was ignited behind scenes a tempestuous activity, to convince the undecided & to replace the opposition, for without unanimous colonial consensus it was felt one or more Colonies could withdraw to the British side.

Right wing of Orginal Draught, Quad 3

Owing to these changes the approving membership then present in Congress rapidly increased from about 41 (July 3), to 46-47 (July 15), to 52-53 (July 20), & to 56 (November 5). Had the portraiture been planned after the end of July, it would have required 53 spaces, but since its design was completed with 49 spaces it would have been fully conceived & the design fixed between July 4 and 19, 1776. From this it is clear that the portraiture was planned soon after the July 4th signing with required space then reserved for the portraiture, excluding the New York Delegation as not supporting, and the new additions from Pennsylvania as not yet approved or selected. The text of the Fair Copy required an exact plan to fit a limited space.

In contrast to the Portraiture of the Fair Copy as the authentic original document, Trumbull in 1791 was still only *planning* his painting and the portraits in it were not started until some 15 years after the signing. Jefferson in consultation with Trumbull in Paris in 1790, advised that signers were to be drawn from life or life-painting & gave him sketches of profiles, & other details of the Statehouse.

Trumbull portraits drawn many years after the event could only resemble aged personages who had endured tragedy of Revolution; and those departed could not be drawn unless from pictures. Several earlier members who were not signers were included by Trumbull in error, including Clinton, Willing, and Dickinson, unlike the Fair Copy's portraiture as correct in the membership represented.

Since the Declaration was the work largely of relatively younger men and its Portraiture reflects this, the Trumbull version has an incongruously post-dated character, more like a 20-year class reunion than actual drama. For those accustomed to the older faces from long familiarity with the historical painting, the vitality as shown in the Fair Copy is startling, - but refreshingly convincing. In the heat of the Revolution it must have been nearly impossible to create 49 portraits in a short time, especially since a few signers had left Congress in early July, or were not re-elected, - or were *in hiding.*

A curious relation between the Committee in the Fair Copy compared with Trumbull's version lies in the Committee profiles, in respect to relative heights and placement, closely together above shoulders, - but the faces differ in the two works by at least two decades of age. It is thus evidently confirmed from similarities of the profiles, that Jefferson in Paris gave Trumbull a sketch of the silhouette of the Committee from his design (without facial details) to show placement & proportions, -- but not the original portraiture, -- when he gave sketches to him of the Statehouse.

The Committee, after Trumbull Painting
(as shown on currency)

The committee, on the Masthead of the Original Draught

The procedure for creating the sketches & drawing the portraiture is unknown. The work could not have been done by an outsider in view of the secrecy imposed upon Congress, - and would necessarily have been planned and executed by one of the members. With the 49 portraits each approximating two inches in size, the portraits can fit the margins as widened at the top. In the confusion during shiftings of membership, it was surely difficult for the sketching to be done artistically without interference in the limited time and several signers apparently could not be drawn.

After preserving margins for the portraiture the faces may have been sketched unobtrusively on separate papers during sessions of Congress, for transfer and completion later, after the comparison of the original text with the later Parchment Copy. The portraiture may not have been seen by Congress, for its security. To the Loyalists it would have comprised a veritable rogues' gallery.

At the masthead the wing-shapes of faces flanking the Committee include influential and key signers. On the right wing the portraits represent those on the Admiralty Board, the Marine and Naval Committee, - those concerned with matters involving *flags & ensigns* - Ellery, Hopkinson, Lewis Morris, Wipple, Williams. As a group they comprise a kind of personal flag made of their own faces, spreading from the vertical *pole* or column of portraits upward.

On the left wing the portraits represent those associated with *educational & public concerns* leading to the founding of colleges & libraries. Hopkins became the first chancellor of Rhode Island College (later Brown University), promoted a public library in Providence, & authored one of the earliest colonial anti-slavery laws (1774) prohibiting importation of slaves into Rhode Island. Rush, as pre-eminent teacher & physician promoted Philadelphia's growth as a medical center, co-founded the Philadelphia College of Physicians, & Dickinson College. Walton rallied Georgia's opposition to British rule and promoted education, co-founding Richmond Academy & Franklin College (University of Georgia). Witherspoon revitalized the College of New Jersey, afterward to be Princeton University.

A feature of primary significance in the Design is the placement of the Committee of Five who were responsible for writing the Declaration of Independence. The full extent to which it was shaped by the dedicated Statesmen at the heart of the Committee is commemorated in its portraiture's great Centerpiece of patriotic, philosophical & magnificent Masters of Eloquence and Principle, unmatched in their steadfastness & integrity at any later time --

⁓ *Thomas Jefferson   John Adams   Benjamin Franklin* ⁓

A St. JAMES'S BEAUTY.

A printed engraving by Bartolozzi from a stippled copper
negative, - an established artform yielding multiple copies.

Reversed technique on Original Draught, stipple inked
as positive: A rare artform for single originals,
largely late 18th century.

As used by many great painters of the past, crayon was old chalk, calcium carbonate or limestone, without the grease or wax added later which destroyed the sensitivity of the medium. In the Renaissance the drawings of the Masters were made with white or red chalk, pastel or lightly tinted, - or with charcoal. These were powdered compacts, to be applied in the *crayon manner*, which meant drawing lines having more or less shading according to the pressure and to the texture of paper.

Old chalk as used in the 18th century adhered sensitively when applied to rough paper - its marks showing variations of densities and discontinuities to indicate light and shadow faithfully. It was the incomparable medium for tonal rendering in the art of drawing, underlying all painting and sculpture and superior to engraving or etching for intimate delineation.

An innovation in the art of drawing occurred in the 18th century which influenced original portraiture. In Italy Francesco Bartolozzi, a goldsmith's son, attracted artists by his talent for design and was apprenticed to a painter. In his knowledge of the goldsmith's trade his use of *multiple dotting by perforation* was an old art, limited to metal design; but from his hand came an original positive dotting method called *Stipple Drawing* to compose delicately toned positive portraits by means of dots, deriving its inspiration from crayon drawing in which the crayon as dry chalk is transferred onto the paper as small marks & short lines but not as fine as true dots. In Bartolozzi's drawings the shadings were fully delineated by controlled concentrations of *positive dots as stipple*.

The dots produced by the pen are applied without pressure, and lie on the surface without having been deeply embedded. Their density comprises a shading akin to that in photography where the dots of the silver emulsion are the counterpart of the ink-dots of drawing. Though less numerous and of coarser grain the ink-stipple achieves modulated shadowing & untouched highlights, - very different from stipple engraving wherein ink is held in cavities engraved in metal as a negative, then transferred as a mechanical copy onto paper in a press.

The stipple drawing technique became prominent only in the last third of the 18th century, to become nearly extinct by the century's close. This rare *stipple drawing method* as used for the Fair Copy's portraiture, is not to be confused with *stipple engraving* for multiple duplications in the common technique of engraving from a master plate, which bears the punched and scored design.

Francis Hopkinson Portrait from Original Draught, Quad 3

After success with portraiture in Italy, Bartolozzi settled in London in 1764 where he made engravings for the great painters, also introducing the art of Stipple Drawing. Francis Hopkinson at that time was to study art in London including Heraldry & the copying of his family coat-of-arms. As a friend of Franklin he met eminent portrait painters & his pursuits led into drawing in the pastel or crayon manner, and a mastering of symbolism in Heraldry.

In the Congress of 1776, Hopkinson was said to have amused himself by *sketching caricatures of the members*. While this description may mislead as to character, it shows that he was laying groundwork for serious portraiture as often preceded by eloquent cartoons. He was the one gifted Artist in Congress.

Having collected preliminary sketches for the borders, the artist could transfer and finish the expressively contoured faces by the stipple method, as the most natural one for the purpose. These as inked originals, show essential differences from ordinary prints where the ink has been transferred from fine depressions in metal surfaces. The stipple dots on smooth paper are quasi three-dimensional, differentiated easily from engraved patterns transferred by their negative in the press. Transfer of his small portraits by copying could have been done after the official comparison of the Documents at table.

On August 26, 1776, John Adams wrote to his wife, Abigail, *"At Mr. Peale's painter's room I met Mr. Francis Hopkinson ... a Counselor of New Jersey, now a member of the Continental Congress, the son of a person much respected...- He is a Painter & Poet. I have a curiosity to penetrate a little deeper into the bosom of this curious gentleman... an ingenious man..."*

The special gifts of the artist of the Fair Copy are shown in Hopkinson's professional work for Congress and the government. He designed the new continental currency from 1777, and created a series of original symbolic devices to be found in the paper money of that period and on the bank notes; he also *designed the initial great seal of the United States, and the unknown initial American flag of 1776* which had replaced the British canton with stars marking the rows in the positions of the British crosses. By the described techniques the presumed artist of the Original Draught produced an entire portraiture in ink, directly from his own hand, uniquely expressive with great economy of means, all within a short time, yet achieving intimate and direct appeal in a permanent form, - an ideal match for the character of the text, in the same ink.

When in the Course of human Events

to advance from that Subordination; in w

and to assume among the Powers of the E

to which the Laws of Nature and of Natur

Respect to the...Opinions of Mankind r

Causes, which impell them to the Change.

We hold these Truths to be self evident,

and independent; that from that equal C

The *Adams copy, with its ghost brackets,*
as the origin of most of the essential changes of text, - hitherto unrecognized

The Declaration - coded & sharpened after the Adams copy...

The Rough Draft is an invaluable Document shaped during the struggle for American independence, and it has long been studied by historians, serving as the source for many deductions about the thinking of the men who created it. Its special value lies in its retention of ideas in stages, with changes retained in full view.

The Adams copy of the Declaration is singularly important as the earliest surviving text before extensive editing, having been copied by John Adams from Jefferson's lost initial paper. It represents the first state before Adams suggested his own corrections but may include a few previously embedded.

Since in the Fair Copy and Rough Draft the initial words remain legible through the lattices of criss-crossing, they show that Adams adopted several previous changes in copying, assumed to be from Franklin, whose practicality is evident where *sacred & undeniable* would have seemed delusive and was replaced by *self-evident*. But that change also raises doubt: -are the truths of line-7 self-evident?

Thomas Acquinas in the 13th century wrote a definition as clear as spring water: --

> *Those truths are self-evident which are at once assented to*
> *when the meaning of their terms is recognized.*

In the Declaration the view cannot be assented to that "all men are created equal", and the assumed Franklin revision is only a weak cover to modify the Declaration's ambiguity, but Adams may have preferred not to dispute an assertion of Franklin's.

It should here be noted that the Adams copy contains numerous faint line-markings possibly unnoticed by some writers of history, but which require scrutiny. They consist of vertical lines isolating individual words or phrases, and they are prominent if enlarged photographically, then appearing as bracketing.

It will be apparent that these markings isolate exactly the phrases and words which were changed or replaced by Jefferson directly after Adams first read the paper. From this indication it is inferred that Adams probably proposed extensive deletions and revisions of text not yet attributed to him. It is plausible that he wrote and discussed his proposed changes separately and then interlineated them in Jefferson's initial paper, fitting them to replace discarded phrases for improved expression. Adams's bracket-like markings thus may provide a basis for his probable authorship of numerous modified parts of the preamble, which outlines partially the philosophy of the Declaration.

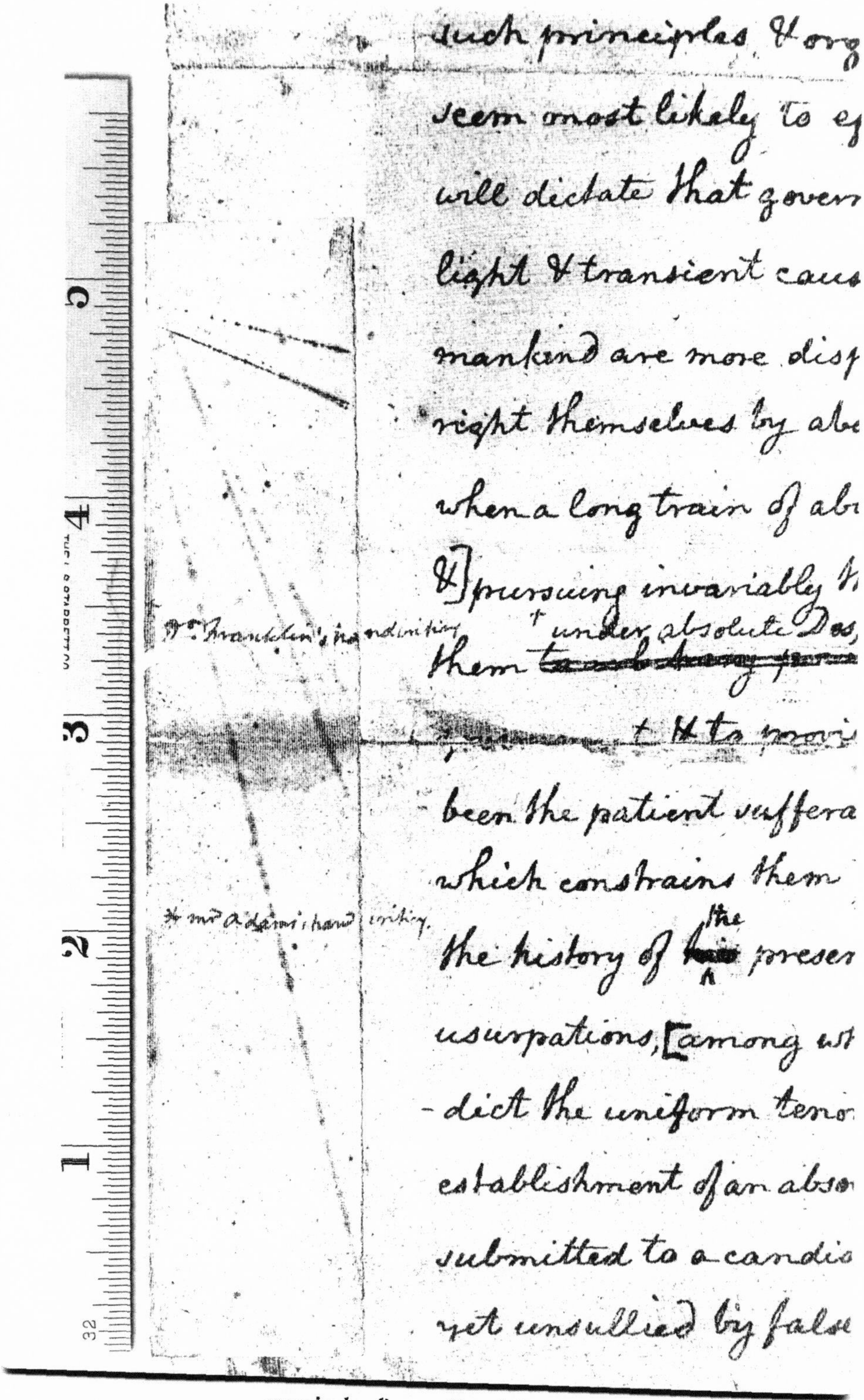

such principles, & org

seem most likely to e

will dictate that govern

light & transient caus

mankind are more disp

right themselves by ab

when a long train of ab

&] pursuing invariably

Dr. Franklin's handwriting   + under absolute Des,

them ~~to a~~ ~~t~~ ~~they~~

~~t H to pro~~

been the patient suffera

which constrains them

the history of ~~his~~ the preser

mr Adams's handwriting   usurpations, [among us

- dict the uniform teno

establishment of an abso

submitted to a candi

yet unsullied by false

marginal codings on Rough Draft

Along the margins of the Rough Draft, entered at a later time, unidentified miniature notations in a few places have been claimed to refer to the actual handwritings of Franklin and Adams. Some writers have accepted these literally as applied to this one copy, and credited corrections mostly to Jefferson as his own afterthoughts.

Evidence is not here found that proves these notations to be more than private accrediting by Jefferson to insertions in his incomplete initial paper, now seemingly lost, where the Committee reportedly did write in or attach their corrections.

The Fair Copy shows no such miniature marginal notations, as it should not, but does show a number of special markings, or codings, close to some of the corrections, viz., plus sign + and asterisk *. These are similar to Rough Draft codings, mostly at the same places, although the Fair Copy has a few markings not shown in the Rough Draft.

It would follow that the marginal notations may be associated with codings, + for Franklin, * for Adams, indicating local original authorship of specific corrections, with marginal notations entered after the Rough Draft was penned to retain sources for designations not evident in the Fair Copy by its markings. These symbols show a very close relationship between the Fair Copy and the Rough Draft.

As stated, in reference to the Adams copy, this had preceded the Rough Draft and indicated for the first time a large number of changes, isolated by Adams with different markings of his own as simple brackets, and identified afterward in the Rough Draft but not apparently originating there.

From this evidence of Adams's initiatives in the editing, it is indicated that Adams may have originated most of the important *changes* in the Declaration as first discussed by the Committee, - but that in the marking of the later Jefferson manuscripts the designations are complete only for a few minor Franklin revisions, where their identity would assure an ample measure of credit for that very senior personage. Jefferson may have overlooked designating, by coding, all of the various probable corrections and rewritings by Adams as indicated with vertical lines in the Adams copy since he and Adams were collaborating closely and merging thoughts on the first drafts. Finally the notations in the Rough Draft are seen as interpreting codings in the Fair Copy as cross-references, although incomplete.

The authenticity of the miniature notations is further supported by their exact transfer into Jefferson's *Memoir copy,* and they formed a permanent part of that document, as *engraved* in 1829. (Ch-17)

Examples of three different handwritings

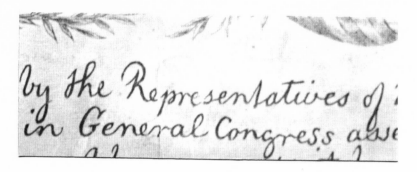

by the Representatives of in General Congress asse

Jefferson

aration by the Represe eral Congress assend

Adams

one Congress immediate

Franklin

Of the miniature notations in the Rough Draft the origin is unknown, and similar ones are not found in the Fair Copy. Of greater importance is handwriting identification of actual revisions of text. Through *macro-photographic enlargement* of revisions the peculiarities of three different writers were not found, - rather the hand of one penman copying changes from a previous paper, influenced by each style, and with usage of alternate letter types as practiced by Jefferson: e.g., '*s*' (old & new); '&' changed with '*and*'.

Handwriting is dynamic and unique in the style of a writer. It depends not only on his grasp of the quill but on his posture, steadiness and muscular control. Inherent in motion are the amplitudes of the fine wobbles. The shape of each letter has a dominant slant and elongation, including pointing of extremities. Combined with the habits of the writer is the nature of the quill, responding to the applied pressure. With these variables combined, handwriting becomes uniquely characteristic.

The slant or inclination of individual letters is a very prominent feature. It is partially governed by the angles of the writer's arm and body, and the quill in hand: - if an elbow is close to a body the slant of words is usually more than if an elbow is far to the side, while the degrees of hand or finger flexing have different leverages. Adams's handwriting appears as written carefully at a desk, and Jefferson's style shows finger motion with roundness as though written in a casual position.

In comparing known handwritings of Jefferson, Adams and Franklin, the slopes are found to be so different that they cannot be confused with each other. In the Fair Copy & the Rough Draft the revisions according to the slopes of the letters are closest to Jefferson's, as would be expected, because as penman he could not permit others to write in an official text.

Thus the handwritings in the Rough Draft, assigned by scholars to Franklin or Adams, when enlarged are found to be not of their penmanship. The slopes and steady elongation of the known Adams hand is nowhere evident. The ellipticity and fullness of the Franklin hand is absent. The handwriting is evidently Jefferson's throughout. The codings may be incomplete, but Adams made his definitive markings. - The Declaration was evidently the work of several minds. Jefferson, believing that men are to be judged, not only by what they receive but what they reject, included all changes of text, in layers, as entered. This cumulative text survives in the Fair Copy and in the Rough Draft, but the initial papers are unknown, except for a few claimed fragments.

This 'one' encompasses concordance among kindred peoples

—— *How the Committee sought Unity, and its Basis* ——

The changes indicated in the Adams copy provide a shift in emphasis. They follow from Adams's education in languages and law and his habit of self-inquiry, through diary writing, for re-shaping of thought increasingly more precise. These habits gave him decisive influence and he was called '*the Atlas for Independence*', as apparently indispensable. His revisions are apparent from his bracketing signs.

His first correction is in the first line where is indicated the switch, *a* to *one*. This unity or *one-ness* is prefigured in the headline where the first three letters of *UNITED* are *connected*, as *UNI* - (Lat. -*one*), to symbolize an *indispensable* harmonizing ideal.

This *One* encompasses compatibility of sentiment and ancestral background in kindred peoples coming together *primarily from the British & European community*, - uniting as descendants of a single race and stock, with a single common language root as *the imperative cornerstone of a national unity*. With a rude diversity of *language roots*, unity is virtually unattainable -- in education, government, and *especially in Science where absolute precision of meaning is crucial:* - otherwise a *babel of misunderstanding* will inevitably intrude.

Along with *exact* language for unity, a basic *scientific & intellectual tradition of many generations is requisite in the modern age*, as practiced for millennia. in Europe and close Mediterranean areas. Alien primitive peoples rarely cope intellectually in modern science and thus should not be in full control of its operations or administration.

The Germanic branch of the Indo-European languages is the common root holding the tongue-related nations of western Europe in a basic link of communication, such that when the Colonies were uniting they inevitably adopted one common speech & writing - and only one - for use in government and business. -Alexis de Toqueville wrote, *the Tie of Language is the most durable that can unite mankind*.

The next change from the Adams copy deleted the ponderous second line - *to advance from that subordination in which they have hitherto remained*, replacing it with - *to dissolve the political* bands *which have connected them with another*. The original lines had suggested suppressed people crawling from obscurity, - but the replacement lines suggest simply a direct political dissolution.

The next change in the Adams copy refers to nations as powers of the Earth, & each holds *equal and independent station*. Liberty is to endow them with a status of *Separate & Equal Station*, - not of Equal strength, size or ability, but only of political equality with others in law. Political *equality in the Law* is the key to the Declaration in the legal sense for Justice, apart from strength or ability.

Now -- as to *All men are created equal,* -- what does this mean?

State House Philadelphia, Second floor meeting room

*State House
Assembly room.
The mind is not unmoved
by the quiet desks....*

Of Independence - and who Illuminated it...

Adams's changes include deletions, insertions and in places also an enhanced rhythm of the prose. His bracketting designates exactly the positions of these changes in the Manuscript, but when asked who *wrote* the Declaration, he said, *Mr. Jefferson was the penman.*

Adams's answer needs insight to be grasped, but inklings may be sensed in the Pennsylvania State House by the vacant chairs of influencing Spirits - Shades of Aristoteles of Greece; Marcus Cato *&* later Leonardo da Vinci of Italy; William Gilbert, Francis Bacon *&* William Shakspere of England; Joh. Gutenberg *&* Martin Luther of Germany; Charles Montesquieu, Diderot *&* the Encyclopédists of France. From these and other blazing minds came inspiration, concepts & inventions for the pursuit of Liberty and Independence.

Aristoteles advanced scientific *&* political domains in organization of Natural Philosophy for many centuries of influence. Cato suspired for Liberty, against Tyranny by Caesar in Rome. Leonardo taught Scientific Truth by experiment *&* invention, - hiding his discoveries from superstitious religious oppressors by reversed mirror-writing.

Gilbert founded magneto-electrical science, and with Bacon set Experimental Method against dogmatic religious scholasticism. Shakspere perfected a noble clarity and power in English Drama as mirrored Histories of Liberty and Tyranny in Conflict. Gutenberg invented the Art of Alphabetical Printing as key to the spreading of Knowledge to all peoples; and Luther bravely exposed religious Superstition *&* the fraud of Indulgences, inspiring the Reformation.

Montesquieu wrote, "*When a legislature becomes corrupt the people lose their Liberty*", illumining this in *Esprit des Lois*. Diderot *&* D'Alembert set Science with Art in rational perspective in *La Encyclopédie.*

Across the table from those aetherial lingering Shadows may be chairs of the Colonial Committee: Thomas Jefferson, John Adams, Benj. Franklin, R.Sherman, Robert Livingston, - Spirits poignantly haunting as time dims recollection of all they thought and wrought.

Hence from the vanished images of those distant souls and the silence of forgotten voices the mind is not unmoved by the quiet desks and motionless quills -- now powerless in our hands but apt then in creating political honesty and designs for courage, with turmoil marking the times by the thundering of cannon -- leading to the creation of the Original Manuscript of Jefferson's work, later to survive suppression for two centuries. If this be mind-stunning - it surely is, but evidence from buried fragments of history show how Ambition and Corruption, driven by Greed and Lust, stifle Liberty to enslave the Spirit of man.

Portrait of James Wilson from the Manuscript

Whether all Men are "Created Equal"-
Or are simply "by Nature Equally Free"?

The focus of critical disfavor on the King alone as the cause of the separation from England became the impetus to change the thinking among the colonial leaders in the period 1763 - 1775. Initially the question may have been whether Parliament had a right to tax the Colonies when they were not represented in it, but further views were gradually shifted to the *Natural Rights Philosophy* as comprising the supreme law of government above all legislative bodies; and in line with this the view soon emerged that there had to be a Supreme Sovereignty above all others.

From this principle in 1770, after ingenious restructuring of ideas of authority by Samuel Adams, Franklin, and John Adams, - James Wilson wrote a paper leading directly to the arguments later to emerge in the Declaration wherein blame was thrust not on Parliament as irrelevant, but directly on the King as the Supreme Sovereign. He alone was being charged with a succession of abuses suffered by the colonists, comprising a tyranny over them. In the necessity of the case in 1774 Wilson published his earlier writings, and by 1776 Liberty through Independence had become inevitable. Wilson had asserted the following:

"All men are, by nature, equal and free: no man has a right to any authority over another without his consent; all lawful government is founded on the consent of those who are subject to it; such consent was given with a view to ensure and to increase the happiness of the governed. The consequence is that the happiness of the society is the first law of every government..."

Wilson declared specifically that all Sovereignty is limited by the superior Law of Nature.

James Wilson was a perceptive lawyer and an important member of the second Continental Congress. He also became a major influence in the writing of the Constitution in 1787.

In view of opinion in writings about *no taxation without representation* as forcing the American Revolution, it is startling that Parliament, and taxation with it, are not mentioned in the Declaration. Those arguments had been thoroughly revised and had been clarified to show that while England and her Colonies had their respective legislatures, none was sovereign in the light of the Natural Rights Philosophy, then under intensive scrutiny. Blame in the controversy could be shifted directly to the sovereign King and his oppressive policies and Acts, and that shift is what had occurred by 1776.

A Declaration of Rights made by the Representatives of the good People of Virginia, assembled in full Convention; and recommended to Posterity as the Basis and Foundation of their Government.

That all men are by nature equally free and independent, and have certain inherent natural Rights, of which they can not, by any Compact, deprive or divest their Posterity; among which are the Enjoyment of Life and Liberty, with the Means of acquiring and possessing Property, and pursueing and obtaining Happiness and Safety.

George Mason: "All men are by nature equally free..."
A general equality of men is not to be considered.

Concepts on Equality derived from the British Constitution & from Wilson's views were written by George Mason, a far-sighted statesman of Virginia. His Declaration of Rights (1776) for the Virginia Constitution was written about May 15 and printed in the *Pennsylvania Evening Post* of June 6 & *Pennsylvania Gazette* of June 12 before the Declaration of Independence was drafted. Acceptance of Mason's text was delayed by Virginia aristocrats who feared a slave uprising might be stirred as a result of sentiments in the Preamble. Mason's third or final draft read:

A Declaration of Rights made by the Representatives of the good People of Virginia, assembled in full convention, and recommended to posterity as the Basis and Foundation of this government: *That all men are by nature equally free and independent and have certain inherent natural Rights, of which they can not by any Compact, deprive or divest their Posterity; among which are the enjoyment of Life and Liberty with the Means of Acquiring & possessing property and pursuing & obtaining Happiness & Safety.*

This final Draft by Mason was similar to his first, except that - *are born equally free* became - *are by nature equally free.*
For a slave-holding Colony to write into its Constitution the principle of *born free* posed conflict in its legal system.

The concepts of born free or born not free had been applied from ancient times to people of one race or of several races, but the plantation owners were not of a mind to change their way of life for a new constitution. They loved their wealth, ease, and protection, but they also quite shamelessly loved their self-imposed privileges, their mistresses and their dark offspring. In the final version, *are by nature equally free,* - not to mean equal - was accepted for the Declaration of Rights. The argument was critically stated as *free.* Equality of men was not then considered. The phrasing refers to states of equal Freedom for all. Nothing here refers to men as equal.
Locke wrote in 1690, *all men are born equal & independent;*
Wilson in 1770 concluded, *all men are by nature equal & free;*
Mason wrote, *all men are by nature equally free & independent;*
Jefferson wrote, *all men are created equal & independent.*
Congress, thinking narrowly, rejected *free* & deleted *independent,* and then concluded - *all men are created equal* (July 1776).
Of Mason's crucially important concept, slavery is not to be a condition of Nature, and neither are persons all equal. But the concept of Liberty and Equality had already been clarified 500 years before it was to be grappled with by these writers.-

Io. cap. XXI. Hic est discipulus ille, qui te stimoniú perhibet de his &c.

Thomas Aquinas (1225-1274) gave a lifetime of thought
to ethical and philosophical questions
some of which were to touch very close
to the unsolved problems of 1776.

He wrote from his meditations
and also from lifelong experience -
By nature all men are equal in Liberty
-- but not in the Endowments

*Wide-spread misinterpretations of "All men are created equal"
force a flood of evil consequences, as though from Pandora's box.*

How the Congress lifted the Lid of Pandora's Box

George Mason wrote for the new Virginia Constitution from long experience and deep insight. His writings were surely in the hands of Jefferson when the Committee first met to outline the proposed Declaration. The basic concepts were familiar but the minds of the Committee held various individual viewpoints.

An overriding concern was the fact that a challenge of *equally free* to prior concepts of born free or born in bondage was a disrupting concern to Colonies tolerating slavery.

George Mason's text had appeared in Philadelphia newspapers, and Jefferson could follow it in form, adapting or appropriating. - But as he felt responsibility for slaves dependent upon him he could not free them without education, *and into jeopardy under the Virginia code whereby freed slaves were forced to leave the Colony within a year and could be retaken elsewhere without trial.*

Jefferson did not copy Mason's expression of equally free, which accorded well with antient ideals of Liberty. He wrote as had Locke in 1690, - *"All men are created equal and independent",* and since slaves were not independent he apparently meant by intention as a lawyer they should be (in the sense of *equality in political status)* and as the law required change, it should appear in the Declaration.

As a basis of free thinking and acting in a new government, correct notions of *equality before the law* was a concept from *Magna Charta,* but in 1776 nothing was meant of equality broadly as to abilities or character. Jefferson did not mean all men are equal in a total sense. In private & public life he denied the notion of total equality of men in their separate endowments.

The Encyclopedia Britannica confirms that - -- *"Both Locke and Jefferson wrote simply of political equality, political freedom".*

The problem in usage of *equal* for comparisons of men was the same then as now: *Equal* cannot be applied totally to one man and another without a basis of comparison. Equal has meaning only when used to measure specific attributes, in particular men, which can be compared on a like basis, - as equal in weight, or in strength, or in height or in hearing, or in memory, - but never all together.

Jefferson's concept was to define all men as being born of equal rank before the law (whereby each is to receive *equal justice* regardless of considerable differences in their *endowments).* This concept is paralleled with that of nations, "when in the course of human events it becomes necessary for a people... *to* assume among the powers of the earth the *Separate & Equal Station".*

In committee the words "& independent" were struck out. This deletion destroyed Jefferson's original meaning which is - No slavery

Thus, nations have separate & equal station in respect to law, but never equality in all powers & abilities, -- and so with men as well.

A consistent modern view of man's equality was given in its true legal sense by Chief Justice Warren Burger in 1971:

"No Person is above the Law. All are Equal as to its Burdens and its Benefits. Just as time extended the reach of Magna Charta, it has also expanded the meaning of the Declaration & the Constitution so as to include all people and to exclude none. Today in our country, as in England, no person is above the law and all are equal as to its burdens and its benefits. This is what is meant by Equal Justice under Law."

Jefferson's phrase - *equal & independent* - means *equality before the law - & not dependent, which is to say, "& free"*; but Congress and the Committee scotched his meaning by striking out *& independent*. This deletion destroyed Jefferson's creation which parallels Mason's axiom - *all men are born equally free.* The abridged phrasing of the Committee and Congress is ambiguous because *equal* by itself is equivocal and invites a gross distortion of meaning if out of context.

The abridged claim -*All men are created equal* - has been stretched beyond reason. In what sense *equal* is not asked, but to say - one man is equal to any other man - is as absurd as to say *a dog is equal to a hog* .

Few expressions are more misleading than the general claim that *all men are created equal.* In the sense of specific endowments *they never are equal.* Tests, qualifyings, competition, & examinations are used universally -- to measure the specific *inequalities* between individuals. A claim of total equality is sheer delusion: - history denies it, experience cancels it, common sense ridicules it. - A general equality of men in all aspects is the delusion of communism.

Owing to this deletion in Jefferson's text and resulting assertion that *all men are created equal*, his attempt to outlaw slavery was blocked, and *equal* is now misused by uneducated people to create a wild and dangerous clamour for universal equality in all things.

In colonial America, discrimination was necessary in the selection of a candidate to assure commitment to office. *Discrimination* (Lat.-*discriminare*) means *to make a distinction between (individuals).* It is not derogatory as charged by uneducated people. Election to office requires the voters' *discrimination* in choice between candidates - distinguishing between good and not good, to decide who should hold office. Never should voting be given to thieves, vagabonds, idiots or illegal impostors under the nonsensical claims of total or general equality in men   - This is the fantasy of the lazy and of the incapable --in pursuit of recognition..

The necessity for leadership in all things proves the inequality of men.

John Adams Portrait
In the Committee; Original Draught, Quad 1

" *These sources of inequality which are common to every people...*
can never be altered by any..."   -- *John Adams*

    While John Adams was in Europe arranging for the payment of interest due Holland *&* France for their loans to the Confederation, he undertook to write a work on the principles underlying the post-colonial governments, which had fallen into an increasingly grave financial crisis after the Revolution; and upon his return to Braintree he was elected as a delegate to a convention for forming a new government and was selected to write the new constitution for Massachusetts Bay, in 1780. (*vide,* Page Smith. *John Adams,* pg-422+438-, 1962)

    In his compositions Adams wrote thoughtfully on *equality* which he considered to be a very superficial term, applied with confusing looseness, far different from its correct relevant meaning as limited to a legal sense before the law, defining only *political equality*: - for in every other way *he viewed all people* as *manifestly unequal* -- in size, beauty, talents, fortune;-- and he wrote:

    " These sources of *inequality*, which are common to every people can never be altered by any, because they are founded in the *constitution of nature*; this natural aristocracy among mankind... is a fact essential to be considered in the institution of government. It forms a body of men which contains the greatest collection of virtues and ability; in a free government it is the brightest ornament and glory of a nation and may always be made the greatest blessing of society if it be judiciously managed in the constitution. But if this be not done, *it is* always *the most dangerous.*"

    For his declaration of rights which preceded the new constitution itself, Adams paralleled closely George Mason's basic statement in the Virginia bill of rights written four years earlier: -

All men are born equally free and independent

    It is important here to note that in the first article, where Adams had initially written; "All men are born equally free & independent". the convention later deleted *equally* and replaced *independent* with *equal*. Thus Adams's wording, to avoid the disturbingly ambiguous phrase, "born free and equal", was rejected by the convention, as had been the case with Jefferson's original parallel wording in 1776. It was clear to Adams that men fundamentally are not born equal, either in intelligence or talents, which makes abridged phrasing misleading and dangerous: "*Free & independent,* yes; *Free & equal,* no".

    While in Paris during this period, Adams dined with the greatest philosophers in Europe, conversed with the Abbé´ Raynal - "the most eloquent man I ever heard speak in French", learned, witty, entertaining with "spirit... eloquence and fire".

effect, men have executed in concert; and with one accord they preserve their work. Such is the origin, such the advantage and the end of all society.

Government owes its birth to the necessity of preventing and repressing the injuries which the associated individuals had to fear from one another. It is the sentinel who watches, in order that the common labours be not disturbed.

Thus society originates in the wants of men, government in their vices. Society tends always to good; government ought always to tend to the repressing of evil. Society is the first; it is, in its origin, independent and free. Government was instituted for it, and is but its instrument. It is for the one to command; it is for the other to obey. Society created the public power; government, which has received it from society, ought to consecrate it entirely to its use. In short, society is essentially good; government, as is well known, may be, and is but too often evil.

It has been said, that we were all born equal; that is not so:—that we had all the same rights; I am ignorant of what are rights, where there is an inequality of talents, or of strength, and no security nor sanction:—that nature offered to us all the same dwelling, and the same resources; that is not so:—that we were all endowed indiscriminately with the same means of defence; that is not so: and I know not in what sense it can be true, that we all enjoy the same qualities of mind and body.

There is amongst men an original inequality for which there is no remedy. It must last for ever; and all that can be obtained by the best legislation, is, not to destroy it, but to prevent the abuse of it.

But in making distinctions between her children like a step-mother, in creating some children strong and others weak, has nature herself formed the germ or principle of tyranny? I do not think it can be denied; especially if we look back to a time anterior to all le-

WM THOS RAYNAL,
Fellow of the Royal Society in London, and of the Academy of Sciences and Belles Lettres in Prussia

The writings of the Abbé Raynal.

They sliced off many of the most valuable heads to level men into a fiendishly enforced Egalité

" There is amongst Men an original Inequality
-- for which there is no Remedy ..." -Abbe′ Raynal

Distantly from the 18th century, echo again some words of the Abbé Raynal, musing upon a lifetime of thought on the nature of man. Raynal's insight was influential to Diderot and D'Alembert in their great French *La Encyclopédie*, published in the 1760's as one of the first comprehensive works of its kind in literature and science, as not accepting superstitious myth, and it became one of the most influential works of that century. In 1781 the Abbe′ Raynal wrote: -

"It has been said, that we were all born equal; that is not so; - that we had all the same rights; I do not know of what are rights, where there is an inequality of talents, or of strength, and no security or approval; that nature offered to us all the same dwelling, and the same resources; that is not so: - that we were all endowed indiscriminately with the same means of defense; that is not so: & I know not in what sense it can be true, that we all enjoy the same qualities of mind and body.

"There is amongst men *an original Inequality* for which there is no remedy. It must last forever; and all that can be obtained by the best legislation, is, not to destroy it, but to prevent the abuse of it.

"What has resulted thence? Why, that the history of civilized man is but the history of his misery. All the pages of it are stained with blood; some with the blood of the oppressors, others with the blood of the oppressed.

"In this point of view, man appears more wicked and more miserable than a wild animal; different species subsist on different species; but societies of men have never ceased to attack each other. Even within the same society, there is no condition but devours & is devoured, whatever may have been or are the forms of the government, or artificial Equality, which have been opposed to primitive or natural Inequality."

Raynal was born in the Age of the *Enlightenment*, and witnessed its flowering in the Arts, Literature, and Sciences. He followed the growth of Science in chemistry with *Lavoisier*, physics with *Ampère & Coulomb*, astronomy and mathematics with *Lalande & LaPlace*, metrology in the invention of the Metric System with *LaGrange, Delambre, Méchain & Condorcet*; - but then he saw this brilliant intellectual constellation from unique minds destroyed in Anarchy by lowly rabble who seized on the *mirage of Equality* by slicing off the heads of some of the world's greatest men, including Lavoisier, a founder of chemistry. This vast tragedy followed false visions and power-usurpations by wildly inflamed, down-trodden, starving people.

The Measure of Inequality

Unequal Weights do tilt the Balance just,
For Nature's differing kinds; - and when assayed
With this Device -- no matter how fairly laid --
All claimed Equalities in truth do fail as dust.

Some say that as alike as Acorns seem
When first, their caps complete, they show new sprout,
'Twould appear that Oaks as from them grown, no doubt
Must weigh alike by girth or height or mien;

Yet 'tis not so, - nor can you weigh man's Being,
His Essence - deftly hid within his Mind
Nor measure the Wise, the deep mysterious Kind,
No two in all the Universe alike are seeming.

'Tis true with men, whate'er they claim to know,
Their Inequalities do always show.

HONORABLE
Mr. JUSTICE BLACKSTONE.

On certain inalienable Rights
—— ⊠ ——

According to Sir William Blackstone the Rights of Englishmen
are usually called their Liberties and they are founded on Nature
and reason. These Rights came down from the antient common law
of the Saxons through the greatCharter of Liberties, Magna Charta,
in 1215 A.D., affirming the common law as the birthright of all
Englishmen. This was declared further in 1688 in the English Bill
of Rights which was then enacted by Parliament. The great
concepts of right & wrong in British Law, refined for a thousand
years, became the basis for government by the Colonists in 1776.

The first English personal Right is "Security, for enjoyment of life,
limb, body, health, and reputation." This is not a Right to Life in
any context but is a Right for *Security for the enjoyment of life.*

The second Right is Liberty, - a free kind as in Nature or a
restrained kind as in society. In this view Liberty provides choices,
with an implied use of wisdom, but as total Liberty in Nature is
perilous, some Liberty must be given up to society for Security.
Rights at times are thus limited, and varying, and cannot be equal as
persons are not equal except before the law. Inequality of men was
recognized in the Declaration by the *expunging* of equal rights.

Disparities appear in the Declaration's *inalienable rights,* - wherein
Pursuit of happiness is not equivalent to the English *Security for the
enjoyment of life...* In addition, the Declaration in the perils of
Revolution, failed to include the English Right of *Property*, -as one's
personal possessions, including land. In reference to this, 'inalienable'
- as *that which cannot be given away, nor taken.* - would mean that
property including land cannot be alienated to aliens. Later Jefferson
amended his omission: - "By our laws, *the same as the English* in this
respect, no alien can hold lands nor maintain an action for money
or other movable thing. Lands acquired or held by aliens become
forfeited to the state".   He clearly viewed the Right of Property as
essential; and to retain our lands he urged us - "To define with
precision the rules whereby aliens should become citizens".

= As aliens acquire our lands they are acquiring our country. =
The spirit of Liberty was deeply held in the English Bill of Rights.
Blackstone wrote (*Commentaries*...Laws of England.1769):"Under these principles
the law of England abhors and will not endure the existence of,
slavery within this nation: so that when an attempt was made to
introduce it, the spirit of the nation could not brook this condition,
even in the most abandoned rogues;therefore this statute was
repealed in two years afterwards. And now it is laid down that a
slave or negro, the instant he lands in England, becomes a free man."

220

The right to pursue happiness...

English personal Rights include *Security* for enjoyment of life, limb, body, health, reputation, -*& Liberty, -& Property*. These require limits to Liberty for *the Security of the Planet*; and to those claiming any Right there is an *Obligation* in the balance as the *Burden*, or English *'duties'*, which pairs with a right as a just compensation.

In our view, Fortune may apply a rule of Obligation when holding *Thorns of Justice* to indolent people who grasp for rights without intention of compensation; - and, justly, Nature often does disdain equal rights by offering *Opportunity - only to the prepared mind*.

Fictitious rights may be hatched, under the claim of equality, and sought by uneducated people, to compensate for their innate inadequacy, without greater Justice than in the aims of ambitious leaders having political or tribal goals for power.

I have a *Right to Life!* may be only the cry of men as egoists, - and self-worshippers of their image in their children: - *over-breeders* who create large progenies as a claimed right. They crowd their people into a people-pollution, leading to poverty. Excess overflow of these over-breeders become land-invaders, asylum seekers, usurpers, destroyers of lands *&* countries of unified peoples beyond borders. By these disruptions the decline of civilization commences. *Nor is asylum a right:-Sovereign nations must block invaders as excess when they are incompatible. Invaders have their land. We have ours. If they are crowded, they must work more by day; sleep more -- breed less -- by night.*

"I have a Right to Liberty", may be only the claim of thieves, filing the bars of jails to vanish into the darkness of stolen freedom.

"A Right to Pursue Happiness" requires definition -- lest it be a whisper of Pan, invading Nature to ravish Beauty's fairest daughter.

Life, Liberty, & the Pursuit of Happiness are increasingly blurred as self-evident, through some definitions having changed since 1776.

Rights not by Nature but by man are to be *defined*, and must be wrought with wisdom. *Equal right s* as first set in the Declaration was canceled in Committee, and wisely not restored by Congress.

The Declaration refers to certain *inalienable* rights, not precisely written as self-evident; but the later *Bill of Rights* as Amendments to the Constitution had been urged by Jefferson as *necessary against every government on earth*. It was blindly opposed by Alexander Hamilton, but was later adopted in necessity, through Jefferson's unremitting written expositions. This Bill of Rights did not spring full-blown by original invention but was drawn primarily from Magna Charta and the *English Bill of Rights*, - and it comprises the first ten crucially important Amendments to the United States Constitution, where it has withstood attacks on its integrity for two centuries.-

✤✦✕✦✤

Queen Elizabeth I

William Goodell wrote, in *The American Slave Code* (1853): -"Sir John Hawkins obtained leave of Queen Elizabeth, in the year 1562, *to transport Africans* into the American Colonies - *with their own free consent*, a condition with which he promised to comply. But he forfeited his word and forced them on board his ships by acts of devastation and slaughter. For this he was denominated a murderer and a robber, even by the historian Edwards, an advocate of the slave trade. This was the beginning of the slave trade by Englishmen. (vide *Clarkson's History*; & Edward's *Hist.. W. Indies*, vol-2).

"By Act of 23 George II, the *trade to Africa was regulated*, including a strict prohibition, under penalties, of the taking on board or carrying away any African *by force, fraud, or violence.*

"Under no other legal sanctions than this, the forcible and fraudulent seizure and transportations of slaves from Africa to the British American Colonies was carried on until the West India and American Colonies were stocked with slaves; and many were introduced into England, held as slaves... and accounted legal.

"But in 1772 it was decided by Lord Mansfield, in the case of James Somerset, a slave, that the whole process in tenure were illegal; that *there was not, and never had been, any legal slavery in England.* This decision was understood by Granville Sharpe, the chief agent in procuring it, *to be applicable to the British Colonies* as well as to the mother country, and undoubtedly it was so. The United States were then Colonies of Great Britain. But the slaves in the Colonies had no Granville Sharpe to bring their cause into the courts and the courts were composed of slave-holders.

"In the great struggle afterwards, in the British Parliament for abolishing African slave trade, William Pitt cited the Act of 23 George II and declared that instead of authorizing the slave trade, as was pretended, it was a direct prohibition of the whole process, as it had actually been carried on by fraud, force, and violence... An elaborate investigation by Parliament sustained the statement; and, after a long struggle the doctrine prevailed, and the traffic was expressly and solemnly abolished, though it has been *secretly carried on* to the present day and is prosecuted still (1853), but Sir William Blackstone had maintained (1783) that any slave setting foot on English soil is at once free."

The slave trade in origin & primary transportation from Africa had been carried on primarily by the Dutch, Portuguese, Spanish, and English, - not by British-American colonists, who in the 18th century acquired their slaves on colonial soil, largely in the West Indies. Germany never resorted to the evil practice. Slavery, as held illegal in Englis h law, commenced through Piracy involving British and European slave-ships.

"American Slavery owes its Origin
neither to American nor European Legislation"

William Goodell also wrote, "The colonial charters which were the colonial constitutions of government expressly provided that the Colonies should exact no laws contrary to the *English common law, the constitution & the fundamental laws of Great Britain.*But these as decided by Lord Mansfield (attested by Coke, Fortescue and Blackstone) are *incompatible with the existence of slavery.*

"Another fact is that the thirteen United States on the 4th of July, 1776, declared that 'all men are created equal and are endowed by their creator with *certain inalienable rights,* among which are *life, liberty, and the pursuit of happiness.'* Similar declarations were incorporated into the original constitutions of the several states, and the courts in Massachusetts decided that *this was equivalent to an act abolishing slavery.*

"In consequence of atrocities committed by a West India slave holder of eminence, a legal investigation took place, which resulted in the discovery and announcement that there was no legalized slavery in the British Colonies. This was made public in England previous to the Act of Parliament terminating the practice of slave-holding. This act accordingly, provides for the suppression of an unlawful custom or practice... Full and explicit is the testimony of Judge Matthews of Louisiana to the fact that both Indians and negroes were originally enslaved in this country in the absence of either European or colonial legislation to sanction or create the relation of owner and slave." {This indicates that habit through long usage may actually take on the appearance of law.]

"In effect, the colonial governments & the initial governments of the United States seem never to have established slavery by legal acts... It is thus affirmed, municipal acts are *in violation of the passages in the Declaration,* and that slavery, being without foundation in nature, is the creature of municipal law, and exists only under its jurisdiction.

"In a specific case of a slave taken to France 'being free for one moment in France, it was not in the power of her former owner to reduce her again to slavery.' The absence of municipal law is fatal to the legality of the claims of the slave holder.

"The Roman civil (slave) law as existing at an early period, before its modification under Christian emperors, is generally referred to in our slave-states, as containing the principles of their peculiar institutions. --- But it is evasion and sophistry to ransack the archives of some other age and nation for the laws and usages which *then* constituted slavery. "   —☙

Benjamin Franklin Portrait in the Committee; Original Draught, Quad 3

When ill-grounded Opinions go unchecked
even a great Nation will regress... and fall

Slavery was at the core of the rising conflicts, - rooted in self-interest, passion, and aggrandizement, with failure of politicians to apply logical and scientific reasoning, a perennial and widespread error producing much irresponsible and ruinous legislation.

Franklin had opposed slavery strenuously, and repeatedly published eloquently against it. His beliefs were original, practical, and clear. --

In 1779 he wrote, "It is an ill-grounded opinion, that by the labor of slaves, America may possibly vie in cheapness of manufactures with Britain. One may compute it. Interest of money is in the Colonies from 6 - 10%. Slaves, one with another, cost 30£ Sterling a head. Reckon then the interest of the first purchase of a slave, the insurance or risk on his life, his clothing and diet, expenses in his sickness, and loss of time, loss by his neglect of business, (neglect is natural in the man who is not to be benefitted by his own care or diligence), expense of a driver to keep him at work, and his pilfering from time to time, almost every slave being from the nature of slavery a thief; and compare the whole amount with the wages of a manufacturer of iron or wool in England, you will see that labor is much cheaper there than it ever can be by negroes here. And why then will Americans purchase slaves?

"The negroes brought into the English sugar islands, have greatly diminished the whites there; the poor are by this means deprived of employment while a few families acquire vast estates, which they spend on foreign luxuries; and educating their children in the habit of those luxuries, the same income is needed for the support of one, that might have maintained one hundred. The whites who have slaves, not labouring, are enfeebled, and therefore not so generally prolific; the slaves being worked too hard, and ill-fed, their constitutions are broken, and the deaths among them are more than the births; so that a continual supply is needed from Africa. The northern Colonies having few slaves increase in whites. Slaves also perjorate the families that use them; the white children become proud, disgusted with labour, and being educated in idleness, are rendered unfit to get a living by industry."

When ill-grounded opinions go unchecked after warnings by men of genius, even a great nation will regress, overpopulate itself into devastating poverty, infected with immigrated drugs, and fall - overwhelmed by enveloping darkness...

"Human nature must shudder at the prospect held up"
- Thomas   Jefferson

It was early known that Africans were *sold freely by their own people* to the European merchants, who claimed they were imported to the Colonies as aborigines without knowledge of the world:-- nothing of electricity, physics, chemistry, mathematics, geography, architecture, law or government; and never having devised any form of writing they were without a literature or any recorded history.

The African slaves in later freedom claimed that they were the Egyptian peoples who had designed and built the great pyramids and other ancient wonders; yet it is said they have not shown the mind, language or habit for that, and are unlike the ancient Egyptian in every attribute. During the slave migrations of the 17th century they were described as a simple tropical race with tremendous physical strength and prowess, extreme agility, and perfected rythmic sensitivity, with protective skin color & eyes, and flattened facial lines with thickened lips and noses termed Negroid as unique tropical and racial attributes. But Egypt is not in the tropics but in the temperate zone, and Cairo & the Gizeh Plateau are nearky 2000 miles too far north from the torrid land under the Equator which alone accounts for the Negro's color and extreme emotionality.

Jefferson from his work with slaves, revealed his painful thoughts: "The first establishment in Virginia which became permanent, was made in 1607. The first (Negroes) brought here as slaves were by a Dutch ship, after which the English commenced the trade, & continued it until the revolutionary war. That suspended, ipso facto, their further importation for the present and the business of the war pressing constantly on the legislature, this subject was not acted on finally until, 1778 when I brought in a bill to prevent further importation. This passed without opposition, & stopped the increase of the evil by importation, leaving to future efforts its.. eradication.

"Early in the session of May '79 I prepared and obtained leave to bring in a bill, declaring who should be deemed citizen, asserting the natural right of expatriation, and prescribing the mode of exercising it. This, when I withdrew from the house on the first of June following, I left in the hands of George Mason, and it was passed on the 26th of that month..."The bill on the subject of slaves, was a mere digest of the existing laws, without intimation of a plan for a future general emancipation. It was thought... this should be attempted by way of amendment, whenever the bill should be brought on. The principles of the amendment, however, were agreed on,– the freedom of all born after a certain day and deportation at a proper age."

" The excessive Multiplying of the Slave Population makes certain that they would greatly outnumber...'

Jefferson objected to racial mixing, and his reasoning was scientific as an anthropologist, linguist and life observer of relations between bi-racial people. He considered the excessively high rates of reproduction of tropical peoples as their fatally insidious threat to temperate peoples, as by over-breeding their numbers in voting power grow to become total ruling power.

In the 18th century social & political incompatibility between the races was clear-cut, & the question became simply - whether two disparate peoples, with origins in different climatic zones for millennia, can ever adapt to each others' habit & temperament.

Jefferson reflecting on long experience with slaves, wrote his concerns: "It is still in our power to direct the process of emancipation and deportation peaceably, and in such slow degree, as that the evil will wear off insensibly, & that their place be, pari possu, filled up by free white laborers. If, on the contrary,it is left to force itself on, human nature must shudder at the prospect held up... ten thousand recollections by the blacks of the injuries they sustained; new provocations; the real distinctions which nature has made; will divide us into parties and produce convulsions which will probably never end but in the extermination of the one or the other race. Hence the races ought to be kept separate, removed beyond the reach of blood mixture."

Jefferson warned further, "Nothing is more certainly written in the book of fate, than that these people are to be free; nor is it less certain that the two races, equally free cannot live in the same government. Nature, habit, opinion have drawn indelible lines of distinction between them... "

Nathan Schachner wrote, "that the subjection of the Negro always had troubled Jefferson, that all of the humanitarian, philosophical and political instincts in him revolted against oppression of one man by another, but that the excessive multiplying of the slave population makes it certain that they would overtake and greatly outnumber the white peoples."

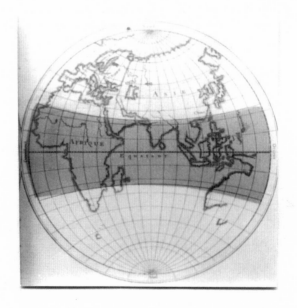

Slavery & the Rule of Numbers - with distant Consequences
‹‹‹‹‹‹‹‹‹

Malthus wrote perceptively in 1806 of population and its control:
"The preventive check so far as it is voluntary is peculiar to man
and arises from the distinctive superiority in his reasoning faculty,
which enables him *to calculate distant consequences.*"

It is plain, that the people who are able to calculate distant
consequences have foresight, and *preserve their Liberty* by voluntary
restraint, -- especially in reproduction, from which excess progeny
despoils Liberty. People without reasoning or restraint cannot
estimate consequences under full liberty, and may reproduce wildly
to their own impoverishment. If charity rescues the starving people
with food, she only regenerates a fresh flood of unchecked births.

Hence, *Liberty must be partially limited,* because not all people
can reason so as to apply essential restraint and may never apply it.

The nature of population is thus fearsome and overpowering. It
cannot be analyzed by opinion or hearsay but requires mathematical
analysis to determine rates of population increase, quantitatively.

Huge numbers of countings have been made in the past century,-
and a harsh fact is that *tropical regions around the globe double
population at far higher rates* than the temperate northern regions.
According to William Peterson, *Population* (1974), the average time
for populations to double was in the range of 22 to 30 years in
tropical America and in the Caribbean regions - and Mexico was
recorded as doubling its population in only 20 years in some areas.

By contrast in Europe & North America , the time for doubling
population ranged from 80 to 700 years, except Albania at 22 years,
where excessively used fertility caused bad population implosions. A
hidden factor was the influence of religious edict: Moslem polygamy
& concubinage have forced huge population growth in their regions.

It is clear without higher mathematics that for two classes of
people in one country of different birth-rates & population
expansion, the sexually wild people of uncontrolled birth-rates will
overwhelm to become a voting majority. Their prize becomes
the *government itself:* -- by the Rule of Numbers, *they overcome by
obsessive procreation.* This dark spectre shows admission of aliens
into a stable country to be fraught with peril. Alien numbers swell
by affinities reaching homelands & by wild birthrates, spurred by
free benefits. Insidious dangers lurk in politicians who seek aliens
as easy votes, and cheap labor for rich corporations that bribe them,
and *they lure aliens* with free welfare, medicine, education & vast
amnesties (fr. Gr. *amnesties* = amnesia.). - An amnesty is literally *a
forgetting*, even forgetting a crime, thus also a crime in itself.

"Foreigners will share with us the Legislation,
infuse into it the principles of the governments they leave,
transmit the principles they left, in their Language, to their Children"

Jefferson in 1782 saw clearly the problem from mixing peoples of unlike qualities and urgencies, as he wrote: "Here I will beg leave to propose a doubt. The present desire of America is to produce rapid population by as great importations of foreigners as possible. But is this founded in good policy? Are there no inconveniences -- from a multiplication of numbers by the importation of foreigners?

"It is for the happiness of those united in society to harmonize as much as possible in matters which they must of necessity transact together. Civil government being the sole object of forming societies, its administration must be conducted by common consent. Every species of government has its specific principles. Ours perhaps are more peculiar than those of any other... It is a composition of *the freest principles of the English constitution*, with others derived from natural right and natural reason. To these nothing can be more opposed than the maxims of absolute monarchies. Yet from such we are to expect the greatest numbers.

" As immigrants they will bring with them - *the principles of the governments they leave, imbibed in their early youth*; or, if able to throw them off, it will be in exchange for an unbounded licentiousness... It would be a miracle were they to stop precisely at the point of temperate liberty. These principles, with their language, they will transmit to their children.

"In proportion to their numbers, they will share with us the legislation. They will infuse into it their spirit, warp and bias its direction, and render it a heterogeneous, incoherent, distracted mass.

"I may appeal to experience, during the present contest, for a verification of these conjectures... Is it not safer to wait with patience longer, - for the population desired ? May not our government be more homogeneous - more peaceable, more durable?

"During the regal government we had at one time obtained a law which imposed such a duty on the importation of slaves as amounted... to a prohibition, when one inconsiderate assembly, repealed the law. This repeal met a joyful sanction from the then reigning Sovereign... and no expedients could succeed in getting the royal assent to a renewal of the duty."

Aliens springing from primitive origins bring with them their recreations; --- animal torture, bull-fighting, cock-fighting, drug-dealing, counterfeiting, kidnapping, medieval superstitions, torture assassination and murder: -- all flourishing under the tyranny of oppressive corrupted regimes ignorant of constitutional government.

Sovereignty - - -
versus the 'Right' of Usurpation & Invasion by Force

Sovereignty is from medieval Latin - '*Supremitas*' - and refers to supreme power, - in an individual or in a council or government. In the rude state of nature the fierce hordes who fell on Europe and usurped countries and provinces often had only primitive or poorly conceived leadership, but when tribally organized they formed weak sovereignties. When tribes of similar language root and ethnic stock came together, they could form a kind of federation with a council, as a confederacy, and a stronger sovereignty could develop out of this, such as when a city-state formed in ancient Greece. According to Aristoteles the supreme power in the city-state rested in an aggregate of citizens, which tended to be self-sufficient.

In the middle ages under the influence of Roman law, trust came to rest on the emperor who thought himself entitled to absolute sway. This sovereignty was further strengthened when church leadership was combined with the emperor, *or became the emperor*, and this enhanced power was absolute and often a form of *despotism*. Later when the church leadership weakened or was limited, the *power of corporations* was added to that of the emperor (*or president*) and this extravagant power drew in vast wealth as had previously been achieved in the church by indulgences, -but becomes more dangerous, *as having neither idealism nor sense of allegiance it is global*.

According to Sir William Blackstone, "Allegiance is the tie or *ligamen,* which binds a subject to a king (or government) in return for that protection which the king affords the subject... Indeed the natural-born may be entangled by subjecting himself to another but it is in his own act that he brings himself into this trouble... the maxim of the law proceeded upon a general principle that every man owes a natural allegiance where he is born and cannot owe two such allegiances, or serve two masters at once."

"The thing itself is founded in reason and to the nature of government and derived from our Gothic ancestry, feudal system, and mutual trust.

"An alien may purchase lands or other estates but not for his own use, for the king (or government) is therefore entitled to them. If an alien could acquire a permanent property in lands, he must owe an allegiance, equally permanent with that property which would probably be inconsistent with which he owes to his own natural liege lord; besides that thereby the nation might in time *be subject to foreign influence* and feel many other inconveniences wherefore by the civil law such contracts were also null and void. "

⊹—⋇—✕—⋇—⊹

As the nature of sovereignty in time became more stable, it developed a harmonious form under the *principle of unity,* wherein the people are *ethnically compatible* and share in a *common language,* with sovereignty resting with the people themselves. This principle of *unification,* including the basic language, inherited principles, and a natural harmony, enabled the people to live peaceably within its government, with a motto - *e pluribus unum* ("from many - *one*").

This principle implies single allegiance to one government. A double allegiance, to separate sovereignties is unacceptable unless by agreement, as two masters would introduce conflicts of interest.

A feature of sovereignty lies in the principle that a unified collection of people in their laws, character & traditions holds a responsibility within themselves over their entire land to specify the privileges to be granted *through their sovereignty,* - whereby aliens entering their land illegally have not that right to define what rights exist from the native sovereignty: because aliens from foreign lands are only under *their sovereignty back at home,* which determines only in their homeland the rights to which they are entitled.

When aliens enter our country therefore, they may not claim or expect to be granted. by *their* sovereign, rights within this realm in which they are here merely as alien visitors. They owe allegiance to *their* sovereign & cannot enter a new allegiance without releasing the old one, as that would entail a double-allegiance, which is no allegiance at all. Our laws naturally require the *pledge of allegiance.*

In the event that an alien enters our land he thus may not claim a *right of asylum* -- of which he has none by our constitution. He has no right of asylum in a foreign country: - only in his homeland. As he is only an alien here and has entered our land illegally, and broken through barriers or entered under cover of darkness, this is a crime, to be treated in accordance with our constitution. Only through *our sovereignty* may he receive asylum, and if his acts violate our laws, he is ineligible for privileges accorded to us as citizens from our constitution, wherein our borders shall be protected.

It is a *sovereign responsibility* that protects a people from intruders. It is the responsibility of our Chief Executive to defend the Constitution carried out under oath -& this protection includes defending our borders as Commander-in-Chief. Failing to protect borders, so that aliens break in, must double the crime of the Chief Executive if he pardons aliens for violating borders which he was obligated to protect. "Right of asylum" is a fiction, an arrogant bluff, with no legitimacy, and in most cases with no factual basis.

Aliens have their native lands & have no right to usurp others.

The fallacy of Asylum --- & the Death of Unity

Asylum means *without right of seizure* and this is the password used by millions of aliens as a mystic key to a better place. The occupation of foreign lands by aliens from overcrowded homelands becomes a *usurpation, or invasion by force,* -- launched through an *assumed right*, claimed by an alien through covetous thinking. Having entered illegally, and temporarily in hiding, his invisible presence gradually dissolves into that of a seeming resident - by the papers he forges, or more openly by a demand of asylum as his right.

He has no such right: only the government has *the right to grant asylum,* through its sovereignty; and if the numbers of aliens seem to politicians too great for examinations, he may receive legalization through the eventual fraud of a mass amnesty. But a mass amnesty is a blind one and evidently null and void, although it may become permanent by governmental neglect of essential duties and law enforcements-- which neglect amounts to a treasonable offence.

The alien's urgency toward his actual *usurpation* of foreign space springs out of *a population overflow, in his homeland* - crowded by an uncontrolled breeding and total failure to see natural consequences, with its inevitable stagnation, poverty and environmental squalor.

The pattern of consequences in this case proceeds through a *geometric progression* of numbers representing a population overflow which will inevitably *infect* usurped foreign space. The real compounding effect of increase is seen in a *geometric series,* e.g. where population doubles in 20 years, as found recently in surveys in parts of Mexico & also in Albania. Through unchecked progression in such regions, three million aliens usurping foreign lands will be doubling their numbers to six million in the first 20 years, as reported, and will re-double to twelve million in the second 20 years, 24 million in the third, 48 million in the fourth, 96 million in the fifth, *and 192 million after 120 years, from an initial 3 million.* By the rule of numbers the aliens will take over the government - by voting power governed solely by numbers growing to ruling power.

A fast-increasing alien population will retain its ties homeward which soon become *a foreign influence in conflict*; and being unwilling or unable in large numbers to adapt to the unifying language, ethnic harmony, and principles of Liberty and Justice of this entered country, they will continue to live by *their* old codes and habit:
"They will infuse into our legislation their spirit, warp and bias its direction, and render it a heterogeneous, incoherent distracted mass." (Ch-43)

They will provide a diversity, foreign and dissonant, and by their infusions will cause - in this once harmonious land -- the Death of Unity.

Der Sündflusz.
De Sondvloedt.

The breaking away of the colonists toward independence was followed with a revision of the Articles of Confederation, but through rigid secrecy in the constitutional convention of 1787 a flawed new Document gave exorbitant powers to the Executive, overriding all considered restraints, and it was said that he would become virtually a king. In the ensuing centuries, the Continent once of incomparable beauty has been devastated through self-interest during the building of a rich, privileged society by the concentration of corporate power and wealth. During this rise of a kind of *neo-Oligarchy*, the American Administrations from 1963 - 67 quietly emasculated our *selective* immigration laws, and this resulted in inundations of *peoples from anywhere*, mostly of lowly origin:, - unschooled in language & law, and retained as the bitter fruit of mass amnesties -- which were often said to hide crimes of bribery, villainy, & criminal invasion, with a resultant destruction of American unity in exchange for unbridled *corporate & political privilege*. During 200 years of growth the insensitivity and avarice of the towering corporations and the groups of ignorant grasping *barbarians* have devastated the Continent with volcanic overflow of waste, poison, pollutions and brutal destruction of natural forests, grasslands, prairies, - swamped under vast highway networks loaded with huge, *roaring, murderous* vehicles, corrupting the atmosphere and exhausting resources which belong to *future generations*; - also driving American Indians to wretched wastelands without resources or adequate agricultural potential and without means for modern education, - those *rightful owners of the continent* not having received a fraction of what has been given to millions of freed Africans with no such claims, who are now suing white peoples for damages conjured up from dead ancestors, without giving any credit for having been taught to read and write out of African illiteracy, and then receiving universal education, affirmative action, welfare, and political equality. FINALLY a clash with the East has come, now as a shock from lack of knowledge in the West of *incessant Invasions* by Tartaric & Arabic tribes over a *thousand year span:--* primitive people spreading by violent oppression of women, polygamy on a wild scale, rapine of the East, and riches by systematic plunder & *"booty" from conquest*. With this barbarism comes militancy in people with no comprehension of radio-activity, nuclear power, or modern science, but only an obsession to destroy the West, *in Envy* rooted in superstitious fantasy, - ratifying *murder* as holy, *rapine* as sanctified by a self-appointed "prophet", *plunder* as the wages of conquest. Those people are lost -- *but remain insidious*.

The Muscle of the gods

Secrecy becomes the hidden chamber of kings
And likewise of elusive presidents: -
'Tis where each holds in hush as resident
His power - in iron hands with mortal sting.

His person sits above all human clod
Presiding over matters grown volcanic;
It pleases him to rule with force titanic
A multi-million people as their god.

If he but lose Divine Rights of a king
Executive privilege then becomes his thing;
And as for Justice, 'tis the same rude story -
He appoints the judges who protect his glory;

He cannot brook restraint nor be impeached: -
He buys his advocates - he can't be reached.

With Bribery thus subservient on his knees
His work will ever Fancy Princes please,
And each corrupt Agreement by Intention
Secures for him his Master's Nomination.

Shifty tilting of Budget-Balance
Will ease the Debt and all its Pain,
While public records in the Book
Shall give his pocket unseen Gain.

The Devil who was called upon before
To seal a Faustian deal with pledge of Soul
Has brought Illegal Aliens quick and cheap, -
But clothed with Presidential Amnesty
They can't be gotten rid of anymore...

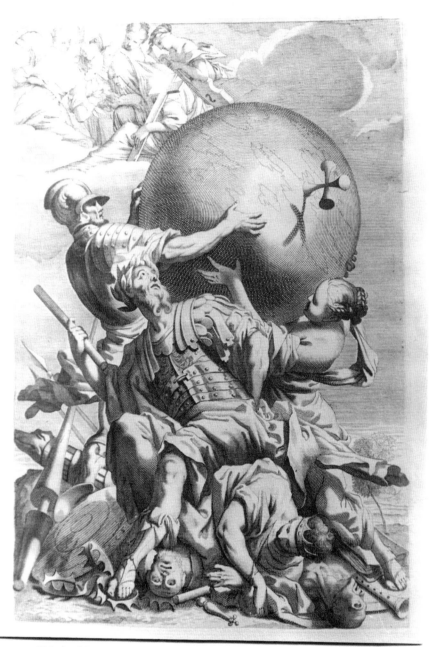

Global Power rests on its bankrupted Victims:
It spreads Inventions promiscuously,
Exports Technology irresponsibly,
Promotes Labor-Abuse profitably,
Imports Corruption politically,
Extinguishes moral Integrity.

WALNUT STREET FRONT OF THE STATE HOUSE IN 1776.[2]

From an old Print of the Period.

Who hid the Fair Copy
... in the Cloak of Night?

With at least 21 known copies of the Broadside as official text printed on the night of July 4th, the years of debate drew toward an uncertain end. The Original Draught (Fair Copy) as framed was smouldering & controversial with a shadow portraiture and hazarded signatures; and to some it was crucially ambiguous in ways that offered inroads toward false interpretations of its intended meanings. Some of its basic deletions in Congress had rent the tough fabric of its integrity, and its message had not been fire-tested nor its vulnerability protected for the future. *We were all in haste* they said.

Nor was that all: - their agreements had not been unanimous and were stained with compromise. They had not been unanimous from the beginning and the political and philosophical rifts, splitting the Colonies north and south, could only be suppressed briefly in an unnatural alliance, compelled under the overriding fear of a tyranny that hovered as a monster over their gathering resistance.

In safeguarding the Original Draught it must have seemed imperative to retain it within hidden security. -- It could not conceivably lie exposed on the table in the State House after hours, with invisible enemies outside and spies within. The Rough Draft lacking title and signatures could have served briefly but the 'States of America' were still separate Colonies having single independent clandestine governments, and without a Confederation there could be a no safe public repository for the Fair Copy itself.

Until July 4th the penman with the committee had held the Fair Copy in their own custody and there it could remain for a while, although it should have disappeared in the early morning hours of July 5th, in the possession of Thomas Jefferson, in whose custody it must reappear secretly for the remaining signers and for 'comparison at the table' with its abridged counterpart.

In 1823 when Jefferson was asked of the whereabouts of the Original Draught he wrote that it should be in the records of Congress but seemed little concerned that it could not be found. As it was a precious document in his life even being named on his tombstone, his unconcern over a disappearance suggests that he had retained possession of it for its security - superseded, but remaining his conception & realization of the work; - and some in Congress would have been relieved by his retention of it during the colonial controversies stretching far into an uncertain future. Further historical investigations especially as in in 1873 and 1943 again failed to provide tangible clues of the Fair Copy's existence.

Thomas Jefferson Portrait
painted in Paris after the American revolution

It would have been apparent to Jefferson that the cynical remarks over the Declaration from some public officials, would have rendered it liable to tampering or even destruction if retained in the future public records.   Such mishandling had been forecast by scheming politicians. The Secretary of State, Pickering, had said - *it should be buried.* By reason of its disappearance the abridged Copy on Parchment manifestly had become the official Document.

With the Fair Copy safely in the hands of its author during the half-century after its signing, Jefferson had the power *&* foresight to secure its preservation most certainly in the faithful hands of his own descendants. This seems the natural sequel, affirmed in the last hours of his life when he was said to have given a morocco leather case to his granddaughter saying, *'This contains some musical strains'.*

The musical strains could refer not to a musical composition which he did not create, but to the opening preamble of the Declaration which had breathed a musical rhythm *&* cadence, in the first two paragraphs - a form that can be scanned as *iambic pentameter or hexameter.*

The preservation of Jefferson's original work could thus be secured for a lifetime in the trusted hands of his granddaughter, *&* from her to 1976 through ensuing descendants. Thence by failure of an inheritance *&* born upon the *Winds of Chance,* it could reappear, only to vanish, even in the hands of some patriot's descendent.

The mysticism of a provenance is unfathomable. Often obscured is the testament that some treasures of civilization are substantiated through incomplete provenances given only in theory, which may be spurious. Several interim drafts of the Declaration have no continuous provenance, and most of the July 4th Broadsides have none, nor has a signed Proclamation of the Louisiana Purchase, but these are valued from internal evidence with logic, and insight.

Toward the end of life Jefferson wrote privately of his thoughts for the future to his favorite granddaughter. - "I received with inexpressible pleasure the information your letter contained... after your own happy establishment which has given me an inestimable friend (Joseph Coolidge, of Boston) to whom *I can leave the care of everything I love...*" Mr. Coolidge was a grandson-in-law *&* the first of a distinguished New England family, who cherished Jefferson, and revered his memory for generations, actively acquiring numerous treasures from Virginia including most of his architectural drawings, and possibly the Fair Copy itself. He built a reduced scale replica of Jefferson's first residence, Monticello, named from the region in Italy where Palladio built the Rotunda, its Renaissance archetype.

Scars of hidden Storage...
▣ ☺ ▣

The thick paper of the Manuscript had been backed originally by a single sheet of finely woven linen, but this had shown long aging; and because of paper cracks along folds, a new backing was added, - a sheet of pure linen attached under the old one, with small stitches of cotton thread linking the two. Also, as protection for the ink on the paper, a sheet of loosely woven white cotton has been placed as a separating layer over the face of the Manuscript, unattached but in place during dark storage. This fabric enables the paper surfaces to glide without abrasion between a double layer of cotton and linen.

During photography of the Manuscript before adoption of protecting fabrics, the paper surface showed small areas with images of threaded patterns. These proved to be stains as of an open-mesh fabric which had stuck in several spots during a remote past, suggesting that fabric layers had been used earlier and then in storage, when damp, had reacted on the paper.

The Rough draft and also the known interim copies of the Declaration in public collections have all shown major destructive attacks from aging or even tampering in storage: 1) the Lee copy with ink notations written upon it by later hands, and loss by mildew; 2) the Wythe copy with scars from plastic tape; 3) the 'Washburn copy', having lost more than one-quarter of the text.

Unlike the interim copies, the Manuscript as the Fair Copy had evidently been strictly protected against tampering after its initial disappearance. No signs of meddling have been found, although an attempt seemed to have been made in the recent past century possibly to re-attach fragments near a lower margin with a sheet of ordinary yellow writing paper attached underneath a torn section of Quad-2, as a support, - but this had failed. Possibly several letters and part of the Wythe portrait are missing. Here the paper had been clearly *torn off* - down to the linen backing!

It is remarkable that a manuscript so fragile, haunted, & misunderstood could have survived for two centuries after Congress had abandoned it. But Jefferson would have foreseen the necessity of a repository, - easily in the faithful hands of his own kin in private trust, rather than in an official file under the eye of his adversaries.

The Manuscript as a secret document must have been moved repeatedly, suffering fissures where fold-lines have fragmented; but preservation of the text's content *&* portraiture have now been secured with precision photography, and under scientific principles the Manuscript emerges as from a lost slumber, - a beautiful original work of art *&* mind - intended to remain that original, *in perpetuo.*

Last two letters of "Independence" *(hand drawn) in the Title of the*
"ORIGINAL DRAUGHT *(or Fair Copy)* OF THE
"DECLARATION OF INDEPENDENCE"

Flinders Petrie once wrote of ancient documents in survival:-

"During the age of the decline of Egyptian power in Syria when the great concepts of Tahutmes-I were all gradually lost, a splendid store of information was laid by for us in the cuneiform correspondence, the *Tell el Amarna*. The clay tablets, mostly from Syria, but with a few duplicates of letters from Egypt, were deposited in the *place of records in the palace of the king*, as it is called upon the stamped bricks which I found still remaining there.   A few years ago the natives, while plundering about the ruins and carrying off Akhenaten's bricks for their modern houses, lit upon this record chamber containing many hundreds of tablets. These were shown to dealers, others sent some to Dr. Oppert, at Paris, who announced them to be forgeries; others were sent to M. Grebaut, then head of the Department of Antiquities, and were treated by him with the customary silence. At last, when they were supposed to be almost worthless, a quantity were carried in sacks to Luxor to hawk among the dealers there, and these were largely ground to pieces on the way. What has been preserved, therefore, is but a wreck of what might have been, had any person equal to the occasion placed his hand upon them in time. The tablets thus reaching the dealers' hands became known, and were bought up mainly by the British Museum and the Berlin Museum. Some drifted to St. Petersburg, Paris, and the Cairo Museum and some into private collections. A similar miserable fate attends all discoveries in Egypt, unless made by a skilled observer, as witness..."

A similar fate seemed to await the Fair Copy:- rescued in a *Place of Records,* tossed to the *Winds of Chance*, offered to an unbelieving crowd for a pittance to be hawked about amongst Dealers and de-accessioned for gold if placed in an Institution. -In searches for a safe Repository, this unique *Record* has repeatedly suffered *the Customary Silence &* been labeled with authoritarian judgment by ten Directors *&* Curators at rich and renowned Institutions: -

an engraving   a silkscreening   a printed paper   a copy of something
a 19th-century souvenir   a lithograph of an original   a forgery

  a nonexistent document   an interesting thing   a priceless Original
If 10 judgments are each different, 9 must be in error. Who is right? -W. M. Flinders Petrie, the great Egyptologist. His quotation is from *The Tell El Amarna Letters* (1898). We reflect on these things...

  "What has been preserved therefore, is but a wreck of what might have been had someone equal to the occasion placed his hand upon them in time".
- Is it not incumbent on Institutions preserving historical materials when sought, with all due respect, to offer responses at least better than hasty disputations, with rejections of requested interviews & generous offers?

Quebec
Montreal
Kingston
L. Champlain
L. Ontario
Niagara Fall
Six Nations
L. Erie
Ohio
Bennington
Portsmouth
Boston
C. Cod
Hartford
Rhode Island
New York
Amboy
LONG ISLAND
Baltimore
Philadelphia
Delaware Bay
Washington
Annapolis
Chesapeek Bay
Richmond
Norfolk
C. Hatteras
New Bern
C. Lookout
Columbia
C. Fear
Augusta
Charlston
STATES
UNITED

Contemporary Authentication

The following contemporary authentication appears in the *"Military Journal during the American Revolutionary War"* by James Thacher, M.D., Surgeon of the American army: --

For July 1776, Pages 55-58: " (July) 12th. The very important intelligence from Philadelphia is now proclaimed, that on the 4th instant the American Congress declared the 13 United Colonies Free, Sovereign, Independent States. --

"(July) 18th. This day the declaration of American Independence has been proclaimed in form from the balcony of the State House in this town. A number of the members of our council and house of representatives, the magistrates, clergymen, selectmen, and a large number of other gentlemen of Boston, and of the neighbouring towns, assembled in the council chamber.

"At 1 o'clock the declaration was proclaimed...

"This highly important transaction of our Congress is the theme of every circle and topic of universal discussion, and it receives the sanction and approbation of a large majority of the community... The history of the world cannot furnish an instance of fortitude and heroic magnanimity parallel to that displayed by the members, whose *signatures are affixed to the declaration of American Independence.* Their venerated names will ornament the brightest pages of American history, and be transmitted to the latest generations. *The instrument was signed by John Hancock, Esq. as President & fifty-four others, delegates from the 13 United States.*

" I am credibly informed that the following anecdote occurred on the *day of signing the declaration*: Mr. Harrison, a delegate from Virginia, is a large portly man, Mr. Gerry of Massachusetts is slender and spare. A little time after the solemn transaction of signing the instrument, Mr. Harrison said smilingly to Mr. Gerry, 'When the hanging scene comes, I shall have the advantage over you on account of my size. All will be over with me in a moment, but you will be kicking in the air half an hour after I am gone.'

" 20th. - It appears by the public papers... a fleet have lately made a furious attack on the town of Charleston, South Carolina... The British fleet has suffered a loss almost beyond example. Their ships shattered almost to total ruin, and one frigate of 28 guns was blown up by her own crew..."

The accuracy of the signing date as of July 4th is confirmed in Thacher's Journal as set between dated events of July 1776.

(ORIGINAL) / DRAUGHT OF THE / DECLARATION
(OF INDEPENDENCE)-
- left side of Title

꩜————⟆

A given name has strange tenacity when it fits its object and may linger long after authoritative attempts to change it. A less fitting name may never stick. The minds of men are taken by the name they like. *Declaration of Independence* was in the air, - about the Colonies and in the halls of the State House in July of 1776; and even though the copies then circulating did not say it, - that was its name from its birth and remained that for two centuries in the minds of the people though never seen publicly, for Congress did artfully hide it.

The Parchment Copy was the first signed official text copied from the *Original Draught*, via the Broadside, to become the standard government document, bearing only the abridged text.

When a new name was invented for the Parchment Copy, few used it. Even that copy like the early derivatives is simply referred to as "the Declaration ..."

As to the fate of the original title, Congress voted on July 19, 1776 to devise an extensively abridged text with a new *unanimous* title, and thereby the original title was to be scuttled by Congress, -- though not by Jefferson, who in due course could faithfully ride off with his Manuscript into a forgotten obscurity.

During two centuries of a turbulent existence it would be inevitable that damage would occur to the large, fragile and much folded paper Document, especially under perennial threat of attack and the necessities of hidden flight. Along its lower border two paper fragments with space for several words and letters had been separated and lost. The missing parts could not be reconstituted from reference to the small drafts as derivatives.

No main title for the Original Draught was to be found near the masthead at the top, where stands only the familiar headline appearing on the early texts -"A Declaration by the Representatives of the United States of America..."

But at the bottom of the Draught, on a solid black inked band, appeared the "lost" Title of the work - as envisioned, designed, and executed - in partially tattered letters of old and venerable style, in the paper's aged color as if hand-stencilled - three time-worn words:-

D E C L A R A T I O N   O F   I N D E P E N D E N C E

The title was flanked by two unfurled ribbons drawn in ink with the remaining lettering in reversed tones as black on white.

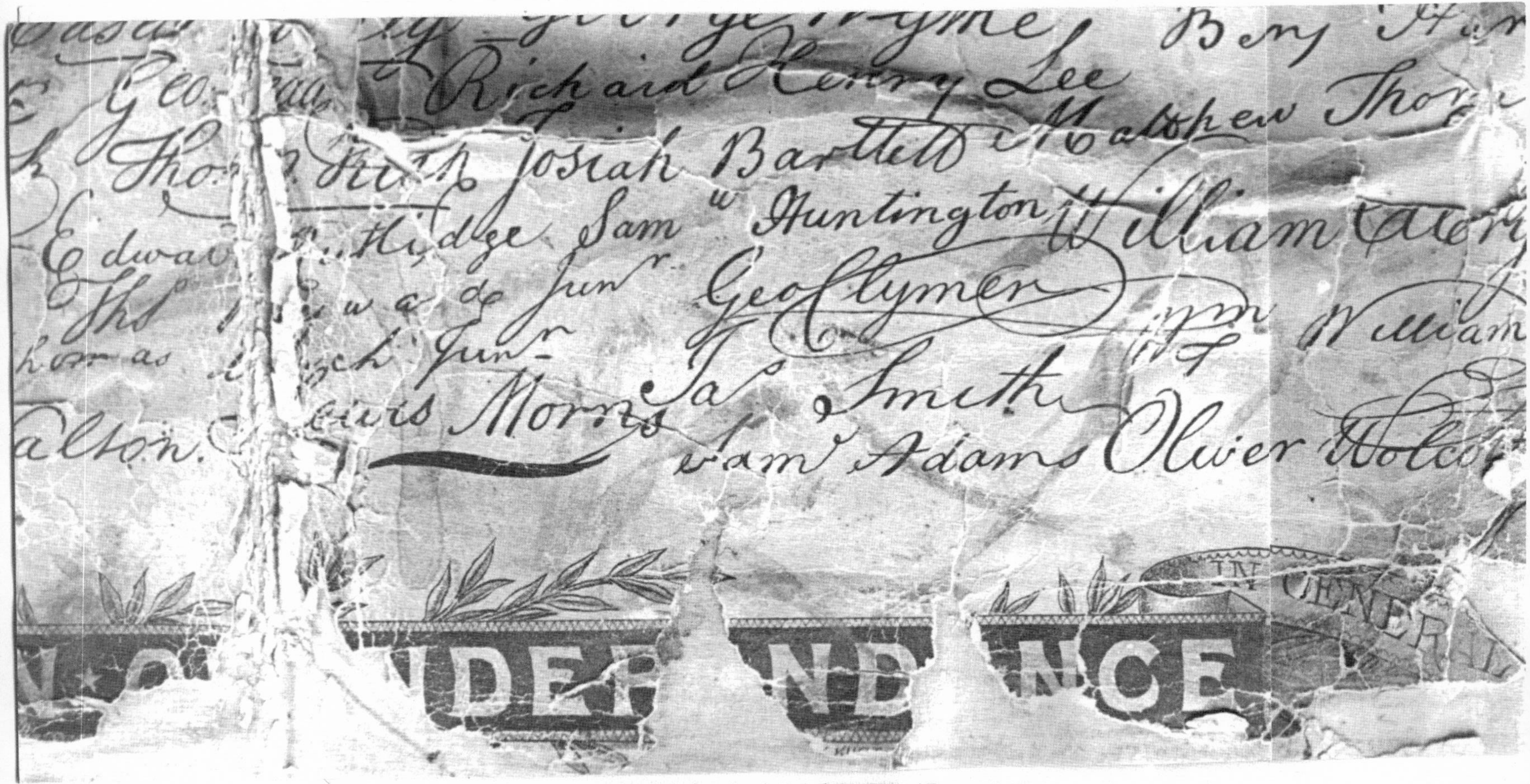

OF INDEPENDENCE / IN GENERAL...(Congress)
right side of Title

On the left the letters show engrossed the first part as "...L DRAUGHT of the DECLARATION****ND*P*NDENCE" followed immediately on the ribbon by "In General Co****** ", now incomplete, the several letters evidently lost *as though torn* from the paper surface, but with space left for about 15 or more letters.

The surviving letters standing alone could not seem sufficient. It would be essential that the date should appear, including the year, also in ink; and could this be reconciled when *compared at the table* with the replacement parchment, already bearing its date falsely as *"July 4, 1776"*?

In the shadows of deception one transgression leads to another; and Congress then could hardly be expected to duplicate dates on two Manuscripts completed four weeks apart. And it is additionally apparent that *Original* would have surely been deleted from the earlier document as a tell-tale of the Parchment as a derivative.

It may have been comprehended that concealment of the act of replacement could be further effected by lifting or peeling the date and the word *Original* from the Draught, separating the upper layer of the paper through the interfaces between layers when peeled back, leaving thus only two scarred bare paper areas still firmly held to the linen backing by the glue.

The actual scarred border of the lower area of the Draught shows damage over two bare spaces where missing words and a date may have been removed. With this assumption, *a facsimile* of the presumed completed title has now been drawn on a photocopy of the original so as to determine the fitting of the date similarly to that shown on the Broadside as the closest derivative. From the fragments thus estimated the complete title may be reconstituted as follows, with 27, 33, *&* 31 spaces per line, and the first 10 & last 15 letters or numbers replaced: (see exemplification >————

The Original Draught of the
DECLARATION OF INDEPENDENCE
In General Congress, July 4, 1776

That this contains the true title of the text as first conceived is shown by Jefferson's references to his work, consistently in his lifetime and on his tombstone, and also from the wording of the Broadside (as the text next of kin), using the same words and date.

Responsibility for the approved later title was not to be Jefferson's choice. As the penman he was responsible for recording the text of the Committee as agreed upon, and as bracketed for abridgment finally by Congress. This he did consistently, in his own hand, and he could do no more.

Beny Harrison   Ths Nelson jr.

...ew Thornton   John Adams

...ger Sherman

...liam... Charles Carroll of Carrollton

...William Rob Treat Paine

...liver Wolcott

CONGRESS JULY 4, 1776

To face the lost original title for the first time after its dark invisibility for two centuries strikes one with a shattering sense of mystical intervention, through seven generations, yet none would tell -- why and where it was , or who saw it and held it, even cherished it. This true title missing since the American Revolution has been a target of repeated speculation *&* controversy. None of the drafts nor the Parchment Copy show any words that this title existed. Its absence created a sense of deception - an enigma amplified by the reference on Jefferson's tombstone:

'Author of the Declaration of American Independence'

Historians challenge - ' *Where is* it ? '

Spirits murmur, ' Hidden... in the security of private hands.'

' Why a different title on the Parchment Copy ? '

' The Parchment Copy is not a Jefferson Manuscript. '

Naturally, a series of small primitive copies could not bear the initially intended title because they were unfinished. Jefferson's headline, "A Declaration by..." was a practical term for the interim copies of the Committee. Jefferson had avoided ambiguity through that headline, reserving his title alone for the final original text approved by the committee.

The Mysterye of the Lost Title -*The Declaration of Independence* thus dissolves into -- *The Mysterye of the Lost Original Manuscript* of the Declaration of Independence -- which vanished with its authentic title in August of 1776, -- never yet having been seen by the public, but referred to by its true name for two centuries.

On Thomas Jefferson's Lost Declaration

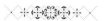

Now look upon me with my signs and scars
And find in me some other tales not read -
But do not stretch my meaning to the stars
Nor interpret me for purposes unsaid...

Do not rewrite me with an unskilled pen
Nor try to fill your need at my expense:
Should you but try with rusty brain to gain
A world unearned - 'twill fail, in recompense.

Mistake not hence my message for your own
Nor compromise my principles - for none,
And never more deny my Author's word
That I was signed, that we did breath as One.

Of Liberty was writ upon his heart,
His hand did write on me - and we did part ...

Thomas Jefferson Portrait from
Original Draught

*"It is while we are young
that the habit of industry is formed. -
- If not then, it never is afterwards..."*

--- *Thomas Jefferson*

Epilogue

The profound changes in the character of the American people and their leadership, in the last 40 years, has afflicted the older generation with a sense of loss of the great American Heritage cherished for two centuries, - & also a sense of impending inescapable tragedy for the future of the Continent. It has been apprehended that a lack of values has been growing in the new generations, -abandoning courtesy, taste, kindness, honesty, chivalry, and even respect of work. At the lowest level the young are increasingly foreign, strange of face and varying in color, with indecipherable speech & habit. They seem of amnestied alien origin. If a Chief Executive grants a mass amnesty it cannot comprise a grant of residency & even citizenship, & if by criminality some of the amnestied are found to be criminals the amnesty is evidently fraudulent & requires court annulment, & an impeachment.

On our traditional side the young are increasingly unkempt, of shabby clothing and unclean habits; they sit on floors, streets, anywhere. Of speech they are careless or semi-coherent, often ungrammatical and cannot write or spell properly; of industry they are above labor, preoccupied with sports or its imitations - fun & games, night prowling, well-equipped with cell-phones, computers, videos, cars, but they disdain simple work, - chores & serious summer jobs when idle for a quarter of the year. They seem adrift, without objective or preparation for problems & difficulties sure to overtake them.

Meanwhile this rich country itself has shipped out to foreign countries our basic manufactures --clothing, household accessories, plumbing, appliances, electronics, - virtually all of our technology as though disdaining the making of it, or interest in the making of it by our emerging generations.

For the first time in 2 centuries there have come the Drugs, with their dealers, and swarms of illegal misfits, suddenly -- by the destruction of our immigration laws in 1963-65 -- as one of the great disasters in the history of Nations, -nor is inundation to be stopped. It is said to be the inexorable power of a chief Executive giving mass amnesties to aliens that he has never seen & knows nothing of, nor ever will see or care who or what they are though they be devil-incarnate -- that is destroying a Nation by corruption within. And it is said to be an Ambition of Administrations, with their legislative bodies in harnessed Appeasement, that launches our numerous wars outside of all constitutional limitations, destroying the good will for us of the World, and rendering us an object of Fear.

Our heritage, including the great inventions of European, English & North American nations and their superb Arts, Literature & Science that have been unique in the world as the great culture of the West, is being sold or given away by a rich privileged corporate & political upper class,- with the destruction of the fairest Continent on the Earth, a loss of pursuits of our creative industrious lives, & thus the abandonment of our Western culture.

First Edition
    First Issue, limited to 76 numbered copies
    Second Issue, limited to 1776 numbered copies

Published in Fort Ticonderoga, New York
July 4th, 2002,
commemorating the 226th Anniversary
of the signing of the
Original Draught of the
Declaration of Independence

Book-List
#*^*#
as References.

***

1776   "ORIGINAL DRAUGHT OF THE
DECLARATION OF INDEPENDENCE",
the secret, unpublished original Document, also called
"Fair Copy" July 4, 1776, in Jefferson's handwriting, signed

<*****>
^*^
*

1574(ca.)   Bernal Diaz del Castillo: "The Conquest of New Spain"
transl. by J.M. Cohen, London, 1974

1624   Capt. John Smith: "General History of Virginia"
(illustrated)

1630   Christophoro Scheiner:
Pantographice sev ars delineandi res
quaslibet per Parallelogrammum sev
cavum, mechanicum, mobile

1635   Ritratti et Elogii di Capitani Illustri
in Roma alle spese di Pompilio totti Libraro
Illustrious personages from the 12th century on,
described with portraits engraved in 1635

1643   Edmund Bohun, Esq. :
"The Character of Queen Elizabeth" London

1675   Edmund Wingate :"An exact Abridgement of all Statutes
from Magna Charta until 1641"

1712   "Ancient and Present State of English History
of its Monarchs from Julius Caesar to this very year"
(has extensive family trees of the kings of England)
London

1748   Charles L. de S. Montesquieu: "Esprit des Lois"

1758   Edmund Burke:(2 vol.)
"An Account of the European Settlements in America"

1759   Johann Huebners
Neu=vermehrtes und verbessertes
reales Staats=Zeitungs-und Conversations-Lexicon.

1762   Diderot-D'Alembert
Encyclopédie des Métiers et Sciences
Recuell de Planches (profusely illustrated)

1774   Arthur Young, Esq. FRS:"Political Arithmetic", London

1776   Thomas Paine
"The Rights of Man"and other Writings, including
"Common Sense"
Modern Reprint, first published Jan. 10, 1776 (2 shillings)

1779   Benjamin Franklin
"Political, Miscellaneous, and Philosophical Pieces"

1783   Sir William Blackstone, Knt
"Commentaries on the Laws of England"
The Ninth edition with the last corrections of the
author, 4 volumes

1785   David Ramsay
Member of the American Congress
"The History of the Revolution of South Carolina
from a British Province to an Independent State",
with numerous maps, 2 volumes

1785   John Andrews L.L.D.
"History of the War with America, France, Spain, and
Holland; commencing 1775 and ending in 1783 "-
with maps and illustrations, 4 volumes

1788   William Gordon D.D.
"The History of the Rise, Progress and Establishment, of
the Independence of the United States of America:
including an account of the late war, and of the thirteen
Colonies from their Origin to that Period", 4 volumes

1789 David Ramsay M.D.
"The History of the American Revolution"
with contemporary maps, in 2 volumes. Philadelphia

1792 Abbe Raynal
"Philosophical and Political History..."
to which is added the
"Revolution of America", Volume 6

1796 John Lendrum
"Concise and impartial
History of the American Revolution ..."

1796 George Washington
Official Letters to the Honorable American Congres etc.
(written during the war between the United Colonies
and Great Britain) by his Excellency George Washington,
Commander in Chief of the Continental forces, then
President of the United States. 2 volumes.

1800 "Journals of Congress: containing the Proceedings
from January 1, 1776, to December 31, 1776
Folwell's Press, Philadelphia, Volume 2

1810 J.J. Stockdale
"History of the Inquisitions; including the secret
Transactions of those horrific Tribunals"
illustrated with 12 plates

1810 "The Mythology of the Pagan World"
illustrated by 52 plates engraved, 4 volumes

1819 "Memoirs of the Life of Thomas Paine"
by W.T.Sherwin, London

1823 James Thacher, M.D., late Surgeon of the American Army
"Military Journal from the American Revolutionary War
from 1775-1783. Historical Facts and Anecdotes from the
original Manuscript", Boston

1830   Thomas Jefferson Randolph
"Memoir, Correspondence and Miscell. from the Papers
of Thomas Jefferson",
edited by T.J. Randolph,(grandson of Mr. Jefferson) Vol.1
Bound in Vol. 1 after page 146 is a printed engraving,
there called the "Memoir Draft"(1829) of the 4 pages
combined into 2 pages as an exact duplicate of the
Rough Draft now in the Library of Congress

1838   Alexis De Toqueville: "Democracy in America"
translated by Henry Reeves, Esq.(friend of de Toqueville)

1843   John L. Stevens
"Incidents of Travel in Yucatan"
New York Harpers Bros. 2 volumes

1847   Jared Sparks
"The Writings of George Washington being his
correspondence, addresses, messages and other papers"
official and private, 12 volumes

1853   William Goodell
New York, American and Foreign Anti-Slavery Society
"The American Slave Code in Theory and Practice:
Its distinctive Features shown by
its Statutes, Judicial Decisions"

1855   B.J.Lossing
"Pictorial Field Book of the Revolution"
1100 engravings

1869   François Pierre Guilleaume Guizot
"History of the French People"
with illustrations by A. De Neuville, 6 vols.

1874   William H. Prescott
"History of the Conquest of Mexico and
the Life of Hernando Cortes" 2 volumes

1876   Unknown copy of the Declaration of Independence,
a Harpers Magazine supplement,
republished by Dover in 1976:
John Grafton "The American Revolution,"
a Picture Source Book, page 44

1884   John Richard Greene
"History of the English People"
4 volumes

1905   "The writings of Thomas Jefferson", Volume 3
edited by Andrew A. Lipscomb (editor in chief)

1906   J.H. Hazleton
"The Declaration of Independence - Its History"

1942   Carl Becker: "The Declaration of Independence,
a study of the History of Political Ideas"

1943   Julian P. Boyd
Published by the Library of Congress, limited edition.
"The Declaration of Independence, the
evolution of the text as shown in facsimiles in various
drafts by its author, Thomas Jefferson."

1944   "The Life and selected Writings of Thomas Jefferson"
edited , and with an introduction by
Adrienne Koch & William Peden

1947   Emile Monnin Chamot, Clyde Walter Mason
"Handbook of Chemical Microscopy" Volume I

1948   Fritz Ephraim, "Inorganic Chemistry"
translated by Thorne & Roberts

1955   George E. Hastings: "Life & Work of Francis Hopkinson"

1961   L.H. Butterfield, Editor
        "Diary & Autobiography of John Adams", 4 volumes
        Belknap Press of Harvard University Press, Cambridge

1962   Page Smith: "John Adams" , 2 volumes

1964   Nathan Schachner: "Thomas Jefferson, A Biography"
        Publisher: Thomas Yoseloff, New York

1971   Peter Tompkins "Secrets of the Great Pyramid"
        appendix by L.C. Stecchini
        Harper & Row, New York

1975   William Petersen
        Professor of Social Demography, "POPULATION"

1976   Julian P. Boyd:
        Pennsylvania Magazine of History and Biography,
        October 1976
        "The Mystery of the Lost Original -
        the Declaration of Independence"

1982   Robert G. Ferris, Richard E. Morris
        National Park Service
        "Signers of the Declaration of Independence"

1982   Helen A. Cooper
        Yale University Art Gallery
        "John Trumbull, the Hand and Spirit of a Painter"

1984   Merrill D. Peterson
        "Thomas Jefferson"
        WRITINGS
        Autobiography, A Summary View of the Rights of
        British America,   Notes on the State of Virginia,
        Public Papers, Addresses, Messages and Replies
        Miscellany, Letters
        Published by The Library of America

1986   Guenter Bayerl/Karl Pichol:
        "Papier", Produkt aus Lumpen, Holz, Wasser
        Deutsches Museum, Muenchen

1987   Grolier
        "American Historical Documents
        from the year 1000 - 1904"

1998   John Balston
        "The Whatmans and Wove (Velin) Paper"
        Its Invention and Development in the West
        Printed in Great Britain by
        St. Edmundsbury Press, Bury St. Edmunds, Suffolk

                        ^****^
                        ^**^
                          *

DICTIONARIES

        11th edition of the Encyclopedia Britannica, New York
        Cambridge Edition

1964   The concise Oxford Dictionary of current English, edited
        by H.W. Fowler & F.G. Fowler, based on the Oxford
        Dictionary

1969   Pictorial Encyclopedia of Science
        Art and Technology
        Diderot and d'Alembert Compact Edition
         Recueil des Planches sur les sciences,
         l'art et livres et les arts mechaniques
        Tomes 18-28, Paris 1762. Microprint 1969, New York

1964,68 Encyclopedia Britannica
        American Editions

1991   Main Dictionary section Librairie Larousse
        The Larousse Illustrated International Encyclopedia
        and Dictionary revised 1990

Glossary

A) Expressions

Parts I & II

Impressment:
> forcibly taking persons, as for military service, especially young men for the British navy; a form of slavery.

Writs of assistance:
> written demands as from George III, including entry and search of private residences on mere suspicion of taxable property (025).

Fascines:
> Tied bundles of brush for disguise in fortification (034).

Part III

Parallelogram:
> Four-sided figure, opposite sides equal and parallel .

Ensign:
> A flag-standard, a flag as an identification of a locality, country, etc. (O.F.enseigne L.Insignia-sign)

Interim copies:
> Small Jefferson copies approximating the Declaration's text as revised by the Committee in late stages before submission to congress showing Jefferson's concepts before major deletions.

Rough Draft:
> Unique copy of the text of the *Original Draught of the Declaration* pantographed by Jefferson at a reduced scale of 3:8, apparently as a "desk copy" showing corrections and alterations cumulatively.

Broadside:
> Unsigned public message printed on a large sheet, especially of the Declaration, July 4, 1776.

Initial or original Paper:
> The first incomplete manuscript sketch, as written by Jefferson and interlined with corrections, and additions in the handwritings of Adams and Franklin; later apparently lost.

Fair Copy;
> Jefferson's "Original Draught of the Declaration of Independence"; the Unknown Manuscript, probably the printer's copy.

Adams copy:
> Earliest surviving text of the Declaration copied by John Adams from Jefferson's initial paper before editing.

Alterations:

Adverts to a change of direction or emphasis.

Corrections:

Improvements in wording.

Quad:

One of 4 contiguous quarter parts of the Fair Copy (Original Draught).

engross:

Make enlarged fair copy in careful handwriting.

Laid paper:

Sheet of writing paper with ladder-like impressions from the supporting wires of the forming mold.

Wove paper:

Sheet of especially smooth paper for map or drawing purposes.

Parchment or Parchment copy:

The abridged Declaration completed on August 2, 1776 entitled the 'Unanimous Declaration of the 13 united States of America", misdated July 4, 1776; in the handwriting of a scribe (not Jefferson) on Parchment; adopted as the official document of the government and engraved in 1823 for reproduction.

Memoir copy:

Precise Fac-simile engraving (1829) of Rough Draft on two fold-out pages published by Jefferson's grandson, T.J. Randolph in "Memoirs of Thomas Jefferson"... Scale 1:1.

Elocution marks:

Jefferson's apostrophe-like signs over words for emphasis in reading (also called diacritical marks); found in the third Quad of the Fair Copy & correspondingly in the Rough Draft. Absent from all other texts.

Reserve copy:

Secret copy of the Committee text of the Declaration, origin and location unknown.

Souvenir copies:

Numerous enlarged copy-texts made by calligraphers according to the abridged text, in pretentious styles, usually with forged signatures and irrelevant pictures. All counterfeits. Fodder for Auction Houses.

PART IV

Gel-size:

Also called "Glue-size" or "sizing". The medium holding the fibers of paper-matrix as a tough flexible sheet without fillers, - the basic component of pre-19th century European long-lasting pure non-acidic fibrous paper.

Alum:

Alum is a natural double-salt of potassium and aluminum sulfate with associated water molecules, essential for stability of old papers, and a component in gel-size.

Ink:

Carbon ink of Fair Copy; the most ancient form of permanent black ink.

Gall ink of Rough Draft and interim copies, the cheap 18th century writing ink generally for impermanent use; subject to oxidation and reaction with paper.

B)   Locations, Artists, Politicians, Authors

PARTS I & II

Houdon, Jean Antoine:

(1740-1828) born in Versailles. Talent inspired by statues in the gardens of Versailles. At age 12 entry to "L'Ecole royale" for sculpture, at age 20 received "Prix de Rome". Spent 10 years in Italy. Houdon executed busts of many famous contemporaries (Catherine II, Denis Diderot, Jean d'Alembert, Prince Henry of Prussia, Moliere) Visited United States in 1785 bringing with him a bust of Franklin. While staying at Mount Vernon, modelled statue of Washington for the capitol of the State of Virginia.

Boyd, Julian, P.:

Distinguished historian and editor of more than 20 volumes of Jefferson's papers & major proponent of the reality of Jeffersons's Original, as "lost" but existing.

State House:

(now "Independence Hall", Philadelphia) -- where the deliberations on independence were held in 1776 by the 2nd Continental Congress

Lexington & Concord:

Villages north of Boston, where first bloodshed of the American Revolution occurred, 19th April 1775.

Breed's Hill:

Quoted as Bunker Hill, Boston; scene of a small battle, at time of burning of Charlestown by the British without provocation.

Olive Branch Petition:

August 1775: Petition to George III in search of reconciliation and resolution of grievances. It was ignored by the King, and his advisers.

Tyconderoga:

(Today Ticonderoga), strategic fort built by the French before 1755 in New France on peninsula overlooking the southern part of Lake Champlain. After heroic stand under their great leader Montcalm, outnumbered against the British, the French retreated in June 1758, blowing up the fort. It was not then rebuilt; major restorations in 20th and 21st century.

Knox, Henry:

A young Boston bookseller and map collector; a dedicated patriot, became a famous general under Washington.

Howe, William:

(1729-1814) British General, commanding (1758) the British in the Revolutionary War.

Beaumarchais, (Pierre Augustin Caron):

Writer, inventor and personal adviser to Louis XVI of France. Persuasive in February 1776 in instigating crucial support for America with huge French war supplies, secret until late 1777.

Magna Charta:

Feudal English charter of liberties, adopted 1215 A.D. at Runnymede by King John under coercion of barons and churchmen. The charter sought to protect the rights of the barony against royal prerogative. In the 17th century its interpretation as the touchstone of English liberty goes back to parliamentarians who sought in it the principles of trial by jury and writs of habeas corpus. It contained the essence of much in the Bill of Rights as added to the United States Constitution.

PART III

Scheiner, Christopher:

German scholar, Jesuit, mathematician and astronomer, contemporary with Galileo, and joint discoverer of sunspots; inventor of the Pantograph of great importance to Jefferson and indispensable in map-making and architecture.

Palladio, Andrea di Pietro:

(1508-80)Italian Renaissance architect, largely influential in revival of classical architecture in Italy, and throughout Europe. His four books on Architecture (1570) became world famous, and a basis for Jefferson's designs for public buildings and his residences, Monticello and Poplar Forest.

Revere, Paul:

(1735-1818) American silversmith, artist and patriot; by a famous night ride (April 18, 1775) his warnings enabled John Hancock and Samuel Adams to escape a fatal capture and to alert the colonists of an impending attack on their defensive supplies by British troops at Lexington.

Boston Teaparty:

An inflammatory incident (December 16, 1773) in which Boston agitators dumped shiploads of British tea into Boston harbor, an unwise provocation for which the Americans later suffered the necessary payment of damages.

Richard Henry Lee:

"Lee Resolution" introduced in Congress 7th June 1776. Lee was in congress from 1774-1780, and was especially prominent in connection with foreign affairs and condemnation of slavery.

PART V

Trumbull, John:

(1756-1843) Artist, historical painter and contemporary of Gilbert Stuart, Benjamin West and Charles Wilson Peale. His most famous paintings are "The signing of the Declaration of Independence", painted after 1790 in two versions and showing several errors in membership and an imagined arrangement of members.

Bartolozzi, Francesco:

(1727-1815) Italian engraver. Practiced as a gold- & silversmith in Venice, later engraver to King George III; distinguished for launching the stipple-drawing techniques.

Hopkinson Francis:

> Writer, poet, designer, musician and artist, member of second continental congress, known for his designs of the American seal, the earliest American flag (1776) and currency upon the orders of congress. Close friend of both Jefferson and Franklin, also the latter's executor. (The Betsy Ross story of the flag's origin is a proven myth).

George Mason:

> (1725-92) U.S. statesman. At the Virginia constitutional convention (1776) he drafted the Declaration of Rights which may have influenced Thomas Jefferson's draft of the Declaration of Independence. A member of the Philadelphia Constitutional Convention of 1787, he opposed ratification of the federal constitution , as did about half of the other members.

Aquinas, Thomas:

> (1225?-74). Italian scholar, writer, philosopher and theologian. His teachings have a profound relation to the Declaration; he does not recognize an equality of men as a total concept but separates attributes of men which can be compared. He makes clear that men are not equal in their endowments but only in their Liberty.

Locke, John:

> (1632-1704) English philosopher. He upholds 'natural rights' (life, liberty, property etc.) & in opposition to the divine rights of kings he bases state power on social contract, with the right to abolish oppressive forms of government. His ideas had profound effects on 18th c. thought (Hume) & on revolutionary movements, esp. France and North America.

Footnote on preliminary entanglements

> Initially, on recommendations, with need of skilled printers, a trial was made at a small printing house near the Northeast corner of Vermont but disastrously the firm had fallen into younger hands; and after initial work on our earlier pictures for this Book-printing, their charges for computer scanning were found to be 9x higher than in New York. Since the Vermont scannings had neglected captions & positioning they were unuseable & our down-payment made in good faith disappeared *unrecoverably* into the Bank of Ireland, - while one of their salesmen, impressed by the Manuscript's remarkable size, overrode confidentiality with disclosures to a *Billboard Collector*.

Signers of the *Declaration of Independence*
*_***********_*

Their Life-spans, Ages at the Signing, Professions, National Origin and Religion

Signer	from-to	State	Life	age/'76	Profession	Origin	Religion
John Hancock	1737-1793	MA	56	36	Merchant	English	Congregational
Button Gwinnett	1735-1777	GA	42	41	Merchant	English	Episcopal
Lyman Hall	1725-1790	"	65	51	Physician	English	Congregational
George Walton	1740-1804	"	64	36	Mechanic-Lawyer	English	Episcopal
William Hooper	1742-1790	NC	48	34	Lawyer	English	Congregational
Joseph Hewes	1730-1779	"	49	46	Merchant	English	Episcopal
John Penn	1741-1788	"	47	35	Lawyer	English	Episcopal
Edward Rutlidge	1749-1800	SC	51	27	Planter/lawyer	English	Episcopal
Thomas Heyward	1746-1779	"	63	30	Lawyer	English	Episcopal
Thomas Lynch	1749-1779	"	30	27	Lawyer	Ir./Dutch/English	Episcopal
Arthur Middleton	1742-1787	"	45	34	Planter	English	Episcopal
Samuel Chase	1741-1811	MD	70	35	Lawyer	English	Episcopal
William Paca	1740-1799	"	59	36	Lawyer	Engl/Ital.	Episcop.
Thomas Stone	1743-1787	"	44	33	Lawyer	English	Episcopal
Charles Carroll of Carrollton	1737-1832	"	95	39	Planter	Irish	Rom/Cathol.
George Wythe	1726-1806	VA	80	50	Lawyer	English	Episcopal
Rich.Henry Lee	1732-1794	"	62	44	Planter	English	Episcopal
Thomas Jefferson	1743-1826	"	83	33	Planter/Lawyer	English	Unitarian
Benjamin Harrison	1740-1791	"	51	26	Planter	English	Episcopal
Thomas Nelson	1738-1789	"	51	38	Merchant/Planter	Scottish /English	Episcopal
Francis Lightfoot Lee	1734-1797	"	63	42	Planter	English	Episcopal
Carter Braxton	1736-1797	"	61	40	Planter	English	Episcopal
Robert Morris	1734-1806	PA	72	42	Merchant	English	Episcopal
Benjamin Rush	1745-1813	"	68	31	Physician	English	Presbyt./Episc

Signer	from-to	State	Life	age/'76	Profession	Origin	Religion
Benj. Franklin	1706-1790	"	84	70	Printer	English	Deist
John Morton	1724-1777	"	5 3	52	Farmer	Swedish/ English	Episcopal.
George Clymer	1739-1813	"	74	37	Merchant	English	Episcopal
James Smith	c.1719-1806	"	87	57	Lawyer	Scotch/ Irish	Presbyt
George Taylor	1716-1781	"	65	60	Ironmaster	Scotch/ Irish	Episcopal
James Wilson	1742-1798	"	56	34	Lawyer	Scottish	Presbyt.
George Ross	1730-1779	"	49	46	Lawyer	Scottish	Presbyt.
Casar Rodney	1728-1784	DE	56	48	Planter	English	Episcopal
George Read	1733-1798	"	65	43	Lawyer	Irish/ Welsh	Episcopal
Thom. McKean	1734-1817	"	83	42	Lawyer	Scotch/ Irish	Presbyt.
William Floyd	1734-1821	NY	87	42	Landowner	Welsh/ English	Presbyt.
Philip Livingston	1716-1778	"	62	60	Merchant	Dutch/ Scottish	Presbyt.
Francis Lewis	1713-1803	"	90	63	Merchant	Welsh	Episcopal
Lewis Morris	1726-1798	"	72	50	Landowner	English/ Dutch	Episcopal
Richard Stockton	1730-1781	"	51	46	Lawyer	English/	Presbyt.
Joh. Witherspoon	1723-1794	NJ	71	53	Clergyman	Scotch	Presbyt.
Francis Hopkinson	1737-1791	"	54	39	Writer/ Lawyer Artist	English	Episcopal
John Hart	c.1711-1779	"	68	65	Farmer	English	Baptist
Abraham Clark	1726-1794		68	50	Surveyor	English	Presbyt.
Josiah Bartlett	1729-1795	NH	66	47	Physician/ Judge	English	Congregation.
William Whipple	1730-1785	"	55	46	Merchant/ Judge	English	Congregation.
Matthew Thornton	1714-1803	"	89	62	Physician/	Scotch/ Irish	Congregat.

Colophon

※——※

It is the fixed policy of Ionian Pictures to secure printing services solely from Printing houses within the United States, as book-printing is an initially Western Institution and one necessarily to be retained by active practice as part of the culture and habit of a Nation == for the preservation of its national Integrity.

Gratitude is here expressed by IONIAN PICTURES, with compliments, to COSMOS COMMUNICATIONS INC., for executing this book-printing with fine attention to detail and excellent procedures, with modern expertise, including advice from long experience, together with prompt responses to requests, in a quiet personal atmosphere; & most importantly, for having maintained the integrity of this work without outside interference or influences.